Acknowledgements

The author and publishers would like to thank the following for their courtesy in providing photographs and/or permission to reproduce images in this book:

Freer Gallery of Art, Smithsonian Institution, Washington DC: 22-3.
Gallery Art Kamigata: 40.
Kyoto Institute of Technology Museum and Archive, collection number AN. 2694-10: 41 bottom left.
From Richard Lane, *Hokusai, Life and Work* (1989): 26.
From Tadashi Masuda, *The Design Heritage of Noren* (1989): 21.
Mitsukoshi Co. Ltd: 36, 37, 46 top.
Morinaga Co. Ltd: 41 bottom right.
Morisawa Typesetting Company: 18 top, 54 top, 214, 225.
Nezu Institute of Fine Arts, Tokyo: 23 top.
Peabody Museum of Salem (photograph Mark Sexton): 25 both.
Philadelphia Museum of Art: Given by Mrs Emile Geyelin, in memory of Anne Hapton Barnes: 27.
Press Arto: 63.
Shiseido Co.: 50-1, 52 top, 53, 67 left, 96 bottom, 160.
Tokiko Sugiura: 35, 44 both, 45.
Suntory Ltd: 43.
Yumeji Takehisa Memorial Museum: 48, 49 both.
Tobacco and Salt Museum, Tokyo: 33.
Tokushu Paper Co. Ltd: 59, 60.
Tokyo Art Directors Club: 29 both, 32 top right, 39 top left, top right and bottom left, 41 top, 47 both, 52 bottom, 54 bottom, 61, 62 both, 72.
From *The Traditional Japanese Dyeing of Happi and Handtowels* (1989): 20 left.
Takamasa Yamada: 46 bottom.

Frontispiece: Tadanori Yokoo, poster promoting the writer Yukio Mishima, about 1966 (1020 x 738 mm). The Japanese flag is in the background of the main picture, featuring a train (the writer?) parting the waves; the woman expressing milk in the top right corner is taken from part of a Mishima story.

Opposite: Ryuichi Yamashiro, *Trees*, poster designed for the Graphic '55 exhibition, 1955 (1052 x 740 mm). This poster received international attention and has since become regarded as one of the classics of Japanese graphic design (see page 83).

Overleaf: Koichi Sato, poster for the Ohara School for Ikebana, 1985 (1030 x 728 mm). Appearing to be both inside and outside the glowing red box is the half-moon shape credited to the seventeenth-century rimpa artist, Sotatsu, a favourite device of Sato. The golden butterfly at the top is the school's symbol, designed by Kuni Kizawa.

Japanese
Graphic
Design

はな、はな、大好き。

小原流 創流90周年

Richard

S. Thornton

Japanese

Graphic

Design

Laurence King

For as long as I can remember, Japanese arts and design have held my fascination. When I began my research I tried to discover those characteristics that give these arts unique visual qualities. There are the obvious uses of Japanese calligraphy and occasional Asian motifs, but I have always believed there is something more basic and internal. Part of my search was to find connections between the heritage of the Japanese and their current practices. Once revealed, those mystical qualities in their graphic design become clear and provide a context for contemporary trends. I hope my Japanese friends will find my observations and assumptions interesting. From my experiences, I know they enjoy reading about themselves and that they are curious about what foreigners think of them. If most of my observations are correct, they may excuse any shortcomings.

Many people have been very helpful in supporting my research over the past twenty years. My sincere appreciation goes to the following graphic designers, art directors and illustrators for providing time for interviews and, in many cases, repeated visits: Masuteru Aoba, Katsumi Asaba, Kiyoshi Awazu, Susumu Endo, Shigeo Fukuda, Tsuyoshi Fukuda, Hiromu Hara, Yoshio Hayakawa, Gan Hosoya, Takenobu Igarashi, Kenji Itoh, Yusaku Kamekura, Takahisa Kamijyo, Toshihiro Katayama, Mitsuo Katsui, Toshifumi Kawahara, Katsu Kimura, Tsunehisa Kimura, Ryohei Kojima, Takashi Kono, Shin Matsunaga, Hiroshi Morishima, Tadahito Nadamoto, Kazumasa Nagai, Michio Nakamoto, Makoto Nakamura, Tadashi Ohashi, Paul Rand, Makoto Saito, Koichi Sato, Henry Steiner, Sadao Sugaya, Kohei Sugiura, Kenichi Tanaami, Ikko Tanaka, Masatoshi Toda, Akira Uno, Kuniomi Uematsu, Makoto Wada, Harumi Yamaguchi, Ryuichi Yamashiro, Yuzo Yamashita, Tadanori Yokoo and Teruhiko Yumura. They have been generous with their time.

During these visits I have had to rely on the interpretive skills of a few individuals in Japan. They not only translated the designers' responses but made sense of my questions and provided the necessary courtesies required in Japan. A special thanks to: Yoshiko Takakawa in 1967 and 1970, Masashi Kimura in 1984 and Noriko Otake in 1987.

In addition, information has been gathered from books, magazine articles, design and art direction annuals, exhibition catalogues, and style books about well known designers and illustrators. Many of these were provided by various Japanese designers and art directors. Others came from people

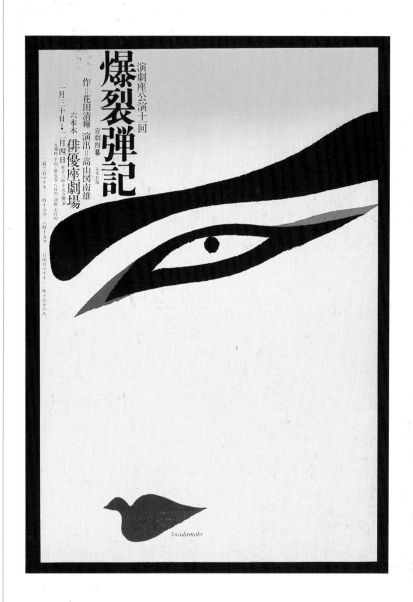

Tadahito Nadamoto, poster for a comedy play *Bakuretsudanki* ("A Story of the Bomb"), 1969 (730 x 515 mm). Designed with his forceful calligraphic style, this poster image is filled with the stylized representation of a woman's face. She is wearing the traditional make-up of the kabuki theatre – exaggeratedly slanted eyes, white skin and small, bright red mouth. The play details are used to outline a frown, and the signature forms a beauty spot. It is an excellent demonstration of the manipulation of space which is one of the most distinctive features of Japanese graphic design.

like editor Masaru Katzumie, writer Tsune Sesoko and, over the past three years, a loyal friend, Nobu Ikeda at Morisawa Typesetting Company, who continues to aid my research with material from Japan. Thanks also to those graduate students at the University of Connecticut in Storrs who translated numerous Japanese publications into English: Sonoko Ogawa, Rumiko Tanaka, Atsu Inoue and Keiko Murasugi; and to Annick Theis-Viemont for French translations.

Grateful acknowledgement is made to the following publications for permission to reprint previously published material: *Design Issues, Aiga Journal* and *Graphics.*

Many of the first generation designers are still actively producing work that is as exciting as that of the younger generation. Some of these designers have accomplishments that span five decades and their names are still listed with every important organization and design event. In many ways this continuity has cushioned the radical industrial and social changes in Japan that have occurred in the last forty years.

One such designer is Yusaku Kamekura. When I first visited Japan in 1967 I met Kamekura and enjoyed his disarming frankness. At that time he was probably the most powerful designer in Japan. Few design organizations or events missed his stamp of approval. I was impressed by the way he sat back in his chair, his chin set high, and how he took control of the interview. A few years later I referred to him in an article as "the boss" of Japanese graphic design, a title that remains with him to this day. I saw Kamekura again in 1970, 1984 and 1987. Each time he maintained that air of confidence and power, and remains a leader in various major design organizations. In spite of his full schedule of business and organizational responsibilities, many of the younger designers credit Kamekura's assistance as a reason for their success. There are many references to him in this book and I owe him a special thanks for his contributions.

Much of the latter part of the book concentrates on designers who have been active in the last 15 years. Without an historical perspective, identifying those significant designers can be a problem. Generally, I have selected designers and art directors who have received considerable recognition from the various national review processes. They are the new generation of individuals who are providing the future spirit of Japanese graphic design.

There were several challenges in organizing the material for this book. One was selecting the right illustrations. Those

from the pre-Sixties were selected on the basis of historical significance and availability. Illustrations by the first and second generation graphic designers represent the best of their early work and those that typify various stages in their careers. Illustrations from younger designers were chosen, with some personal bias, to characterize current design trends. Chronologically arranged, the illustrations should provide a broad view of the best from Japan's graphic design history. Regrettably, I was not able to obtain examples from a few important designers. The problems of language and distance were insurmountable.

There has been a conscious effort on my part to include information about important women designers and art directors. However, Japan is a very male-dominated society, in spite of political efforts to provide professional equality. In recent conversations with two designers, Tsuyoshi Fukuda and the venerable Yusaku Kamekura, they tell of their colleagues' almost complete rejection of women as art directors. Fukuda and Kamekura said that women do not have the right qualities to gain respect from clients and to provide the kind of forceful negotiations necessary in today's profession. There are, however, subtle changes occurring which indicate that Japanese men may be beginning to recognize the validity of women designers.

Another dilemma I faced in putting this book together was the issue of how to list Japanese names in Roman letters, and whether to use the Japanese form of family name followed by given names, or the Western form of given name first then family name. Currently, most publications in Japan use the Western format; I have joined the majority. A few exceptions to this are early artists whose names are generally acceptable in the Japanese format. Where dates are concerned, I have included both major Japanese eras based on emperors, and the Western lunar calendar.

Geographic identification also presented a problem for me. At first it seemed acceptable to refer to Japanese as "Oriental," but friends told me this term does not translate favourably. So the more generic term "Asian" was substituted. In addition, the word "Western" is both overused and weighted. The original map-makers in Europe conveniently placed Britain on the left and Japan on the right. "Western" countries took up only one quarter of the space and the rest is identified as "Middle East," "East," "South East" and "Far East." No matter how hard I tried to avoid the directional designations, they kept reappearing. It does not seem to matter that from the Japanese perspective the country directly east is the United States, and Japan's western neighbours are the Chinese and Koreans.

Many individuals have been extraordinarily helpful in preparing this book. Thanks go to Professor Shinichi Watanabe at Nihon University and to those friends who assisted in making Japanese arrangements in Tokyo, Yukio Aki and Yasunobu Shimasaki. Masashi Kimura and his wife provided some last-minute assistance in locating illustrations when communication and translation were a problem. The competent organizational skills of Eriko Osaka at the Institute of Contemporary Art, Tokyo, were instrumental in locating many historical works and in sending transparencies.

Thanks to the University of Connecticut's Research Foundation for financial assistance in preparing materials for this book. And thanks to Rachael Lent for suggesting that it was time for me to write it. At John Calmann and King, Laurence King and Jane Havell were patient and helpful; Junko Popham provided invaluable assistance with the captions. Lilly Kaufman at Van Nostrand Reinhold provided early encouragement. A special thanks to my wife Juanita for her many years of support, assistance and encouragement. She was there from start to finish, from helping with travel to organizing the illustrations.

This book is dedicated to the memory of my friend and mentor, the late Masaru Katzumie. His inspiration and commitment to accuracy have been my constant companions.

Richard S. Thornton
Storrs, Connecticut
1990

Graphic designer Kohei Sugiura said that when the Japanese examine their heritage they find little that is original. Using the metaphor of the Japanese body, Sugiura said that if everything were removed that had its origin in other countries, only their hair would be left. This bold statement could be accepted as just another example of humble Japanese deference to foreigners. Yet Sugiura is a very confident and proud graphic designer who has a considerable ego. His statement was not made without extensive thought and research into the foundations of Japanese religion and culture, providing him with a credibility that is unquestionable.

Sugiura was repeating what was said a little over a hundred years ago by the nineteenth-century scholar of Japanese history Basil Hall Chamberlain. A British citizen who held the unprecedented status of emeritus professor at the Imperial University of Tokyo, Chamberlain wrote in 1880 that Japan was a "nation of imitators." From his research he noted that Japanese religion, philosophy, laws, administration, writing, all arts – just about everything – were imported from neighbouring continents. Chamberlain could find only two things that the Japanese did not borrow from other countries: their poetry and their hot baths. His observation was made at a time when Japan was emerging from 215 years of self-imposed isolation, when the people realized that the world had changed and they were being left behind. This time Japan was not influenced by its Asian neighbours but by those from the West, creating an environment of intense industrialization and a single-minded concentration on modernization.

Edwin O. Reischauer, in his book *The Japanese* (1977), pointed out that many people mistakenly think that these radical changes were an effort to Westernize Japan. He made the point that the Japanese simply took over modern aspects of Western culture – railroads, factories, mass education, great newspapers, television and mass democracy. Reischauer wrote: "In this sense Japan has more significantly become modernized, not Westernized, and the process of modernization has taken place on the basis of Japan's own traditional culture, just as it happened in the West, with the same sort of resulting contrasts and strains."

Basing their historical tradition on borrowing ideas, the Japanese have not regarded invention and the need to be original as important. Instead, they were able to adopt and synthesize, to create a new reality that is uniquely their own. For example, take the name of their country, which we call

Eiko Ishioka, poster for Parco, 1979 (1030 x 729 mm). The American actress Faye Dunaway, dressed in fantasy Japanese style, frames two Japanese children wearing kabuki make-up and kimono skirts; the copy reads "Can West wear East." One of her best known images, she chose it for the cover of her influential style book, *Eiko by Eiko* (1983).

Japan. The first historical references are unclear on the origins of the name. Two early books – *Kojiki*, a "Record of Ancient Things," written in 712 AD, and *Nihon shoki*, written in 720 AD as a genealogy of emperors and empresses from 585 BC to 628 AD – use Chinese calligraphy for their country's name. The Japanese pronounced this "Nihon" – at that time a eulogistic expression for Yamato, the original name of the central kingdom. Nihon means "origin of the sun" or "sunrise," taken from the country's position to the east of the Asiatic continent. *Nihon shoki* states that in 670 AD the government officially designated the name to be pronounced Nihon or Nippon, and notified the Koreans and Chinese.

Apparently there was a misunderstanding. Some of the many Korean scholars who crossed the Japan Sea during the early part of the seventh century, and the Chinese, when they read calligraphy for these islands, pronounced the country's name "Jih-pen." During Marco Polo's visit to China in the thirteenth century, he reported on a series of small islands lying just east of China, which he was told were called "Zhipan-gu." Japan was named. Instead of restricting themselves to a constant, single designation, Japanese still use all three names – Nihon, Nippon and Japan – with seemingly equal frequency. They have the Nippon Design Center, Nihon University and Japan Graphic Designers Association. This openness reflects their casual attitude to language formalities and their receptiveness to the invention of new words.

Trying to document the origin of the name is like gathering most of the information for this book: its historical reference to graphic design revolves around Japan's social, political and cultural history. With less than 140 years since America's "discovery" of Japan, the relevant connections with Japan's rich history, added to related materials from several sources, reveal a fascinating story that may or may not demystify the Orient.

Any research activity on Japan is relatively easy. As a small country, about the size of California and with a population half that of the United States, compared to the ethnic make-up of other countries it is unbelievably homogeneous. As Robert Christopher wrote in his book, *The Japanese Mind* (1983): "Ninety seven per cent of the Japanese are members of a single great tribe united not just by common citizenship or common language but by common bloodlines, common racial memory and common tribal codes, some of which stretch back into prehistory." It is this "family" relationship that provides for a unique social interaction, influencing acceptable behaviour in the home and business.

Most Japanese designers know each other as if they were one family. The hundreds of weekly and monthly magazines, daily newspapers and television have given many graphic designers a national recognition that would not be possible in America. There is also the unique practice of printing both vanity and trade books on the collected works of historically successful or currently stylish designers, illustrators and art directors. In no other country is there such an opportunity for individuals to honour themselves.

There are many compelling reasons to prepare a publication as a design reference for Western people. Recent social and political changes in the Far East, combined with aggressive industrial production, have focused international attention on the Pacific. Japanese have become a dominant force among the Pacific Rim countries and a leading economic power in the world. They know that at least the last two decades of this century belong to them.

The calligraphic character *wa*, artist unknown (270 x 240 mm). It means "peace" or "harmony": there is no better image to convey the true graphic spirit of Japan. It is painted on a shikishi, a square piece of paper which is displayed in the home.

一

1

Origins of design

What began as a trickle of curious explorers from ancient China, Korea and India grew to a stream of uninvited guests. Native Japanese greeted these visitors with various levels of welcome, and then absorbed every useful idea they had. A mixture of art and culture from Japan's Asian neighbours created a fusion of exotic Far Eastern art concepts, an aesthetic synthesis that clouded the unique character of Japanese artistic achievements. At first glance there appear to be considerable similarities between Chinese and Japanese art. Traditional paintings from China, Korea and Japan share the same materials, spatial concepts and a spontaneity expressed with bold brushstrokes. It is such a blending of traditions that only those who know Asian art can identify the origins of individual aspects. As Sherman E. Lee explains in *The Genius of Japanese Design* (1981): "Where Chinese art reveals balance and rational sequence, the art of Japan delights in asymmetry and intuitive placement. Where the Chinese tended to rely upon the purity and separation of color, the Japanese delighted in mixtures, off-tints and blending."

The Buddhist religion was introduced to Japan in 530, providing a foundation for the Japanese belief in art and design as an essential part of life. During the Heian period (794-1185), famous for its courtly aristocratic life styles, the arts flourished. Particular arts developed during these eras that influenced graphic design are an expressive calligraphy and identifying monsho, family crests.

Calligraphy

One of the first major imports from China was calligraphy, with the forms reportedly invented by Ts-ang Chieh in 1800 BC. The Chinese had already developed a complex system of graphic characters or signs that represented words or concepts and their phonetic renderings. The Japanese copied this calligraphy and other fundamentals of Chinese civilization during the Asuka and Nara periods (552-749 AD), and transformed them for their own use. They gave many characters different sounds and meanings, to make the imported Chinese texts easier to understand. Once the transformation process began, it was not long before the original Chinese phonetic system was completely abandoned.

The Japanese developed three principal styles of calligraphy from the Chinese. One, designated kaisho, the standard or "regular script," is primarily used for official records and sutra, writing on Buddhist texts. The second, a loose, more

御家流重法正韓

甘肉の書を習ひ対は上達

遠書お仏へーんを渺書を戮

習まぐし

Hiragana calligraphy (bolder, on the right) and kanji, which is more free-flowing. Each character is drawn left to right with brush and ink, but reads top to bottom, right to left. This traditional directional style began to disappear after World War II and is now never used except deliberately to evoke earlier eras.

百福自来
いろはにほへとちりぬるを
イロハニホヘトチリヌルヲ

Top: kanji (top), hiragana (centre) and katakana (bottom) typeset in the mincho style to mimic the traditional brush calligraphy. Katakana is the style used for writing foreign languages into the Japanese syllabary.

Centre: a spread from a standard dictionary of monsho forms, arranged by subject matter and showing almost five thousand different crests.

Above: a monsho used as a decorative element on the end of the roof tiles of a building in Kyoto: the versatility of this design form is one of its most marvellous qualities.

abbreviated form, known as gyosho or "running script," has an informal use. The third style, sosho or "cursive script," is the more expressive form used for personal correspondence and poetry. All three scripts, called kanji, have over 13,000 characters, with about 6,000 in constant use, and about 2,500 as the essential part of modern Japanese writing and printing.

To broaden their calligraphic forms and to provide an alternative to the complicated kanji script, in the tenth century the Japanese developed two syllabaries, also based on Chinese characters, that are still in use today. Each of these forms has 46 characters which represent signs for phonetic sounds. The katakana characters are angular with short chop-like marks and are used primarily for words of foreign origin (other than Chinese or Korean). The other, hiragana, a cursive style that looks like loose knots, has a more general use, sometimes to be printed next to a complicated kanji so that readers can sound out words. At the present time, printed matter uses four forms – kanji, hiragana, katakana and romaji (Roman characters) – each with their individual typographic character and colour.

Monsho: Japanese Family Crests

The monsho is one of those devices which had a simple, inconsequential beginning, to add identity and decoration as a sign of influence and wealth. It first appeared in the middle of the tenth century during the Heian Era, noted as a flourishing period for Japanese literature, painting and architecture. Tiny decorative monsho were first used by the gracious-living aristocracy to identify their family possessions. These early designs were based on simple things that brought beauty to life – butterflies, flowers and other plant images. Modest, symbolic representations were drawn with a minimum of line to create flat motifs, which were used as decoration, for example on carriages and clothing.

During the Kamakura and Muromachi eras (1192-1568) – distinguished as five centuries of disorder and civil wars – the crests attained their peak of perfection. Used as identity for various warlords during battle, the monsho became characteristically larger, bolder and more masculine, to be clearly identified on the banners of bow-men. By the end of the fifteenth century, the *Kenbun Shokamon* book of family emblems listed 255 different monsho. From the middle to the end of the sixteenth century the ruling class built several large castles throughout Japan; craftsmen applied the monsho to roof tiles, stone lanterns, gates and gravestones in addition to battle equipment, such as armour, swords and shields. Stone, clay, metal and paint transformed the early delicate designs into bold, solid form.

As the Edo period began in 1603 feuds between lords ceased, creating a period of tranquillity that lasted for over 260 years. During this period the shogun assigned his retainers and servants to use monsho as status symbols and in the daimyo parades that took place at ceremonial events and festivals: the monsho would be carried on a tall standard as identification of the clan. Kabuki actors had their own monsho on fans and towels for publicity purposes. Firemen painted them on their short coats and matoi – hand-held standards with 48 streamers: each monsho designated a particular block assigned to the firemen.

Soon monsho were adopted by the general public as family emblems to be applied to formal clothing. By this time, the motifs embraced a wide range of subjects – plants, animals, natural phenomena, geometric forms, even articles of everyday life – reaching an amazing total of over five thousand designs. Examples of typical motifs include flora designs that could be considered conventionally Japanese, such as the chrysanthemum, wild pink, morning glory, bluebell, lotus, cherry blossom, plum blossom and narcissus. Familiar domestic articles are candles, spools, feather brushes, scissors, sake flasks, keys and coins. Those crests derived from fauna are the pigeon, hawk, sparrow, crane, wild goose, butterfly, rabbit, horse, tortoise, shellfish and carp. Farm crops include the aubergine, beans, millet, rice and grapes. Natural phenomena based on the sun, moon, stars, clouds, snow, waves and thunder are also used. The most famous monsho is the 16-petal chrysanthemum, representing the Imperial family.

The popularity of the monsho gradually spread during the eighteenth and nineteenth centuries. Contributing to its increased use was the rise of the merchant class who adopted crests as trademarks for their companies. This application was originally made during Japan's isolation when almost no Western influence was allowed. Merchants used monsho on packages, ship sails, paper lanterns and as identity on store houses. Symbols began to decorate entrances to shops on either kanban (signboards) or on noren, dyed cloths that hung over entrance doors, an idea brought from China in the twelfth century. Made of large squares of fabric, many dyed indigo blue with a white business monsho, noren were hung

Left: two participants at a festival wearing happi coats bearing the monsho of the renowned kabuki actor Danjuro Ichikawa, based on the gyogyo peony. Ichikawa was the first of a long line of actors who took the name Danjuro: the name and monsho appeared in 1660 and were passed down from father to son for nine generations over three centuries.

at eye level at the front of a shop to identify the entrance and announce that the shop was open for business.

As the monsho evolved into simple forms contained in a geometric shape defined by a bold line, they were easily adopted as trademarks for modern merchants. Three large department stores still use their original monsho – Sogo Stores Limited designed in 1830, Takashimaya in 1886, and Mitsukoshi in 1904. Kikkoman Soy Sauce Company has used its monsho since 1765. Many other old Japanese companies have, unfortunately, recently discarded these more appropriate marks for the nondescript, ubiquitous Roman letterforms.

Reduction and Refinement, 1600-1850

In the seventeenth century, following a history filled with a series of brutal feudal battles and the eventual expulsion of Christian missionaries, Japan settled into 260 years of almost complete, peaceful isolation. During the rule of the Tokugawa shoguns, called the Edo Period (1603-1867), Japan limited its foreign contact to commerce with China and Holland through a small settlement on the artificial island of Deshima in the port of Nagasaki. The remarkably harmonious isolation from both the advances and failures of the West provided time for all areas of Japanese art and design to reach a high degree of refinement and systematization. With no outside influences, its national cultures were nurtured from sources and inspirations within the Japanese people. Those few foreign ideas that penetrated the barriers were carefully tempered according to Japanese tastes and then incorporated as intrinsic elements in the culture.

One early element of Japan's artistic history, originating in the seventeenth century, had a major influence on several contemporary graphic designers. Rimpa is included here because its indigenous shapes, patterns and colours have been recently repeated on posters produced from 1970 through to the present time.

Rimpa

With a cultural heritage as rich as Japan's, it is unusual for one fine art movement to have such a major influence on graphic design. Contrary to most foreign opinion, rimpa has had more influence than the popular ukiyo-e woodblock prints on the illustrative motifs used in advertising and packaging. One reason is that rimpa was reserved for the highest social level and ukiyo-e was its counterpart at the lowest level.

Facing page, top: monsho, traditional family crests, possess both elegance and strength: this selection makes use of customary images such as flowers, fans, sails, waves and coins.

Facing page, centre: the trademark for Takashimaya Department Store, which is a stylized version of the kanji character for the first syllable of the family name, *taka*. The suffix *-ya* means shop. Dating from 1886, the mark originated at a time when Japanese kimono shops were beginning to promote Western apparel and household items.

Noren of the Kyoto restaurant Shiruko, which provides boxed lunches and soup. The black monsho, printed on undyed cloth, hangs in the doorway and serves as a shield against the wind as well as an identifying mark for the shop. The illustration is from a collection of photographs of noren by designer Tadashi Masuda.

Another is that rimpa, with its highly decorative and complicated design motifs, approached art as abstract design and not as representational illustration.

The name rimpa, meaning "the School of Korin" after its most famous practitioner, Ogata Korin (1658-1716), is commonly associated with a dozen decorative artists who worked in Japan from the early seventeenth century into the nineteenth century. It is highly unusual for such a small colony of artists, some of whom have gained more popularity than others, to be held together by a common art movement for over two hundred years. Their revival of classical Heian arts during the Edo period provided a rich assortment of motifs, which were to influence future directions of Japanese decorative arts and crafts.

Honami Koetsu (1558-1637), generally accepted as the group's founder, was first listed as a master-painter. However, since 1950 some scholars have concluded that no paintings can be attributed to him. He is now credited as the source of inspiration and catalyst for many significant artists and designers who are identified with rimpa. Koetsu's contribution was as a master-calligrapher, applying his art as poems in paintings and as letterforms on tea bowls. Other more important members of the group were Nonomura Sotatsu (active in 1615-1635), noted for his beautifully composed cranes, wisteria, azalea and lions painted on folding screens, and Ogata Korin himself, who created highly decorative and elegant lacquer boxes, fabrics, baskets and screens.

Rimpa artists are identified as more decorative than earlier painters. Sotatsu contrasted bright, bold colours clearly defined as shapes with no concern for shadows or dimensional shading. Korin used decorative swirling patterns on gold-leaf ground. Their work expressed the Japanese love of life during the two and a half centuries of peaceful, isolated rule by the shogunal government.

In reviewing their simple but exquisite designs, rimpa's commanding influence on today's designers can be seen: the tilted half-moon shape found in several rimpa paintings is favoured by Koichi Sato; clearly defined shapes with linear patterns are used by Kazumasa Nagai; textured patterns contrasted with simple shapes are often repeated by Tadanori Yokoo; and deep earth colours – rich browns, earth greens and burnt oranges – placed on layered textures, and simple, flat, geometric shapes for plants and flowers can all be found in the works of several contemporary designers.

Nonomura Sotatsu, screen, *Pine Islands*, dating from about 1600 and made for the Yogen-in temple at Kyoto (twelve panels; each panel 1520 x 3550 mm). Pine trees, rocks and the force of the sea unite to become decorative elements.

Top: Ogata Korin, screen, *Irises*,
dating from about 1710. Korin, said to
be more refined than Sotatsu, put
more emphasis on precise outline and
an even application of colour. The
purple blossoms are not so much
realistic illustrations as a structure to
provide space for the green stalks to
dance across the surface.

During the first part of the Tokugawas' rule in the seventeenth century, two important forms of visual communication were developed and allowed to flourish – kanban, or shop signs, and ukiyo-e, a special genre of painting and woodblock printmaking. Both still receive considerable attention from Western art collectors and are highly influential on modern graphic design.

Kanban: Shop Signs

Japanese kanban, literally translated as "signboard," is an inventive folk art developed by the merchant classes in the Edo and Meiji periods (1650-1914). These hand-crafted signs, hung outside shops in villages and along popular routes, are simple pictographic representations of the goods and services provided by individual shopkeepers. Some of the more complex sculptured and painted signs had calligraphic designs adorned with elaborate gold and silver embellishments, but most used only limited colour to decorate the simply carved, flat boards.

Frank B. Gibney, in his book *Kanban, Shop Signs of Japan* (1982), describes these signs as ingenious, with their simplified shapes of evocative images and visual puns that "testify not merely to the abiding Japanese fascination with form and style, even above content, but with symbol more than substance." Gibney writes that by the early eighteenth century, the signs "reached a new high in their size and the imaginativeness of their decoration. Whether for medicine, fans, cosmetics, food and drink, a kabuki program or a geisha teahouse, the kanban hanging outside was designed to convey a sense of assurance and opulence to the prospective customer."

The use of kanban continued in Japan throughout the Meiji Restoration, with several surviving the devastation of earthquakes and wars in the twentieth century. Today, when walking down narrow streets in towns and cities, it is a thrill to discover some of the survivors still hanging outside small shops. Fortunately, many Japanese consumers still use small speciality stores that are reached by foot, which encourages the use of smaller, more personal signs. But, by nightfall, many of these small shops are transformed into another world with spectacular neon and incandescent lights that crowd the narrow streets.

Ukiyo-e: Woodblock Prints

Beginning as black-and-white illustrations depicting the sensuous life of the pleasure quarter in Edo (the early name for Tokyo), the woodcut art of ukiyo-e quickly grew into a popular art form of the sixteenth century. Early work was generally expensive and available only to the upper class in society. Later, the prevalent characteristics of ukiyo-e were that they were mass-produced and sold cheaply, making them accessible to the general public.

Hishikawa Moronobu (1618-1694) is credited as the founder and one of the most creative artists of the "pictures of the floating world." Moronobu lived among the common people and succeeded in heightening the aesthetic value of this genre art to a popular form. Much of his work consisted of book illustrations, with almost half devoted to erotica for sex manuals and guides to courtesans. Another favourite use of ukiyo-e was to promote the popular theatre, kabuki. A leading woodblock artist for the theatre was Toshusai Sharaku, possibly himself an actor, who produced a number of highly expressive actor prints in a period of ten months in 1794-5.

During the latter part of the eighteenth century, at the height of ukiyo-e's popularity, the work of Kitagawa Utamaro (1754-1806) captured the interest of the public. He is best known for his elegant portraits of women, and a refined taste in eroticism. Richard Lane, in his book *Masters of the Japanese Print* (1982), describes Utamaro's skill: "His girls and women speak directly to the viewer in terms of a frankly sensual beauty; and, behind this surface attraction, in Utamaro's finest works we sense the mind of the 'eternal female,' seemingly oblivious of her own charms, yet well aware of their effect upon her male audience and of their profound influence upon her own life and her concept of happiness."

Later masters, such as Suzuki Harunobu (1725-1770), Katsushika Hokusai (1760-1849) and Ando Hiroshige (1787-1858), became important influences on French Impressionist painters in the second half of the nineteenth century. What attracted the Europeans was the absence of sculptured effects and shadows to suggest a three-dimensional quality. This was not a depiction of what the Japanese artists saw in nature, but of the concept of it. The Van Gogh brothers, Theo and Vincent, were avid collectors of ukiyo-e prints, and amassed over four hundred between them.

As foreign interest in Japanese crafts grew, a few prints from the private collection of Sir Rutherford Alcock, first British Consul-General to Japan, were included in the 1862

Wood kanban, maker unknown, dating from about 1700 (740 x 650 mm). After the wars of the Momoyama period, the early part of the Edo era was peaceful, and helmets came to be regarded as more ceremonial than military. This kanban is carved and painted to resemble metal and corded silk.

Kanban for a geta, or clog-shop, dating from about 1890, Meiji period (285 x 266 mm). It depicts Okame-san, a symbol of womanhood and beauty, and a popular choice for signs appealing to the working classes. The ideal female face was very round, with a small mouth; here, the cloth thongs of the wooden clog represent the hair-line.

Katsushika Hokusai, landscape at
Nikko, from *A Guide to Nikko*, 1837.
The line quality and repetition of
details are reminiscent of Hokusai's
famous wave print from *Thirty-Six
Views of Mount Fuji*, completed a
few years earlier.

World Exhibition held in England. The next international exposition was held in Paris in 1867, by which time Japan's representation – organized by the then shogun, Tokugawa Yoshinobu – included lacquerware, ceramics, swords, tools, instruments, armour, fans and 5,600 ukiyo-e prints. Westerners were fascinated by Japanese products because they were produced by a culture that had matured completely independent of European influence.

Equally important was the influence of these prints on European and American poster designers of that period, such as Maxfield Parrish, Edmond Penfield, Ludwig Honhoein and Jules Cheret. Cheret was particularly impressed with the elimination or subjugation of backgrounds, which projected the subject into the foreground – an ideal design for a poster. Early European poster designers were also excited by the artificially raised background and simple graphic image. Toulouse-Lautrec borrowed from ukiyo-e and based his monogram on the Japanese signature seal or "chop."

Ukiyo-e artists produced prints much like today's graphic designers. The artist acted as an art director in supervising the printing process. Artists drew original sketches with brush in black-and-white, made appropriate notations on patterns for carvers to cut, and on choice of colours for printers. Several woodblocks, one for each colour, were cut and organized for mass production of multicoloured pictures, a process that was rare in the Western world at that time (chromolithographers used a similar production-line process in Europe during the early part of the nineteenth century). Another interesting element of ukiyo-e for graphic designers was the combination of calligraphy and pictorial image on a single print. The idea of calligraphy as part of the print came from China and has a long history as part of a total aesthetic image and not just an addition.

As previously noted, early prints had sexually explicit views of life in Tokyo's yoshiwara, an area designated for legalized prostitution. The straightforward depiction of genitalia, particularly the exaggerated male images, must have shocked European society. Even today, the prints cannot receive open public showing in Japan and are banned by strict censorship. Yet the yoshiwara district continued into the twentieth century; it was closed only a few years before the Tokyo Olympics in 1964 to avoid embarrassing foreign visitors. This dualistic approach to sex has been a major influence on the use of sensuous images in present-day Japanese advertising.

Kitagawa Utamaro, woodcut showing the courtesan Shinonara of Tsuruya, from the series *The Seven Komachi of the Green Houses*, about 1800 (378 x 226 mm). Utamaro was one of the most famous of ukiyo-e woodblock artists; in this example he painstakingly illustrates every detail of the hair and facial features.

The Meiji Restoration, 1850-1900

Towards the end of the Edo period – which included 15 Tokugawa shoguns – many Japanese intellectuals became aware of progress beyond their borders. During those years of isolation, Europe had passed through the glories of the Renaissance and the Age of Discovery, and had experienced a surge of modern inventions during the industrial revolution. No wonder that, once news of these changes reached Japan, there were some who questioned their country's isolation, but it took a military threat to accelerate change. At about the time of this enlightenment, Japan had a very unexpected visitor in 1853. An American navy commodore, Matthew Perry, boldly sailed an armada of black ships into a central harbour and demanded a meeting with the governing shogun.

Perry was there not just to open commerce to the West, but to express a modern military strength that was unknown to the Japanese. The resulting treaties signed by the two countries in 1858 favoured America, which was more interested in establishing ports to shelter American ships engaged in trade with China than in trading with relatively poor Japan. Later the shogun signed similar treaties with European countries, who dominated Japanese relations while America was busy with a civil war.

The Tokugawa were toppled in 1868 by a combination of anti-foreignism, which in fact lasted only a few years, and first-hand observation of modern military strength. By the middle of the century, the shogun had begun to lose power, and strong nationalism among the people led to opposition to any relationships with foreign countries. At the same time the role of the Emperor was heightened with the battle cry "Revere the Emperor and Expel the Barbarians." Once the Tokugawa had gone, Emperor Meiji established a new government and changed the name of the capital city from Edo to Tokyo. Anti-foreign feelings diminished, and a revolutionary attitude swept the people in favour of an active importation of European and American culture. With that came an absorption in the study of Western political, judicial and economic systems; and, more important to this book, a preoccupation with Western advertising and visual communication.

From the beginning of the Meiji Restoration, the assimilation of foreign ways was as much creative as it was imitative. The intent was more to modernize, not just Westernize. When changes did occur, every attempt was made to retain "the spirit of old Japan," an attitude that continues through to the present time. Because of this major social turmoil, the first visitors during the 1870s reported back to their home countries that Japan was in a state of transition. Later visitors, in the twentieth century, continued with that same sentiment, not recognizing that Japan had been in a constant state of transition from the beginning of the Restoration. Many of today's visitors would agree with one early tourist, Rudyard Kipling, who visited Japan in 1889 and was completely taken in by the charm and beauty of the people and country. With glowing observations, he expressed considerable anxiety about the damaging effects of Western influences. In his essay "From Sea to Sea" he wrote, "It would pay us to put the whole Empire in a glass case and mark it *Hors Concours*, Exhibit A."

Kipling's wish is, in essence, a confusion over the dualism shown by Japanese in continuing certain traditional mores and at the same time adopting foreign accomplishments and imitating Western social fads. As Masaru Katzumie wrote in *Japan Style* (1980): "The result [is] a kind of dichotomy – a dichotomy by which, for the past one hundred years, we have been in a state of perpetual oscillation between the opposed phenomena of tradition and progress, Japanese and Western." It is this oscillation that has created a hybrid culture, exemplified by its graphic design.

Transitional Design

The most important transitional design produced during late Edo and early Meiji eras was an early form of poster, called ekanban: advertisements with pictures and letters painted on paper or cloth. Some were individually painted on cloth and others printed on paper. Their origins in ukiyo-e are evident, from their bold illustrations and expressive brush calligraphy. The major distinction between ukiyo-e and ekanban is the latter's obvious promotion of goods or services. During the early Meiji period ekanban remained popular: as the merchant class gained more influence, promotion for goods and services was an integral part of the expanding economy. Unfortunately, because of their fragile character, few ekanban survived; but the name continued to be used by the public even when the printing process changed from woodblocks to lithography in the early twentieth century.

Ekanban were also used to promote the favourite sport in Japan – sumo. Attending sumo matches in Edo was a popular recreational activity and attracted visitors from all over Japan, as it still does. Before each match, a banzuke, or hierarchical

Above right: ekanban for a sandal shop, artist unknown, 1860s. Reducing the size of the illustrations allowed the designer to place more emphasis on the copy that promoted the merchant. This example shows a typical bird's-eye view of a shop front opened to the street, with animated passers-by and customers trying on shoes. At the left of the print the name of the shop is given in large letters, and beneath it the banner hanging by the shop gives the name of the craftsman who made the shoes.

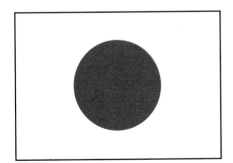

The Japanese flag, *hi-no maru,* "the rising sun." One of the most powerful, and best known, examples of the country's graphic design, it is believed to date from 1850 and is credited to the Lord of Satsuma, Nariakira Shimazu. The bold red sun on a white ground was first flown on the ships of an Edo-era shogun; it became the official flag in January 1870.

Kunisada, ekanban for perfume, about 1860. The delicate beauty of the ukiyo-e print is transformed into an advertisement for perfume which, the copy unambiguously claims, will increase the wearer's sexual attraction to men.

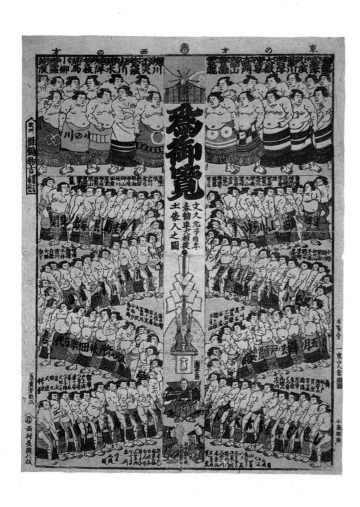

list of wrestlers, was printed as an ekanban and posted through-out the country. Many were a wonderful combination of ukiyo-e style illustration and calligraphy often found in the more informal style of ekanban known as bira.

Ekanban produced between 1868 and 1900 had calligra-phy written both vertically and horizontally. These later forms of posters with their woodblock illustrations took on an ap-pearance of comic book art, with simple line drawings defin-ing everyday life surrounded by balloon-less captions. But they lacked the refined spirit and careful attention to tex-tures, shapes and colours found in the best of the images of the floating world.

While posters continued in the tradition of woodblock art, newspapers adopted modern technology and set advertise-ments with typography and a few small wood and, later, steel engravings. The general trend was to fill all white space with information and use very little variation in type size. These type designs are interesting for Westerners because of the decorative patterns created by exotic Japanese letterforms. By 1890, bolder headlines began to appear, as did more concern for design through contrasts in size and weight of letter-forms and the addition of recently imported Western type fonts that included arrows, squares, triangles, dots and other non-alphabetical characters.

English words were often used on traditional Japanese products to make them seem more modern. Some early food and soap labels had wonderful phonetic English: "Rimonaede Searop," "Best Soented Toilet Soap," "Finest Laundby," "Chat Bland." Early medicine labels often used Roman letters to imply that the medicine may have been formulated in the West. Actually, the English words were usually meaningless; they were deployed to be more fashionable and not to de-ceive the public into thinking the product was in fact West-ern. It was generally accepted that to appear "modern" was to adopt Western words and culture.

As Emperor Meiji moved Japan into the twentieth century, he mixed East with West, producing a hybrid culture. In pro-moting this new life style, Japan's graphic designers attempted to find the best in both cultures, thus creating their own hybrid design.

Yoshiiku Ichikeisai (1829-1904), ekanban for sumo wrestlers, 1861 (512 x 380 mm). The symmetrical design, reminiscent of the rope-like belt worn by sumo wrestlers, grades them with the leading contenders at the top standing shoulder to shoulder. Below them are the complete teams, East on the left and West on the right - a total of 124. In the centre, marked by bold calligraphy, stand the umpires. Posters for sumo continue today in similar designs that date from the Edo period.

Masanobu Baido, poster advertising a travelling Western circus troupe, 1886. "Western acrobatic teams," as they were known, were very popular in the Meiji period, and the entertainers and animal handlers from Italy, France, the UK and America attracted as much attention as the animals themselves.

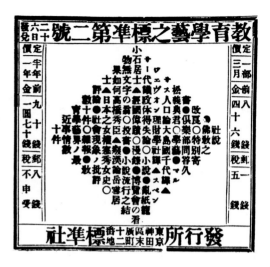

Kenji Inoue, poster for an exhibition of a century of posters, held at the Matsuya Department Store in 1967 (1030 x 728 mm). The artist has adapted an 1881 poster by Yoshitoshi Tsukioka, advertising a comedy play.

Modern banzuke handbill advertising a spring kabuki theatre programme, 1967. It is traditionally printed on rice paper with the same complicated calligraphic forms as were used in the Edo era, and contains the names of the actors, musicians and chorus, with the location and size of the calligraphy indicating their status, popularity and even their salaries.

Newspaper adverisement for an educational publication, 1888 (88 x 95 mm). The even size of kanji characters, which form a perfect square, lend themselves easily to elegant and geometric design.

Poster advertising cigarettes, artist unknown, 1890 (746 x 510 mm). Modern officers in their finest uniforms promote the masculine appeal of smoking, as well as conveying the high-class qualities of the brand on offer. The hawk, the battle flag and the cannon are all male symbols, and the two characters in red proclaim the words "honest" and "brave." The copy in black describes the cigarettes in detail: the idea of inhaling tobacco directly through the mouth was new to the Japanese, who until the Meiji restoration had only smoked pipes.

2

apan's hybrid design
1900-1950

Emperor Meiji, who began his reign in 1868 at the age of 17, generated the most important era in Japan's history. It was during his reign that Japan was transformed from an isolated feudal society to a recognized world power. By the end of the nineteenth century, these political and social changes in Japan had had a major impact on graphic design. Encouraged by the policies of Emperor Meiji, Japanese packaging design, newspaper advertisements and posters showed considerable influence from Europe and America. Another major influence for printed materials was the replacement of woodblock printing with modern lithography, radically changing the look and quality of the printed image. In spite of these technical improvements, poster design suffered from a confusion of identity. Artists replaced feudal motifs with pseudo-Western images in garish colours which lacked Japanese spirit. They could not decide whether they should continue with traditional imagery and remain provincial, or adopt Western views to show how international the country could be. The public chose the international image.

It was important that Japan's system of higher education should meet the international challenge. Early in the Meiji Restoration, Japanese art schools adopted European and American forms of teaching art and design. Tokyo School of Art, founded in 1887 as part of the Tokyo Imperial University, opened new departments of design and architecture in 1901. In 1949 the "Imperial" designation was dropped and Tokyo School of Art combined with the music school to form Tokyo University of Fine Arts and Music, or Tokyo Geijutsu. Kansai Academy of Arts in Osaka was founded in 1905 and Kyoto Painting School was founded in 1909. Wasada University, organized in 1882, founded the "Society for the Study of Advertisements" in 1914. These schools became the training ground for future designers.

One event in 1901 that prompted more attention to advertising as a legitimate area of academic study was a battle over cigarette sales between two emerging tobacco companies, Iwai and Murai. Cigarettes had been introduced in Japan before a national tobacco regulating commission was established; these two companies were in confrontation to achieve dominance. What is unusual is that the battle involved a new public forum – newspaper advertising. Advertising thus became established as an acceptable form of communication and the result was that it soon gained a place in the university curriculum.

Hisui Sugiura, poster for Mitsukoshi Department Store, 1914 (1060 x 770 mm). Sugiura developed the Art Nouveau style to the full: here, a distinctly Art Nouveau kimono blends with the patterns on the cushions, upholstery and wallpaper, and the carving of the table reflects the forms of the tulips in the vase. On the wall is a framed European print, to express the woman's cosmopolitan personality, and she holds a Mitsukoshi catalogue in her hand, its cover also designed by Sugiura. Flowers were a favourite motif of Sugiura and he promoted them in a ten-volume publication, *One Hundred Flowers*.

In addition to the Meiji policy of modernization, the next most important influence on graphic design at the beginning of the twentieth century was a change in the printing process from relief to lithography. This brought about a radical transformation in Japanese visual communication similar to that in America and Europe. In 1902, three-colour lithography printing became practical and was used for the first time to print the cover of a popular magazine. Next year, the first chromolithographic poster was produced to advertise Kirin beer. Both the cover and poster image showed a beautiful Japanese woman, signalling a trend that continues even today and spawning the bijin-ga, which translates as "beautiful person picture" or just "beauty picture." These posters provided Japan's first hybrid design that rivalled ukiyo-e in popularity.

Bijin-ga: Beauty Pictures

A pretty female figure has always been a useful poster standby in the West; and the same is true in Japan. At the beginning of the century, a series of realistic illustrations of women in elegant kimonos and traditional hair styles adorned posters that promoted a variety of products such as beer, tooth powder, dry goods and cosmetics. Most posters pictured a woman from the waist up, looking directly towards the viewer with a slight Mona Lisa smile and light skin, as if she wore a hint of traditional geisha white make-up. They were called beauty pictures because the emphasis was on an attractive Japanese woman and only slight reference was made to an advertised product. The use of the documentary style peaked just before the social and economic upheaval of the Twenties and continued with less emphasis and minor variations until World War II. It reappeared in photographic form after the war and is still popular today.

The content of these posters has its origin in ukiyo-e prints, particularly Utamaro's prints of courtesans and actresses. The images are similar in their honesty of presentation, but there is a major difference – ukiyo-e represented Japan's feudal past. Modern Japanese were trying to put these eighteenth- and nineteenth-century art forms behind them and direct their attention to a new, non-Asian, style of painting technique based on observation and the presentation of everyday life in natural colours as an illusion of three-dimensional form. Chiaroscuro was a new discovery for the Japanese and artists were anxious to apply it to their own native images.

Saburosuke Okada, *Portrait of a Lady*, 1907, with copy and their monsho added by the Mitsukoshi Department Store (760 x 600 mm). The original oil painting, now at the Bridgestone Museum of Art in Tokyo, was reproduced as a poster by chromolithography to advertise the store's kimonos. The painting shows a pensive lady playing a seventeenth-century drum, an imitation of Western art styles.

Goyo Hashiguchi, poster for Mitsukoshi Department Store, 1907. Making an interesting comparison with the poster by Okada, this image is a more obvious statement of the combination of old and new, West and East. The subject is wearing a very modern kimono, its fashionableness emphasised by the contrast of the illustrations in the old book of kimono open on her lap. The poster was printed by a new chromolithography process, requiring thirty-five separate runs to produce the stunning Art Nouveau colours.

Catalysts for this style of painting were reproductions by European Realists and instructions from European artists who came to Japan to teach. Japanese artists who studied with painters in Europe returned to Japan with a naturalistic way of depicting scenes of modern life. Some early twentieth-century Japanese travellers saw posters illustrated by the French poster designer Jules Cheret, who was infatuated with romantic images of women. Maurice Rickards, in *Posters at the Turn of the Century* (1968), has written that "among the thousand or so posters Cheret produced, it is said that 988 of them featured women. He created the 'Cheret girl' and made her sell everything that came his way." Yet few of Cheret's posters featured women as prominently as did those in Japan. There were other differences between these Japanese figurative images and those produced in France. Where European women, with their fulsome figures, were created in a spirit of self-conscious naughtiness, Japanese women were the essence of quiet dignity and youthful innocence. Instead of ebullience, they expressed oriental serenity.

Since images of women were most important, there was no need to clutter the posters with any information about the client or the product, other than a simple greeting to the viewer. Typography was held at a minimum and, in some cases, almost completely disappeared into the background. Even as American and European posters became more influential – with their concentration on words over images – Japanese posters continued their quiet pictorial emphasis. Kanji characters seemed to take on an illustrative quality that blended with the images, while Roman letterforms set themselves apart on a level separate from the illustration. The popularity of these new images, reproductions of paintings in a Western style, provided visibility for many previously unknown illustrators who would not otherwise have achieved substantial recognition for their efforts.

A leading exponent of romantic beauty pictures was the Mitsukoshi Department Store. As one of the major chains and most active advertisers at the beginning of the century, it established its identity as a style leader through these posters. It was the first, for example, to reproduce non-Asian style oil paintings of young women painted by Saburosuke Okada (1896-1939), a professor at Tokyo Art School. To discover additional new artists Mitsukoshi held a competition in 1911 to find the best beauty picture, announcing that the prize-winning painting would be printed as one of its posters. The

response was unprecedented, with over three hundred entries received; the first prize went to Goyo Hashiguchi (1880-1921). Such posters inspired other firms and department stores to match the elegance and colour expressed in beauty pictures through the technical possibilities of the chromolithography process.

The Art Nouveau qualities shown in Hashiguchi's posters had come full circle and returned to the country of origin. Japanese illustrators who painted in this flat, decorative style were providing an Eastern version of a popular European illustrative style whose forms had originated in Japanese woodblock prints, kimonos, fans and blue-and-white china. Unfortunately, when the Japanese attempted to copy the Art Nouveau styles, they referred to European surface elements and not to the original Japanese motifs, but, ironically, the woman in one Hashiguchi poster is looking at a picture book of ukiyo-e prints (see page 37).

The era of the beauty pictures continued through the Twenties. As various American and European design movements and advertising techniques influenced Japanese graphic design, the impact of these posters depicting beautiful women diminished. Popularity for bijin-ga was not universal. Some critics felt Japanese artists were too provincial in their imagery and lacked the modern enthusiasm for the abstract found in foreign-produced posters. Even today the reaction is mixed. In looking back to those posters, museum director Masataka Ogawa stated in an article in 1967, "A Memorandum of One Hundred Years of Posters", that this romantic, pictorial style was produced in the golden years of Japanese poster history, but because of its popularity, it "delayed a more complete development of Japanese graphic design." Twenty years later, when Japan is rushing into the twenty-first century, those wonderful serene images are refreshing memories of a peaceful period in Japan's society.

The Romantic Taisho Era, 1912-1926

Emperor Meiji's death in 1912 came at a time when Japan was in the middle of a political and military expansion that established foreign allies and enemies. His third son, Yoshihito, succeeded as emperor in July 1912 and called his reign Taisho, meaning "Great Justice." Unlike his politically active father, his limited involvement resulted in a reduction in the status of the emperor to little more than a symbolic ruler. Early in his tenure, Emperor Yoshihito suffered from debilitating mental

Facing page, top left: Hajime Okita, newspaper advertisement for Club cosmetics, 1920 (290 x 210 mm). The regular blocks of type emphasise the illustrated figure in a design that is both simple and very elegant. Both the artwork and the copy promote the idea of more freedom for women. The company conveys modernity with a catchy name written in katakana.

Facing page, top right: Toshira Kataoka, newspaper advertisement for caramels from the Morinaga confectionery company, 1918 (295 x 260 mm). This expressive advertisement uses reversed out type from a handprint said to come from a popular sumo wrestler of the time. Kataoka worked for the advertising group that eventually became Dentsu.

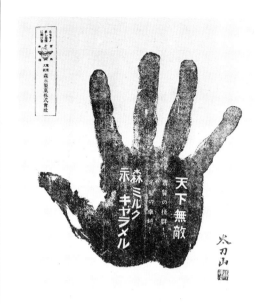

Newspaper advertisement for a cinema programme, 1922 (259 x 360 mm). The large kanji characters give the names of the films, almost all of which are imports from the West, with titles translated from English. Proper names of characters and actors, however, cannot be translated and can be spotted in katakana, including the name "Sherlock Holmes" which appears at the left near the bottom of the advertisement.

Otto Dunkelsbuehler, poster for Calpis soft drinks, 1923. This was the third prize winner (from 1,400 entries) in a competition sponsored by the Calpis Food Industry Company to aid German, French and Italian artists and designers after World War I. The stylized illustration of a blue-eyed black man dressed like a vaudeville character showed the influence of Modernism, and reflected the company's philosophy of "Health and Communication" in its depiction of an active, healthy black person. Calpis discontinued the image as its brandmark in 1989 as a response to complaints that the caricature was racially discriminatory.

and physical illnesses and lived in seclusion to the end of his short reign. His eldest son, Hirohito, appointed regent in 1921, succeeded his father in December 1926 to become the 124th emperor of Japan. He reigned for 63 years, calling his reign Showa, or "Enlightened Peace."

Within two years of the start of Taisho, Europe had entered World War I, followed by America. This had little effect on Japan, other than a short-term stimulation of the economy with the demand for consumer goods for those involved in the war. More important to Japan's future were the repercussions produced by the Great Kanto Earthquake on 1 September 1923. This massive eruption and the resulting fires destroyed half of Tokyo and almost all of Yokohama. The fires and tremors lasted for three days, creating a horrendous disaster that at the same time proved to be a uniquely advantageous event for Japan. The improved economic conditions and high productivity of the Twenties gave people an opportunity to build over the destruction with modern, Western-style buildings, thereby burying a feudal past with the latest international architectural design. It was Japan's chance to show the world that Tokyo was as modern as London, Paris or New York.

Importation of automatic offset printing presses from the United States in 1914 provided major improvements in the appearance of Japan's graphic design. Advertisements that appeared in newspapers during this time were unable to match the illustrative energy of posters because of limited letterpress printing technology. Generally they were uninspired typographic solutions with some small graphic images. A few hold interest for their decorative social content more than for their inventive design quality.

As Japan began to expand into the international market, one major company decided that it could provide a more international look for its products if it hired a foreign designer. Calpis, a leading Japanese food company, held a contest in Germany to find a designer to produce an advertisement poster for its soft drink. This was the first time a Japanese client paid for a design by a foreign artist. The poster, designed in 1923 by Otto Dunkelsbuehler, has become a classic in Japanese design history, and was reproduced in newspaper advertisements and neon signs for sixty years (see page 39).

The Taisho era was noted for changes in social fashions and modes of living, particularly for women, who became economically independent as secretaries and office workers.

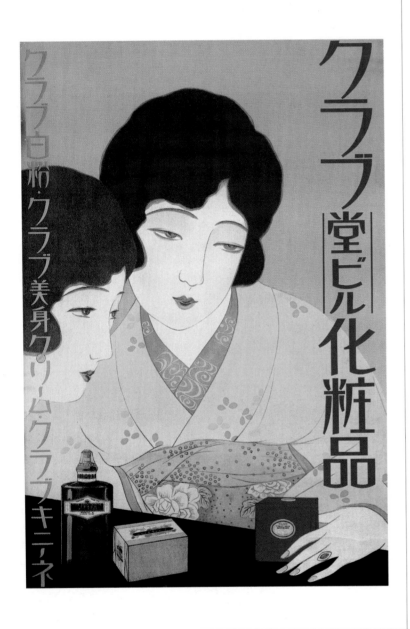

Poster advertising a range of Club cosmetics, artist unknown, 1920 (778 x 520 mm). Traditional ukiyo-e flat composition is blended here with modern, stylized figures, the mixture of old and new being further enhanced by the use of both kanji and katakana characters. Interestingly, the company's name is written only in Japanese on the poster, but the boxes and bottle containing the cosmetics proclaim it in English.

Top: newspaper advertisement for
skin-care products, 1909 (60 x 163
mm). The man in his Western fedora
eyes the shyly smiling kimono-clad
woman in an effective blend of old
and new. The typography blends
bold and light faces, large and small,
kanji and hiragana.

Tsunetomi Kitano, poster advertising
kimono fabric, 1927 (1101 x 605
mm). Unlike many of his
contemporaries, Kitano continued in
the traditional Japanese style of
bijin-ga into the late Twenties,
showing his customary richness of
imagery and style and careful
attention to detail.

Poster promoting confectionery,
artist unknown, 1922 (1060 x 375
mm). Illustrated with bijin-ga realism,
this poster shows a half-Western
woman, with a wholly Western
hairstyle, enjoying a new type of
candy which, though made in Japan,
is packaged in the Western style.

It was also the time when Japanese people became the greatest newspaper-reading public in the world. They had more leisure time for sports and books; there was time to organize symphony orchestras to play Western classical music, and young people became interested in jazz, café life and materialism. This life style was very much like that of the 1980s teenager, with its emphasis on youth, affluence and the good life; it made a major contribution to changes in the appearance of contemporary Japanese graphic design.

Life styles and social attitudes in the Twenties can be traced in images used in posters. Japanese design imagery remained passive, while European and American graphic design depicted a fast-paced culture enamoured of the speed of automobiles, boats and aeroplanes. Japanese posters continued to concentrate on the simple conveniences that made life pleasurable – candy, beer, soft drinks, cosmetics, medicines, exhibitions and movies. Designers who became well known during this time had their training in beauty pictures, but gained popularity when they developed a more modern image. Three early romantic designer-illustrators who are identified with the Taisho era are Hisui Sugiura, Hokuu Tada and Yumeji Takehisa. Although they also concentrated on the painted images of beautiful women, these designers experimented with design, type and the stylized figure.

Hisui Sugiura

One of the most inventive and talented designer-illustrators was Hisui Sugiura (1876-1965), who worked for the Mitsukoshi Department Store in 1914. Among his achievements was a series of elegant posters whose quality was facilitated by the advent of four-colour offset printing. Sugiura quickly moved beyond the characteristic beauty picture to be the most prolific designer in the first half of the twentieth century, clearly one of the leaders of the early Japanese designers. His illustrations, always created over precise drawings, matured from realistic paintings, through intricate Art Nouveau details and work reminiscent of Matisse, to more experimental forms in the Thirties that were influenced by the Cubists and early Bauhaus artists. He used typography as an integral part of composition, initially as a secondary element in his early posters and later as an element equal to the figure. This change in emphasis must have been influenced by European designers whose work Sugiura would have seen in Tokyo exhibitions.

Top: Tsunetomi Kitano, poster promoting an export trade fair at Kobe, 1911 (775 x 530 mm). With the beautiful port of Kobe in the background, Kitano depicts a Japanese woman in Western Art Nouveau style.

Above: Tsunetomi Kitano, poster promoting tooth powder, 1910 (940 x 635 mm). A recognized painter, Kitano (1880-1947) directed his energy to producing bijin-ga for twenty years. He painted women realistically in traditional kimono with great style and elegance - in this example, the subject is wearing a nightwear kimono, indicating that she has just got up.

Toshiro Kataoka (art director) and Mokuda Inoue (designer), poster promoting Suntory port wine, 1922 (820 x 580 mm); photograph by Kawaguchi Photo Studio. This was the first Japanese poster to be made using photogravure, and also the first ever to show a nude; it won first prize at the World Poster Contest in Germany.

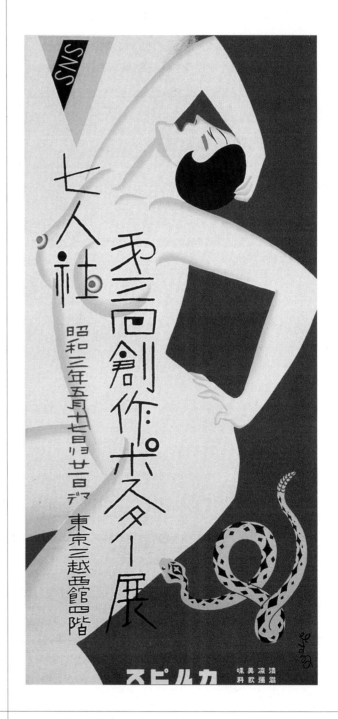

Hisui Sugiura, magazine advertisement for an exhibition of posters and other graphic design, 1927 (600 x 220 mm). As Sugiura became influenced by European artists he began to emphasise design over illustration. His women changed from realistic paintings to more stylized studies: this free-spirited woman is not the typical shy Asian seen in his earlier work.

Hisui Sugiura, poster advertising a poster exhibition at Mitsukoshi Department Store Art Gallery, 1928 (770 x 350 mm). The shape of the rectangle is carefully composed to accentuate the figure and the typography.

Hisui Sugiura, poster for a department store advertising a new subway line, 1927 (1060 x 770 mm). Sugiura clearly shows the influence of Western graphic design, particularly the style of transport posters developed by the London Underground (he had travelled in Europe during 1926). The scene is drawn in striking European perspective, and could come from almost any modern city of the Twenties, except for the two women dressed in kimono. This poster was reproduced for the fiftieth anniversary of the Ginza Subway.

Midway in his career, in 1926, Sugiura organized Tokyo designers into a group entitled Shichinin sha, or "Seven People's Club." Sugiura had just returned from a European trip and he brought news of similar groups there. He felt it would provide recognition for professional artists and introduced the idea of an organization of commercial artists; one offshoot was the publication of a magazine entitled *Official*. Sugiura continued to be a leading figure in design for forty years. Always interested in organizations, in 1952 he set up the Tokyo Commercial Artists Association, with Hideyuki Oka and others. In 1980, it was renamed the Tokyo Graphic Design Club, or TGDC.

By 1927 he had organized and published *Affiches*, a research magazine on posters which gave recognition to international and leading Japanese designers. This publication is credited with providing national recognition for commercial artists. Sugiura finished his years teaching new generations of designers at the Imperial School of Art and Tama Imperial University of Fine Arts; his students bestowed on him the title "Founder of Commercial Art."

Hokuu Tada

Another designer-illustrator who continued the production of beauty pictures throughout the Twenties and Thirties was Hokuu Tada (1889-1948), who is best known for his softly edged paintings of romantic looking young women. Born in Nagoya, Tada quickly became known for his exceptional drafting skills. At first he depicted women in traditional kimono; later, during the Twenties, a few were shown in modern clothes. They were illustrated holding candy, cookies and sometimes a glass of beer. A unique identifying style for Tada was his extremely short depth of field and a wonderful play with shadows in the close background.

As Tada's beauty pictures evolved into the socially active and more liberated Twenties, they pictured women with more animation and open smiles who were very cosmopolitan in appearance. Women were still the primary interest; modern conveniences – electric fans, magazines, bicycle tyres – seemed to enter the posters as if they were afterthoughts. Tada shared Hisui Sugiura's interest in promoting the design profession through active participation in commercial art organizations.

Hokuu Tada, poster advertising the opening of a renovated branch of the Mitsukoshi Department Store, 1935. The elegant interior has clearly been redesigned in the most up-to-date style of the mid- Thirties. Red and gold - the traditional colours for gift wrapping - predominate, and the red carpet is a further expression of formality.

Hokuu Tada, poster for Kirin beer, 1917 (890 x 590 mm). A master of composition and draftsmanship, Hokuu Tada painted many bijin-ga posters. The animated features of the subject, such as her slightly open mouth, is a signature of his work.

Hokuu Tada, magazine advertisement for skin-care products, 1931 (210 x 148 mm). It shows the artist's preference for a closely cropped background, enhanced in this case by a dominant shadow around the figure, stylishly dressed in Western clothes. The advertisement appeared during the period of Japan's worst depression of modern times.

Hokuu Tada, poster for Kirin beer, 1937. The modern style of the composition, with its unusually plain, dark foreground, is enhanced by the very modern concept, which would at this time have been unfamiliar to Japanese, of men and women socializing together. Kirin was one of the new companies in the early years of the twentieth century to emphasise their modern outlook by inventing a brand name that was not the family name of the proprietor, and proclaiming it in the new katakana characters.

Yumeji Takehisa, poster advertising an exhibition of his own work, 1918 (580 x 270 mm). Takehisa was responsible for the quintessential "Taisho" look, featuring romantic young women dressed in traditional Japanese style.

Yumeji Takehisa

No other artist is identified so closely with the Taisho look than Yumeji Takehisa (1884-1934). His work is characterized by carefully crafted illustrations of women dressed in modern kimono that were stylish during the Twenties and Thirties. He used strong blacks, simplified compositions and lively colours in combinations that recall the finest tradition of ukiyo-e artists during their prime in the nineteenth century.

Takehisa's illustrations did not have the overworked, painted quality of his contemporaries' work. He also seemed to place himself in an era untouched by industrial change and political upheaval, in depicting women and children engaged in everyday, almost rural, activity. Most of his paintings and prints have a fresh, direct approach that is natural for his favourite media – sumi-e (ink drawings) and woodblock prints. Art Nouveau stylizations were completely ignored in favour of simple, naturalistic drawings rendered in soft colours, such as pinks, reds and light blues, contrasted by rich greys and blacks.

Born in the southern part of Japan, Takehisa had no formal art training. Early in his career he was encouraged by the painter Saburosuke Okada who regarded him as a genius. Takehisa moved to Tokyo where he designed and illustrated numerous children's books, book covers, sheet music covers, posters and other promotional material. During his most productive years in the Twenties he rarely illustrated people in modern apparel, with the exception of the sandy-haired boys and girls in European landscapes pictured in his children's books.

Shiseido Sets the Style

The romantic images of Sugiura, Tada and Takehisa were reinforced by an extensive advertising campaign by a cosmetics firm that was established in 1872 as a medicine company. Very few corporations have had as much influence on international graphic design as Shiseido. Early in its history Shiseido decided to reject any provincial appearance and before 1900 it had adopted the foreign style in illustrations for its products – soap, cosmetics, perfume and toiletries. By 1910 its publicity and packaging design were purposely directed to appear European. Recognizing the need for a professional approach to visual communication, in 1916 Shiseido formed a full-time, three-person design staff to create packaging design, newspaper and magazine advertisements and window displays. One identifying feature was the use of illustration

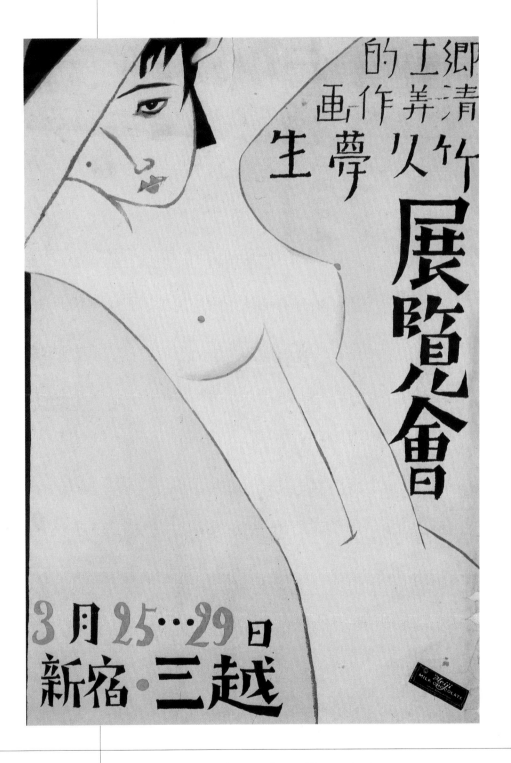

Yumeji Takehisa, sheet music cover for the song "Evening Primrose," 1928 (305 x 230 mm). As well as his many posters, Takehisa was known for decorative book and sheet music covers and film advertisements, all in a distinctive romantic style which brought him considerable recognition, especially from young women.

Yumeji Takehisa, poster for an exhibition of his own drawings, 1931 (550 x 380 mm). Towards the end of his career, Takehisa's approach became more stylized, although he retained the romantic look. As is customary, this exhibition, presented by Mitsukoshi, had a sponsor. The traditional place for the sponsor's name on a poster is at the bottom right; instead of the name Meiji, the artist has used a strategically placed image of a Meiji chocolate wrapper, probably just large enough to satisfy an alert censor.

SHISEIDO

Shinzo Fukuhara, trademarks for
Shiseido, 1915; revised by Ayao
Yamana in 1974. Fukuhara was the
company's first president; his
monsho-like drawing of two flowers
and sans serif trade name with the
stretched "s" have remained in use,
only slightly amended, to this day.

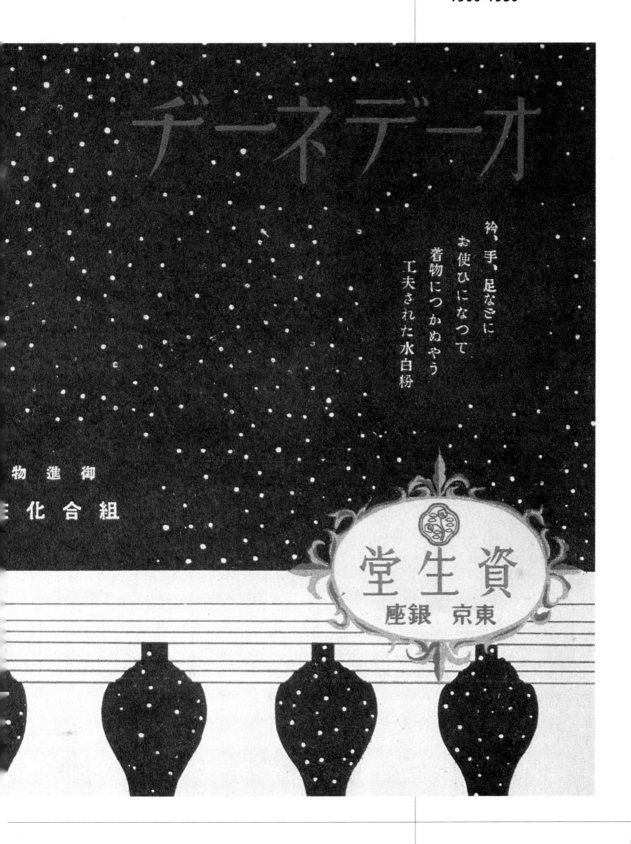

Reika Sawa, poster for Shiseido
cosmetics, 1926 (174 x 248 mm).
Typically late Twenties in style, with
its elongated figures and flat,
decorative design, the poster
matches the elegance of the fashion
and the setting with the lushness of
the design. The red katakana
characters read, in French, "eau de
neige," snow-water.

instead of photography in posters and publicity until shortly after World War II. Shiseido's influence is most evident in its portrayal of women. Illustrations were obviously of European women with soft blonde or auburn hair, blue eyes and sharp noses. Images of non-Asian women dominated Shiseido's publicity before World War II and from 1946 until the late Sixties. From that period, first mixed Eurasians, and later Japanese models had almost exclusive domain.

Shinzo Fukuhara, the first president of the company who was credited as being Shiseido's first art director, gathered many talented young artists around him to design publicity. In 1929 he invited Ayao Yamana to join the company, and he became the designer most identified with Shiseido up to the late Fifties, establishing what is now called "the Shiseido Style." It was his ambition to match the national recognition given to Hisui Sugiura.

Ayao Yamana

Ayao Yamana (1897-1980), was born in Hiroshima Prefecture, and studied European painting and Bauhaus typographic theories at school. His first major position was with Nihon Kobo, a publisher of an English-language magazine used to promote Japanese culture. His tenure there was short and he was hired by Shiseido in 1929 where he stayed for four years, before returning to Nihon Kobo for three more years. By 1936 he was back at Shiseido and from then until 1943 produced for them what is acknowledged to be his best work.

Yamana is noted by his Japanese colleagues for his delicate, elegant, Beardsley-type illustrations. He said that he was an early fan of Aubrey Beardsley and always felt that his death one year after Yamana's birth created a special tie between them. Comparison shows that Beardsley's erotic grotesquerie makes a great contrast with Yamana's romantic innocence. While Beardsley despised society and depicted it as more than slightly sinister, Yamana wanted to show the beauty of women, with delicate features that epitomized a rational, good-natured human race. His newspaper advertisements show him at his best in line drawings. Most picture only the woman's face, either full front or side view, handled as a flat design. Other drawings have elongated figures that some say are in the Beardsley style, but Yamana's delicate lines describe a feminine beauty rarely seen in Beardsley.

When World War II was at its height, Yamana left Shiseido and designed a series of propaganda posters for the Ministry

Top: Takeo Yamamoto, corporate image promotion poster for Shiseido, 1938 (665 x 520 mm). Yamamoto, born in 1910, was closely associated with Shiseido in the Thirties and Forties, when he helped to shape the company's image. He shared Yamana's approach, but differed in his preference for Western subjects, usually softly modelled and painted in full colour with a modern effect; the women were usually depicted as inanimate store mannequins. In 1964 he designed a package for "Zen" perfume using a flower motif dating back to the rimpa artists (see page 67).

Ayao Yamana, cover of *Nippon* magazine, 1932. This popular international magazine was founded by the photographer Yonosuke Natori, who had studied art in Germany and brought Bauhaus principles of design to Japan as well as new forms of photography. Yamana designed several of the early issues.

of Finance and other governmental agencies, in his typically clear graphic style which was dominated by typography. Following the war he rejoined Shiseido in 1948, staying until his retirement ten years later. Yamana continued his involvement in graphic design on a limited basis, sometimes brought in as a consultant for Shiseido, until his death in 1980.

Modern Design Comes to Japan, 1926-1940

It must have been quite an experience for Japanese designers to travel abroad during the first half of the twentieth century. After visiting culturally active countries, they recognized the need to share their experiences with fellow professionals at home. Travellers to Europe and America returned with copies of current posters and illustrations, observations of the latest professional developments and, if they were lucky, examples of pedagogy from some of the leading educational institutions. The free and easy flow of design exchange between Europe and America had difficulty reaching Japan. First there was the factor of distance from Japan to the West, and then there were formidable language problems for most Japanese. Ideas could easily cross borders in Europe and into America, crystallizing unique concepts into international trends. After the De Stijl movement took root in The Netherlands, Bauhaus in Germany and Constructivism in Russia, there was a ten-year lag before any of them reached Japan.

It was not unusual for modern movements from Europe, such as Art Nouveau, Vienna Secession and, to a greater extent, Bauhaus, to be absorbed by Japanese designers and illustrators, providing considerable influence on their images. However, at the time they were introduced, Japan was not fully developed nor ready for them, so the movements failed to flourish. Generally, Japanese solutions reflected more attention to technique than concept, and somehow they lacked the commitment found in many European ideas.

In an attempt to facilitate modern influences, several organizations introduced American and European designs in Japan. In 1921, Asahi and Mainichi newspapers promoted an exhibition of World War I military posters. Five years later, the Mitsukoshi Department Store held its first exhibition of posters, an annual event that continued for the next decade. These exhibitions brought national attention to the new poster medium, prompting the end of the Japanese word ekanban and adoption of the English word poster. Another, more comprehensive, poster exhibition was held in 1927. It repre-

Ayao Yamana, advertisement for Shiseido cold cream, 1936. Yamana is said to have been strongly influenced by the graphic art of Aubrey Beardsley, but his style is softer and much more romantic. The Shiseido monsho is positioned on the bodice of the blonde, Western figure's dress.

sented a collection by Yukio Koriyama, which he gathered on a trip made through the United States and several European countries – England, Germany, France, Italy, Austria and Switzerland. The posters included those produced from the workshops held at the Bauhaus. Additional attention to European and American graphic design, interior design, signs, photographs, magazine design and shop windows was shown in the twenty-four volume publication, *The Complete Works on Modern Commercial Arts*, edited by Hisui Sugiura and five others, and printed between 1928 and 1930.

At the time of this interest in international graphic design, a special genre of newspaper advertising originated to promote two new social and technical innovations – weekly magazines and movies. These advertisements were packed with bold headlines and small body copy, a profusion of superlatives that crowded out all white space. Information could be read in traditional Japanese style (top to bottom, right to left) and Western style (left to right) for occasional English words. Later in the Thirties, these designs would include little illustrations and photographs tucked into corners. Headlines printed in kanji characters were specifically drawn to fit the space, some overlapping others to provide maximum use of the area. The overall effect was very much like nineteenth-century circus publicity or American supermarket advertisements produced after the Fifties. This jumbled, excited style of design to advertise magazines was renewed in Japan after World War II and now thrives in nakazuri, transport posters. Attention to letterforms signalled a new emphasis on Japanese typography.

Typography and the Printed Page

The influence of European typographical images based on the Bauhaus principles taught by Herbert Bayer and Joost Schmidt, and American emphasis on letterforms in the Twenties, promoted further improvements in Japanese typesetting capabilities. Typesetting originated in Japan during the Meiji Restoration when modern equipment was imported from Europe and America, and very quickly all magazines and newspapers were typeset. Even with over four thousand separate characters in the Japanese language, typesetting by hand was relatively simple. In setting the Chinese characters, which are designed to fit tightly within a square of space, there is no need to add spacers or worry about kerning (the spacing between characters). A body of Japanese copy does

日本の文字を美しく伝えてゆく

日本の文字を美しく伝えてゆく。最近でこそ活字や写植用の書体デザインがさまざまな形で紹介されることがあるが、それでも依然として印刷文字の楽屋は裏方であり一般に知られることは少ないのである。たまたま書体制作の現場を見学した人たちの持つ感想の第一は、同

日本の文字を美しく伝えてゆく

日本の文字を美しく伝えてゆく。最近でこそ活字や写植用の書体デザインがさまざまな形で紹介されることがあるが、それでも依然として印刷文字の楽屋は裏方であり一般に知られることは少ないのである。たまたま書体制作の現場を見学した人たちの持つ感想の第一は、同

Top: mincho (top) and goshikku, the two most popular type forms. Mincho expresses the original brush forms of Japanese calligraphy, while goshikku was developed to provide a more modern appearance. These samples show kanji, hiragana and katakana characters.

Above: press advertisement for a popular women's magazine, designer unknown, 1935 (505 x 385 mm). Advertisements such as this were routinely filled with typography and small photographs to illustrate different features or stories; the busy, crowded style survives today in nakazuri posters (see page 132).

not have any word spacing and only a few punctuation marks. When hiragana and katakana characters are run together they can be difficult to read because the end of one word runs into the beginning of the next; by adding the more complicated kanji letterforms, the number of characters is reduced and communication is improved. By 1915 a Japanese language typewriter was invented and four years later a mono-typesetter was developed.

The first type style, called mincho, was derived from the ancient kanji characters, duplicating their calligraphic thick and thin brush characteristics. It is equivalent to the European typefaces with serifs called "roman." Like our standard typeface, mincho became the basic typeface and is still used in most Japanese publications. Its original form has been altered to produce a variety of families such as bold, italic, outline, condensed, shaded and almost as many other variations as found in roman type. As an alternative to the classical character mincho, a new face that corresponds to modern sans serif was developed in Osaka in 1916. Called goshikku, a name derived from "gothic," it also has many varieties.

By 1929 the first Japanese typesetting machine was invented and major improvements were made in 1935 for its expanded use. The major technological change in 1960 was the development of the first photosetter by Morisawa Typesetting Company. An operator had access to 2,304 characters and could set 300 characters a minute. Called shashoku, phototype has its own system of size designation that is different from hot type or katsuji.

Designing text with Japan's four distinct letterforms is one problem for the graphic designer. Another is deciding the direction in which it should be read. Originally the three Japanese scripts were written vertically in columns arranged from right to left, a form that continued up to the Meiji Restoration in the late nineteenth century. This writing problem was explained by the late design critic, Masaru Katzumie, in *Japan Style* (1980):

Probably the first attempts at writing pure Japanese horizontally were inspired by the notes taken by Japanese learning English or French or by bank and company ledgers that made use of Arabic numerals. But even when a decision has been made to write Japanese horizontally, there remains another choice – whether to write from right to left or from left to right. Traditionally, when large signs (for

example, the framed notices put up at the entrances to Buddhist temples) were written horizontally, they were written from right to left. To begin with, placards and street signs followed the same practice, but inconsistencies occurred when Roman and Japanese script were used together – for instance, in signs giving the names of railroad stations – since the Japanese read from right to left and the Roman script from left to right; such inconsistencies often give rise to argument and debate.

By the Twenties typesetters were asked to set type horizontally, but with no consistency in direction. In 1928 the *Yomiuri Shimbun*, a major Tokyo newspaper, recognized this problem and how it affected readers. Its solution was to hold a competition for the best design of an advertisement that used left to right writing. Inconsistencies continued, however, until soon after World War II when the government, with American influence, adopted a rule that horizontal writing should read from left to right.

This problem also affects the pagination of books and magazines. Should the publication open from right to left, Western style, or left to right, traditional Japanese style? Modern Japanese magazines use both forms. The decision on which one to use seems almost quixotic, with those magazines that have a modern content usually opening Western style, and those that are older, with traditional content, opening Japanese style. Generally, inside pages of Japanese-style binding have copy printed in both Western and Japanese style, with no apparent confusion for the reader.

Katzumie emphasized one distinct design advantage of the Japanese writing system: "Japanese script is usually arranged in a grid layout, which takes the uniformly square shape of the Chinese-derived kanji as its basic unit. This layout permits free interchange between vertical and horizontal writing. It is not possible at present to be certain if this will prove to be much of an advantage in the long run: but, for the time being, the acceptance of a mixed writing system has a powerful effect on our modern culture in general."

Today, modern Japanese designers are not sure whether there is a design advantage to the Japanese language and feel frustrated with the complexity and variety of the scripts. As recently as 1985, art director Susume Sakane wrote in *Graphic Design in Japan, 4*: "Japanese design and ads have been handicapped by their reliance on the Japanese language."

This philosophy accounts for the frequent use of English on posters, flyers and packaging, not because the product is exported, but in order that the company will appear less provincial in its design to Japanese consumers.

Bauhaus Influence

Of all the foreign design theories that influenced Japan, the teaching theories of the Bauhaus workshops had the greatest impact. Japanese readily joined the movement of German artists who believed that they could work for industry without personal or creative compromise to make what was called commercial art a respectable profession. In addition to this philosophy, Japanese designers adopted the emphasis on typography as a major design element rather than as information that was secondary to the illustration. Several Japanese posters produced in the early Thirties show the influence of typographic experiments by European graphic designers such as Herbert Bayer and Jan Tschichold.

Bauhaus concepts developed in Weimar and Dessau were brought back by Japanese travellers primarily in the form of posters and other printed material, as well as books that were later translated. They were first introduced to Japan by Sadanosuke Nakada in a 1925 article for *Mizue* art magazine. Japanese art schools specializing in commercial art courses were aggressive in assigning Bauhaus problems and objectives to their classes. By the mid-Thirties the most influential schools, such as Tokyo Industrial School, Kyoto Industrial School and Tokyo Geijutsu, had projects that came from various Bauhaus workshops.

A pinion in the mechanism for the new visual communication developed during the Bauhaus years was the acknowledgement of two new images. Described by Mildred Friedman in *The 20th Century Poster* (1984), "[the] first was toward pictorial modernism in which widely recognized images became the means of communicating with a diverse audience from all walks of life...The other direction was toward abstraction, and led to the design of easily recognizable visual symbols that conveyed political and social messages." Two Japanese designers who expressed Friedman's ideas began their careers early in the Thirties while the romantic image was still the dominant motif in posters. Takashi Kono and Hiromu Hara both had a European vision of design, with Kono stressing "pictorial modernism" and Hara leaning towards abstraction.

Takashi Kono
Building on the transition from illustrative solutions to a modernist approach, as defined by Hisui Sugiura, the next most important designer in Japan's history is Takashi Kono. He is recognized as one who began his career by moving against the painterly approach taken by most Japanese who were popular in the Thirties. He established himself first as an exceptionally creative designer, and emphasized composition and typography rather than illustration. His medium in the early Thirties was the movie poster, a modern Western import that provided complete latitude for contemporary imagery. The job also presented him with an opportunity to create an international look through design and illustrated European faces.

Born in Tokyo in 1906, he studied craft and illustration from Edo artisans and finished his design course at Tokyo Art School. After graduation he joined Shochiku Cinema Company to take charge of newspaper advertisements, posters and stage settings. From 1929 to the early Thirties he produced posters that reflect considerable influence from German designers with their well composed type, graphic images and inventive use of colour.

During the mid-Thirties, Kono met Yonosuke Natori who had worked as a news cameraman for the German newspaper *Ullstein*. They cooperated in editing and designing the Japanese cultural magazine *Nippon*, published by Nihon Kobo, a company Natori created for overseas publicity. The magazine used striking photographs by Japanese photographer Ken Domon to create a European-style publication.

In 1943 Kono was honoured with a one-man exhibition of his poster designs held in the Ginza of Tokyo. Unfortunately, he was unable to see the opening because he was drafted into World War II and served until 1947 as a member of the press corps stationed in Djakarta. After the war, he became art director for *New Japan*, published by the Mainichi newspaper. He provided leadership in the formation of the Japan Advertising Artists Club and the Japan Design Committee, and participated in the World Design Conference and the various Olympic Games Design Committees. He served as President of Aichi Prefecture University of Arts until 1989.

Takashi Kono, poster advertising a Japanese film, *Lady and Beard*, directed by Yasujiro Ozu, 1931 (1060 x 730 mm). The European faces are drawn bold and flat in the style of Picasso. Many later graphic designers - notably Tadanori Yokoo, Ikko Tanaka and Tadashi Ohashi - regard this poster as having a critical influence on their own development.

督監郎二安津小・作原松小村北

子弘﨑川・彦時田岡

共演　子蝶田飯・雄達藤齊
　　　子里達伊・郎一田月

叔と髪曲女影

Koh.

Hiromu Hara

A year older than Kono, Hiromu Hara (1905-1985) approached graphic design with a better grasp of abstract imagery. Hara was one of the first Japanese designers to understand European theoretical qualities and use them in his posters. He dismissed romantic imagery in his work and rarely used illustration or any decorative elements. Born in Nagano Prefecture in the central highlands of Japan, he went to Tokyo to study at the Tokyo Technological School and graduated in 1921. Typically, his designs gave equal weight to typography and photographs, following the finest tradition of Bauhaus teaching. His work is considered to be in the mainstream of Japanese graphic design, neither flamboyant nor inventive in concept, but well crafted in the International Style.

Especially known for his publications design, Hara received early training in 1938 when he joined *Nippon* magazine as its art director; he stayed there throughout the war and at the same time served as art director for *Front* magazine. He designed several of the first issues of *Graphic Design* magazine and continued to be associated with it for several years. He was also art director for *New Japan* and *Taiyo* magazines in the 1960s. When he designed books, he involved himself with the total process, including the selection of paper colour and quality, type style, method of printing and final binding.

There are several reasons for Hara and a few of his contemporaries to subscribe to the Bauhaus theories on photography in graphic design. Photographs lack the romantic overtones often found in illustration. They are authentic and more immediately recognized for their iconographic images. The photomontages of Moholy-Nagy, Gyorgy Kepes and Herbert Bayer, with their juxtapositions of narrative content, influenced a few Japanese designers. Herbert Bayer wrote: "the photo was not much used as a squared conventional image but was cut out and treated to bring forth the essentials."

Hara became one of the foremost leaders of Japanese design, a designation that continued for 25 years. His role as founder and long-time president of Nippon Design Center and his leadership of many national and international groups give testament to his exceptional organizational skills. A quiet and unpretentious personality, he played down his role as an intelligent and effective leader who commanded respect from all who knew him. He received many awards and honours, the finest being the Japanese Government Purple Ribbon Award in 1971.

Hiromu Hara, poster for a government-sponsored exhibition of photographs taken in Manchuria, then a Japanese colony, 1938 (790 x 550 mm). Hara arranged the exhibition, which displayed the work of two famous press photographers, Yoshio Watanabe and Ihei Kimura. Leicas, then the most valued cameras, were used for all the photographs.

Hiromu Hara, poster for an exhibition of mannequins made by Shimadzu held at a Sapporo hotel, 1935 (462 x 388 mm). Hara was one of the first leading Japanese designers to concentrate on photography in graphic images. The photomontage and sans serif lower case type follow Herbert Bayer's teaching at the Bauhaus.

島津マネキン新作品展覧會
5月5・6日 於・札幌駅前グランドホテル2階大宴會場

Exhibition of
Mannequins Shimadzu

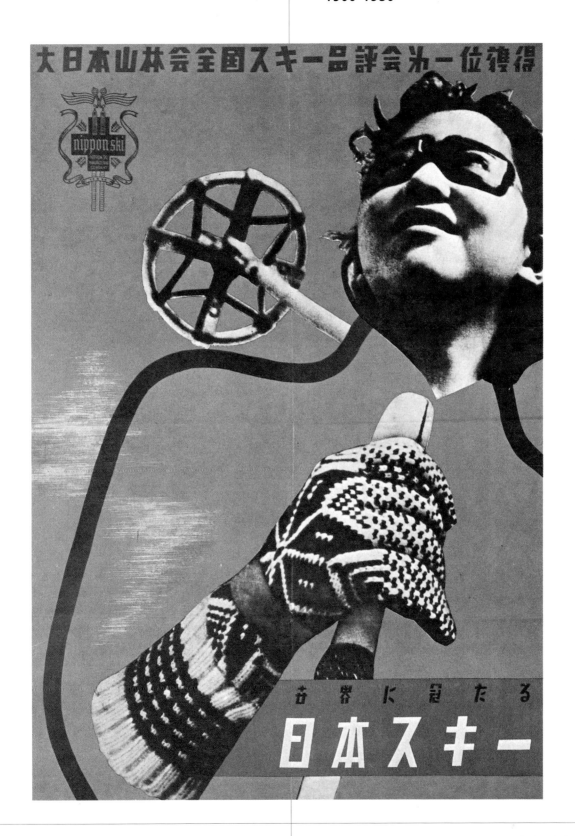

Gihachiro Okuyama, poster for Nikke clothing, 1936 (752 x 532 mm). Okuyama (1907-1981) combined the flat, simple shapes of the Edo woodblock artist with the spirit of German Expressionism; his work shows an affinity with that of the artist George Grosz. He produced a remarkable series of posters for Nikke clothing and for Nikka brandy, with block-like typography or hand-drawn calligraphy perfectly matching the forceful quality of his figures, which could be either European or Asian.

Kinkichi Takahisi, poster for ski clothing, 1939. Takahisa (born in 1911) followed the trend in the Thirties in using photomontage, here emphasising the blue sky by cutting out the figure and restricting the type to the edges of the frame.

The War Years

During the late Thirties, before the full war effort, these early professional commercial artists were called, in Japanese, zuan-ka – a difficult word to translate, but roughly meaning "those involved in the craft of design." It was not surprising that young artists at that time did not like the word zuan-ka: it looked strange, and sounded too provincial and old-fashioned. Students who graduated in the late Thirties from universities with European-style commercial art programmes looked for a more modern word. But their efforts were side-tracked in 1941 with the beginning of World War II when a spirit of nationalism enveloped the country and a ban was imposed on the use of all English words.

With the frenzy of war restrictions in 1941, there was complete military control over magazines and newspapers. This control remained until after the war, shifting to governmental control until 1950. During the early and successful part of the war, newspapers were filled with advertisements to benefit the military campaign. There was an agreement in the industry that advertising should show restraint in colour and design. Advertisements for cosmetics and pharmaceuticals increased until 1944, when the Japanese suffered their first major defeat at Midway Island. Severe restrictions were imposed until 1945, when a full prohibition of advertisements for merchandise was imposed. To help the war effort, a tax was placed on advertisements in 1942.

Several designers were active during the war producing propaganda to promote national interests. Tadashi Ohashi recalls working with Ayao Yamana, Hiromu Hara and Seiichiro Arai on special design projects that had an unofficial association with the government. Ohashi said this experience of making design decisions with more established designers influenced his future direction to be more modern. Other professionals joined the largest advertising agency, Japan Telegram and News Agency (later renamed Dentsu), and organized a full-scale group of advertising technicians to provide posters and other propaganda for the government.

The catastrophic destruction of Hiroshima and Nagasaki permanently embittered the Japanese about the realities of atomic warfare. The Hiroshima Appeals posters, jointly produced by the Hiroshima International Cultural Foundation and Japan Graphic Designers Association, were started as an annual event in 1983 to focus international attention on peace.

Top: Kiyoshi Hachiya, recruitment poster for the Navy, 1942. This memorable poster was produced when the artist was only 17; he lived for just two more years, and could well have been a war casualty.

Above: press advertisement for an insurance company's savings bonds, 1944 (70 x 55 mm). During the war severe restrictions were placed on press advertisements, which were only allowed if they were very small.

Kumi Sugai, poster promoting an air defence exhibition, 1943 (733 x 513 mm). The crippled American aircraft becomes a bomb as it plummets to earth - a powerful visual statement with effective combination of illustration and type.

決戰防空
博覽會
主催
中部軍司令部
大阪府
兵庫縣
協賛
毎日新聞社
四月十五日
五月廿一日
會場
阪急西宮球場及外園
觀覽無料
第二會場
大阪市主催
市民防衛展
(大阪高島屋)

3

The rush towards international recognition
1950-1960

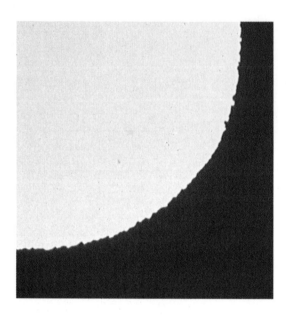

The Japanese people had never experienced invasion by a foreign power or military defeat until World War II. The devastation caused by bombs and complete economic collapse brought severe physical and mental depression as well as a psychological "loss of face." The Japanese expected to be plundered and humiliated by the invading Americans. Instead, the occupation between 1945 and 1952 is said to have been the best prepared and best conducted in the history of warfare. Gen. Douglas MacArthur became the supreme arbiter and an effective ruler in the style of the Tokugawa shoguns. Strict in observation of all formalities in relation to his duties, he was dignified and aloof – precisely the conduct expected and appreciated by the Japanese.

Under American rule, a new constitution was passed in 1946 that took effect in May 1947. It provided coeducation beyond primary school and voting rights for women. During occupation some highly influential professional graphic designers and illustrators were taught that they could be successful at any vocation they desired. Eiko Ishioka and Harumi Yamaguchi are two examples of this new educational policy.

Early in 1946, amid post-war confusion, Japanese designers turned their attention towards the future and established the Japan Advertising Society. Its first exhibition was in 1947. Dentsu Advertising Agency awarded the first Dentsu Prize for advertisements in 1948. During military occupation, design influences from America and Europe were best seen in the Shimbashi section of Tokyo where news-stands would be filled with American magazines, such as *Look, Life* and the *Saturday Evening Post*. Tadashi Ohashi remembers seeing copies of the German design magazine *Gebrauchsgraphics*. Yusaku Kamekura recalls being influenced by the design of the American candy-wrappers he would find on the streets. Encouraged by these non-Asian images, Japanese designers knew it was time to reassert their position in the world.

Most Japanese designers attribute the introduction of the words "graphic designer" as a replacement for zuan-ka to Yusaku Kamekura, who first used them in 1951. Before this time the word "design" had generally been understood to mean fashion design and was not related to commercial art. Kamekura said that after reading about European graphic designers, he decided that that was what he was, and began using these more appropriate words to describe his profession.

Following World War II, it took several years for financial conditions to improve and for the country to turn from a

Tadashi Kono, poster advertising a magazine for those who study the tea ceremony, 1955 (727 x 515 mm). The rich black field contains a symbolic illustration of a white fruit, topped with a stem and a green leaf. Both the illustration and the type have rough edges that may be the result of enlarging a very small original artwork. This was the first Japanese poster selected for inclusion in the permanent collection of the Museum of Modern Art, New York.

dependent economy to one that was more self-sufficient. During this time, when shortage of materials combined with a rush to improve the economy by providing goods for export, Japan failed to meet its own historical standards of quality. The words "Made in Japan" suddenly meant poor quality and shoddy workmanship; cheap goods from Japan seemed to flood the world markets. It was unlike any earlier period of manufacturing. During the 260 years of Edo, when Japanese were isolated from foreign imports, they had a long history of an economy of scarcity. Their material goods, particularly the most utilitarian, had to be produced with the highest standards of workmanship and elegant simplicity of design. It was this aesthetic, whether rooted in Zen Buddhism or inherent in Japanese social mores, that again took over once the psychological and material ravages of World War II had subsided. As the economy improved, quality improved, but it required over ten years to erase the stigma of exported rubbish.

One surprising catalyst for more production was America's involvement in Korea, from 1950 to 1953. This undeclared war hastened Japan's recovery by providing for the purchase of military and other requirements for the United Nations forces. Japan became a convenient location for rest and recreation for American servicemen who needed to travel only a few hours from Korean battlefields. As American occupation in Japan was phased out, the role of the Yanks changed from beneficent occupants to aggressive consumers.

To encourage the demand for products and meet the international challenge for exports, businesses became dependent on graphic designers and art directors. Graphic design production for this chapter in Japan's history was best described by Yusaku Kamekura in a statement at the 1960 World Design Conference held in Tokyo. Kamekura said, "Japanese lack a modern tradition of their own and usually lag a step or two behind their colleagues in America and Europe. But in ten years, we have been exerting an almost superhuman effort to catch up." Kamekura's claim accurately identifies the primary activity of Japanese graphic designers following the war as a compulsive need to reach internationally recognized status equal to that of the United States and Europe. He predicted that "Japan's design is about to reach an international level," and was one hundred per cent correct.

To achieve this goal, Japanese designers had to adopt a comprehensive plan that would raise the level of design consciousness and acceptance from major Japanese corporations and the general public and, at the same time, organize themselves to improve design production. The culmination of the decade would be the organization of a world design conference to attract international attention to Japan. It is not known if such a plan existed, but this was exactly what they did. If there was a plan, one person would have received much of the credit – a former designer and active "design critic" who had a major influence on the future of design in Japan and the world. No other person has had such a grasp of global design activity and was as dedicated to the improvement of design as Masaru Katzumie.

Masaru Katzumie

Masaru Katzumie was the benevolent tsar of Japan's designers. Born in Tokyo in 1909, he attended the most important university in Japan, Tokyo Imperial University, receiving a Master of Arts degree in Aesthetics and Art History. After graduation he taught at Yokohama College of Social Sciences until 1940. Following the war, Katzumie became an art and design critic and joined the Paris International Association of Art Critics. Very soon he was involved with nearly every design activity in Japan, beginning in 1951 as exhibition adviser to the World Graphic Design Exhibitions sponsored by Tokyo Metropolitan Government for nine years. He was also exhibition adviser for the Gropius and Bauhaus Exhibition and the 20th Century Design Exhibition, held at the Tokyo National Museum of Modern Art in 1954 and 1957. He assisted in establishing the Craft Center Japan in 1957, was exhibition commissioner for La Belle Epoque in Tokyo in 1963, and was commissioner for the Japan Style Exhibition held at London's Victoria and Albert Museum in 1980.

Katzumie has been involved in every major Japanese design organization since 1952, including the Japan Advertising Artists Club, the Tokyo Art Directors Club, the Japan Design Committee and the Japan Graphic Designers Association. In 1975 the Japanese government awarded him the coveted Purple Ribbon Award.

One of his major contributions to visual communication was his promotion of pictographic signs, a policy that has become standard for international events. As Design Coordinator and Art Director of the Tokyo Olympic Games he gathered the best young Japanese graphic designers to create simple pictograms that would communicate each of the competitive sports. As a tireless traveller lecturing in many

Takeo Yamamoto, poster for Shiseido cosmetics, 1954. The name "Zen," meaningless in Japan, is clearly designed to appeal to the export market. Yamamoto based his decorative motifs on those of Edo lacquer ware, which are still used today to provide a timeless identity for Japanese products.

Kenichi Kuriyagawa, travel poster, 1954 (1030 x 728 mm). Kuriyagawa (born in 1911) uses an impasto technique to depict a member of the Ainu minority group in traditional dress on their island of Hokkaido; the group remains a tourist attraction to this day.

languages thoughout the world, he understood at first hand the problems of international communication. To promote graphic design in the form he wanted Japan to adopt, he wrote several important design books and translated the works of authors such as Herbert Read and Henry Dreyfus.

He was also on the faculty of various universities from 1954 to 1969 and was a professor and member of the board of directors at Kuwazawa Design School from 1962 to 1965. He founded Tokyo Zokei Daigaku (Tokyo University of Art and Design) in 1966 and became one of its professors.

Despite his books and translations, Katzumie still needed a vehicle to proselytize his design theories throughout Japan and the rest of the world. The Swiss magazine *Graphis*, started in 1952, and a Japanese magazine *Idea*, started in 1954, featured American and European art directors and designers, but neither held the design philosophy that was important to Katzumie. So in November 1959 he founded a quarterly magazine called *Graphic Design*. Its purpose, as he admitted in a 1969 issue, was "first of all to establish constructivism" as a way to free Japanese graphic designers from the schools of applied arts. Katzumie chose the title of the magazine over the more popular "commercial design" or the more avant-garde "visual design" in order to promote constructivism as "firmly connected with printing." To reinforce this, he chose to promote those designers who voiced the same constructivist theories – Joseph Muller-Brockman, Karl Gerstner, Max Bill, El Lissitzky and Alvin Lustig – rather than those whose philosophy was more subjective, such as Raymond Savignac, Herbert Leupin and Hans Erni. His selections were not based on relative superiority, but instead his emphasis was "on the introduction of designers with a frankly constructivist style."

When the time came to promote Japanese designers in his magazine, Katzumie featured every important designer and had an uncanny ability to recognize rising young stars, many of whom were introduced in *Graphic Design*. Although much of his attention was on Japanese design and historical art movements, Katzumie usually included a foreign designer or group in each issue. In the Seventies, he had a running feature entitled "Global New Waves in the '70s" to introduce young foreign designers who had received little recognition in other magazines.

Graphic Design added a plus symbol to its title on its fiftieth issue in recognition that it would include other areas of interest for designers. During the late Seventies the magazine suffered financial difficulties and almost ceased publication, but Katzumie rallied international attention and it continued. When Masaru Katzumie died suddenly in his sleep on 10 November 1983, his able and very loyal associates, Kazuko Sasaki and Yoshiko Kato, continued the magazine until Number 100 in March 1986, which was the final issue.

Katzumie was involved with so many organizations that his business card had to have a foldout to include them all. This tells not only of his personal involvement in design but also of the Japanese need for organizations. Japanese are almost compulsive about organizations and clubs: every profession, hobby or special interest group seems to have several organizations. One reason for this is that Japanese society recognizes the value of group acceptance over individuality – it is through collective group efforts that individuals receive acceptance in society. Ikko Tanaka offered another reason by explaining that throughout history the Japanese have organized themselves around various cultural interest groups. For example, those who study tea ceremony and flower arranging participate in groups that are organized at each level of accomplishment; as the practitioner advances, he or she joins a new group. Designers and art directors are as much attracted to social acceptance as those who study tea ceremony. To chronicle the organizations involved in commercial art, advertising design and graphic design would be arduous. Some of the more important have a legacy dating from 1926 when Tokyo members of the Seven People's Club formed a national group of sixteen artists, called the Japanese Association of Commercial Artists, the first time the words "commercial artist" were used in an organization. A few years later the group was renamed the Japanese Commercial Art Association, but was dissolved in 1941. Similar organizations were formed throughout the early Forties, such as the Association for New Designers; Japan Association for Poster Artists; Tokyo Ad Art Association, later renamed Tokyo Ad Art Club; New Design Association, formed by Tokyo Industrial Arts School (now Chiba University); New Designer Group, formed by the Tama University; New Visual Designers Association, and the Association of Japanese Industrial Artists – a group that included Tadashi Ohashi, Ayao Yamana, Yusaku Kamekura and Takashi Kono. Of all these organizations, two formed in the early Fifties had a commanding influence on Japanese graphic design – Nissembi, the Japan Advertising Artist Club, and the Tokyo Art Directors Club.

Nissembi: Japan Advertising Artist Club

With so many similar design groups overlapping, it is hard to trace the beginning of any one organization. Tadashi Ohashi, a young designer in the late Thirties, recalled that an informal gathering of designers in 1938 loosely called "the conversation group for advertising artists" gathered to share information, and was the forerunner of Nissembi. The "conversation group" was not formal enough to write a charter but was organized more to promote the camaraderie of professionals who sought national recognition. After the war, the group reformed as the Japan Designers Association. It was destined to be the beginning of a truly national organization that would speak for designers as a vital force between the people and industry. The active professional designers in Tokyo, led by Yusaku Kamekura, provided the organizational skills. Named Nihon Senden Bijutsu-kai, and known more familiarly as Nissembi or JAAC for its English title of Japan Advertising Artist Club, it was set up in 1951 with a nucleus of 55 members.

At first it was difficult to build the membership. Kamekura recalls that so many Tokyo designers had left the city during the war that he made recruiting trips to Osaka, where industry had progressed faster and provided more activity for graphic designers; they included Yoshio Hayakawa, who was quickly recruited by Kamekura. Membership was open to all who called themselves "advertising artists" and no other requirements were made. Artists could stay in the organization as long as they liked, even if they were not professionally active. Ayao Yamana designed the symbol, which was based on an abstract monsho with five small squares within a larger square to create a constructivist's play with figure and ground. Kamekura and Masaru Katzumie selected it in 1978 as one of Japan's hundred best symbol marks.

JAAC appealed to all designers in Japan and not just those who had their offices in Tokyo. The number of members from greater Tokyo was always about 45 per cent of the total membership; Osaka came a distant second with about 20 per cent. With chapter offices in other major cities, JAAC provided a national support group for design.

Two distinct philosophies operated in JAAC from the beginning. One group was interested in forming a guild that would improve living standards for graphic designers, while the other was primarily concerned with elevating the quality of design. The first idea seemed to be the primary goal of most members, while the leadership tried to promote the

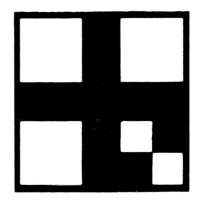

Top: Ayao Yamana, logo for the Japan Advertising Artists Club, 1952. It has no relationship to typography or calligraphy, but promotes a general interest in geometric design trends popular with the young design group of the time.

Above: Kenji Itoh, poster for the first exhibition held by the Japan Advertising Artists Club, 1953. The initials JAAC, artfully placed to represent a face, and the English title direct the poster to an international audience.

second. This difference in purpose continued throughout JAAC's life and was eventually one of the contributing factors to its demise in 1970. But both groups recognized that the one important goal of JAAC was to clarify the reasons for the existence of the profession of graphic designer. If graphic designers were to have legitimacy, then they needed recognition from Japanese industry who would hire them, as well as recognition from their international peers. JAAC's first joint effort was a non-competitive exhibition in 1951 of 88 works produced by the 70 members, held at Matsuzakaya Department Store in Tokyo. It continued on an annual basis and became the organization's leading activity.

The leadership at JAAC kept graphic designers together in relative harmony for twenty years; by the end of the Sixties the membership numbered almost four hundred. By the mid-Sixties confusion about its purpose and lack of a recognized professional status for those who paid membership dues created more divisions within the group. The final blow was a challenge to authority led by young people caught up in the Sixties international atmosphere of social and political change. At the time when a group of Tokyo University students calling themselves the "All-Campus Joint Struggle Committee" closed their university in 1969, a related event occurred at JAAC. The organization's screening committee was forced to cancel selections for the 1969 annual exhibition because of protests by a student-run "Anti-JAAC Joint Struggle Committee." Tadanori Yokoo recalled the event in terms of his role as the only well known member of JAAC who stood with the students. As Yokoo's voice was raised, Ikko Tanaka and Yusaku Kamekura urged him to tone down his objections, reminding him that his early career had been boosted by the club's leaders as well as by organizations such as the Nippon Design Center: approval by these establishments had helped to make him a popular independent designer.

The students identified the individuals who had power within JAAC, and distrusted the impact the organization had on young designers beginning their careers, who needed recognition. Older members, meanwhile, felt that their reputations were assured and that they did not need JAAC at all. After a considerable number of meetings and thoughtful discussions, JAAC was not able to counteract the negative feelings created by Yokoo and the rebels, and it was dissolved by a vote of the membership in 1970. The life of the organization was commemorated by a book entitled *JAAC 1951-70*.

Tokyo Art Directors Club

What started with the discovery of the American position of "art director" led to the formation of the most élite design organization in Japan. In the early Fifties Seiichiro Arai travelled to the United States and learned of these English words to describe the function of the advertising artist. When he returned to Tokyo in the summer of 1952 he joined with Ayao Yamana, Michio Fujimoto and 15 others (including several leaders of JAAC) to form the Tokyo Advertising Art Directors Club, modelled on the New York Art Directors Club. The name was soon shortened to Tokyo Art Directors Club or, more familiarly, ADC.

One early goal of ADC was to bring art directors and industry together. In 1954 it sponsored an exhibition entitled "Serving as an Intermediary between Art and Business," and in 1955 another entitled "Giving Expression to Business." Instead of concentrating on individual work, members operated as a group to establish a recognizable design policy. They organized an annual exhibition that featured various awards and was commemorated in the *Japanese Annual of Advertising Art*. Its first issue, published in 1957, was designed by Yusaku Kamekura. Still in publication today under its new name *Tokyo Art Directors' Annual*, it provides an impressive record of the work and accomplishments of Japanese art directors, designers and copywriters.

In these early years, the title "art director" was used with little regard to actual duties. Most members were managers in corporate public relations with no special training in design. As ADC grew, it included those who were art directors for books, magazines and, later, television. It was reorganized in 1970 to emphasize the professional nature of the membership, stipulating that only active art directors would qualify to be invited as members and that it would purposely be kept an élite group. An award system was devised with one award reserved for members, and the rest for non-members. Recent reorganization in the Eighties added other changes in awards and pushed ADC into more international activity, such as joining ICOGRADA (International Congress of Graphic Designer Associations) and cooperating in the mounting of international exhibitions.

ADC members have been very successful in maintaining it as a small organization. There were 28 members in 1960, 44 in 1972 and by the end of the Eighties, membership numbered 72. Considering that there are approximately 20,000 art directors in Tokyo, selection for new members is rigorous. In a 1987 interview, Masuteru Aoba, art director and leader of ADC, claimed that the selection process was fair and open. At the conclusion of the annual exhibition, non-members who have won prizes are proposed for membership. The entire membership votes, but it is not clear if a majority is necessary or how the final determination is made. ADC was and still is an "old boys' club." Presently only two of the members are women: Eiko Ishioka was invited to join in 1972, and her sister Ryoko joined in 1982. Aoba's explanation is that there are currently no successful female art directors who have achieved sufficient recognition to be considered as members.

Japan Design Committee

In addition to JAAC and ADC, another group was formed in 1953 that had a global perspective. Organized with a manifesto that would impress foreigners, which was written in English so that they could read it, the Japan Design Committee had an auspicious beginning. The manifesto was a little defensive in declaring that "fine art, design and architecture must be interacting components of human activity, searching for good forms." The group vowed to ally architects, designers and artists in a "cooperative effort for global and homo sapiens culture."

The committee's membership consisted of three architects, including Kenzo Tange; an industrial designer; two interior designers; one graphic designer, Yusaku Kamekura; a photographer; a painter; and three critics, including Masaru Katzumie who provided the English translation of the manifesto. At first the committee intended to engage in international activities: the architect Walter Gropius and the French furniture designer Charlotte Perriand were advisers. There was participation in the 1953 International Design Conference in Aspen, Colorado, and the group coordinated Japan's representation at exhibitions in Boston and Milan. This led to outside pressure for Japan to sponsor an international design conference, which was scheduled for May 1960.

The group, renamed the "Good Design Committee," then confined its activity to selecting and popularizing good design in Japan through exhibitions and awarding prizes. Their selection of international products with design excellence was exhibited and sold in the Matsuya Department Store's "Good Design Corner" on the Ginza as well as in two branch stores. This activity, started in the Fifties, is successfully con-

Top: logo for the Tokyo Art Directors Club, 1953. There is some disagreement about who designed this distinctive logo. Tetsuya Ohta in his book *History of Trademarks* (1989) credits Tekeharu Imaizumi and Tamimasa Kawasaki. Masutera Aoba, on the other hand, claims that everyone wanted to design the logo, and that the result was a compromise.

Above: Yusaku Kamekura, "G" mark for good design, 1959. A by-product of the Japan Design Committee was the designation of products as excellent in design; the mark is printed as a small label attached to the goods.

tinuing forty years later. Items selected include stationery goods, household items such as scissors, cutlery, tools and kitchen equipment, and small electronics. In addition to being excellent in design, the items selected must be mass-produced. Katzumie reported on the success of the group in 1963 when he wrote: "There is no denying the fact that good designs selected and recommended by the committee are gradually becoming popular with the public."

Another programme to improve Japanese design was the dissemination of printed reproductions of current designs from foreign designers. This information was provided in the 1951 six-volume publication *World's Commercial Design*, printed by Kyodo News Service. It provided an influential experience for young Japanese designers to see reproductions of the best design from Europe and America. The material was organized by Masaru Katzumie, Hiromu Hara, Yusaku Kamekura, Takashi Kono, Ayao Yamana and others. Each volume measured about 6 ½ x 10 in (16 x 25 cm) and contained small black-and-white reproductions that filled the pages, giving it the appearance of a mail order catalogue. The publication was updated and expanded in 1953 into eight volumes and, in 1974, was published in seven volumes as *Graphic Design of the World*, edited by Hiromu Hara and Masaru Katzumie.

International Recognition
Following World War II Japanese designers made a concentrated effort to gain international recognition for their work. They realized that if Japan's graphic design was to be recognized then their work had to appear in international publications. The 1950 issue of the *International Poster Annual*, published in England, had no posters from Japan. The 1951 annual, featuring works from famous European and American designers, had seven posters from Japan (one unfortunately printed upside down) by lesser known designers, none of whom achieved future prominence.

In the 1953/54 annual, Japan was better prepared. Designer Hiroshi Ohchi, who was born in 1908, organized the showing that included 32 impressive posters with works from leading designers, including ten by Ohchi himself (in this issue, two posters were published upside down). Designer-publisher Walter Herdeg included about a dozen Japanese posters in his 1952/53 *Graphis Annual* and double that number in the next two. His early favourites were the softly painted images of

Hiroshi Ohchi, poster for the Russian Don Cossack Chorus, 1952 (1030 x 728 mm). The repeated rectangles, resembling musical notation, and the simple colour scheme brought Ochi considerable recognition for this poster.

Yoshio Hayakawa, poster for a kimono show at Kintetsu Department Store, 1951 (788 x 515 mm). This well known poster shows an elongated, Giacometti-like figure clad in a kimono. This was the second Japanese poster added to the permanent collection of the Museum of Modern Art in New York (the first is shown on page 65).

Yoshio Hayakawa. When he did show the more prevalent geometric abstract posters, such as a promotion by Yusaku Kamekura for the peaceful use of nuclear energy, they were reproduced as small black-and-white illustrations. Herdeg had invited Kamekura to design the cover of a 1953 issue of *Graphis* magazine; he produced a geometric design in two colours avoiding any reference to Japanese tradition.

Many of the early posters selected for inclusion in international annuals and journals had a distinctly provincial look to them. This is not how the Japanese wanted to be viewed. Writing about this problem in his introduction to the 1953/54 *International Poster Annual*, entitled "On Japanese Posters," Hiroshi Ohchi identified the difficulty in satisfying the foreign design community. He said foreigners wanted to see views of Mount Fuji, pictures of geisha, pagoda, chrysanthemums, pine trees, plum trees and bamboo – all "distorted remnants of old traditions that in no way represent modern commercial art so closely linked with modern industry." Designers in Japan had no interest in promoting these "souvenir style" images because they represented history and not modern technology. If they were to receive international recognition for their accomplishments they needed to show a modern, industrially active Japan. Other than kanji letterforms, designers used few graphic images that provided recognition of their native country. European models were favoured over Asian, and abstract symbols for modern technology were more evident than views of traditional Japanese folk art – a trend that continued for another twenty years, until Japanese designers became more confident and proud of their heritage.

In a further effort to remove the provincial appearance of their designs, some major corporations hired American designers. In 1952 Raymond Loewy was commissioned to design the package for Peace cigarettes; his widely reported fee of $4,000 was unheard of in Japan. The process was repeated in 1959 when Asahi Brewery commissioned Walter Landor to design their symbol. His design simplified two Japanese clichés that had been on the label since 1897 – the rising sun from the military flag and a Hokusai wave. He was paid a design fee of $10,000, much higher than fees paid to local designers. Japanese designers had and still have two views on competition with foreign designers. They would prefer that their own designers were recognized but, at the same time, are overjoyed that such high fees *are* paid, because it increases Japanese designers' status as professionals.

Walter Landor, redesign of the Asahi Brewery trademark, 1959. Landor kept the two elements of the earlier design, the battle flag sun and the wave pattern.

Individual Japanese designers organized a series of one-man exhibitions in 1951 to provide recognition for their profession and their work. The first exhibitor was Kenji Itoh; a year later, work by Yoshio Hayakawa was exhibited and, in 1953, Yusaku Kamekura. Kamekura remembers that while most other design exhibitions were limited to original art, some of his printed pieces were added to his show, which was called "The Graphic Design of Yusaku Kamekura." By 1955, major graphic design exhibitions were occurring more frequently, including the annual JAAC exhibition as well as other one-man shows. One special exhibition, Graphic '55, recognized leading Japanese designers and played an important part in Japanese design history.

Graphic '55: The First Generation

Led by Yusaku Kamekura, who provided the title, a small group of successful designers staged the Graphic '55 exhibition in Tokyo's Takashimaya Department Store. Joining Kamekura were Yoshio Hayakawa, Kenji Itoh, Takashi Kono, Hiromu Hara, Ryuichi Yamashiro and Tadashi Ohashi. They also invited American designer Paul Rand to join them; he was represented but was unable to visit Japan to see the exhibition, although he did meet Kamekura in Connecticut a few years later. During Rand's first trip to Japan in 1958, he met many of the other participants of Graphic '55.

This exhibition had one quality which was different from any previous poster exhibitions – its emphasis on printed works. Earlier JAAC exhibitions always displayed original art and it was expected that Graphic '55 participants would do the same. But Kamekura insisted that corporations paid money for printed work and that this was what the public wanted to see. The group also wanted recognition as professional designers rather than as artists concerned with the craft of their work, and recognition of the professional qualities of others – typesetters, platemakers, printers – who are involved in the production process. Participants understood that poster exhibitions in Europe and America showed only printed pieces and not original art. Since some of the younger designers were too early in their careers to have a good selection of commissioned posters from clients, they were invited to prepare special posters for the show – limited edition silk screen prints. In addition to posters, the exhibition included book design, packaging, wrapping paper, book covers, trademarks and calendars. The artists represented are considered to be the

Ikko Tanaka, concert poster for an Argentine orchestra and dance company, 1953 (728 x 515 mm). Tanaka designed this poster at the age of 23 for his employer, an Osaka newspaper; the sophisticated design has several references to the composition of Paul Rand, while the colours draw on the pale blue and white of the Argentine flag.

unequalled "first generation" of Japanese graphic designers. Hiromu Hara (see page 58) was the oldest, at 45, and Ryuichi Yamashiro the youngest, at 35.

Yusaku Kamekura

Hiromu Hara wrote about Yusaku Kamekura in 1972: "no other designer has won as many awards." This statement is still true today. Not only had Kamekura won almost every Japanese design award possible from his colleagues by 1972, but since then recognition has continued including in 1980 the Medal of Honour with Purple Ribbon. In 1985 he became the only graphic designer to be awarded the Third Order of the Sacred Treasure by the Japanese Government. Masaru Katzumie, in his article "Pro et Contra" in *Yusaku Kamekura: His Works* (1971), commended him for his "instinctive political sense" that made it possible for him to "envision ideas, give energy to them to develop into movements in which he was able to occupy the position of a most persuasive leader. We can hardly find any big event in the design field since the end of the war where he did not play an important role." Twenty years later Katzumie's statement is as valid as Hara's. No other Japanese designer has had a career as long and as distinguished.

Yusaku Kamekura was born in 1915 and grew up in Nigata Prefecture, northwest of Tokyo on the Sea of Japan. When he was 17 he knew he wanted to be a graphic designer. After finishing high school he learned of a new school, Shin Kenchiku Kogei Gakuin (New Architecture and Industrial Arts School), established in 1931 as a Japanese version of the Bauhaus. In 1938, a year after he graduated, he joined the publishing firm Nihon Kobo as a designer with Ayoa Yamana and photographer Ken Domon. While there, he was fortunate to study alphabet letters from Erna Mechlenburg Natori, the wife of the publisher. In 1939, at the age of 24, he was appointed editor-in-chief of a Thailand magazine titled *Kaupapu*. The following year Nihon Kobo changed its name to International Industrial Arts Information Company and designated Kamekura as chief of the art department where he supervised about ten people. After the war he continued his work in publications as art director of *Commerce Japan* magazine.

A scholarly interest in monsho contributed to Kamekura's skills in designing trademarks, his most consistent work. To further his knowledge of symbol design he planned and organized two books: *Trademarks of the World* (1956) and

Top: Yusaku Kamekura, logo for the Japan Industrial Designers Association, 1953. This was Kamekura's first important symbol design, a simple geometric form with an appropriately industrial appearance.

Above: Yusaku Kamekura, poster for Daido Worsted Mills, 1954 (1030 x 728 mm). The textile industry was one of the first Japanese industries to be revitalized after the war. For this early and important commission, Kamekura produced a poster very European in appearance, with a carefully composed still life and the use of English type.

Right: Yusaku Kamekura, poster for Nikon cameras, 1955 (1030 x 729 mm). This is one of a series of geometrically based designs for Nikon made during the Fifties, which he regards as his most significant work. Simple forms are accented with bold, flat colours; the elements are reminiscent of decorative motifs from the Edo era.

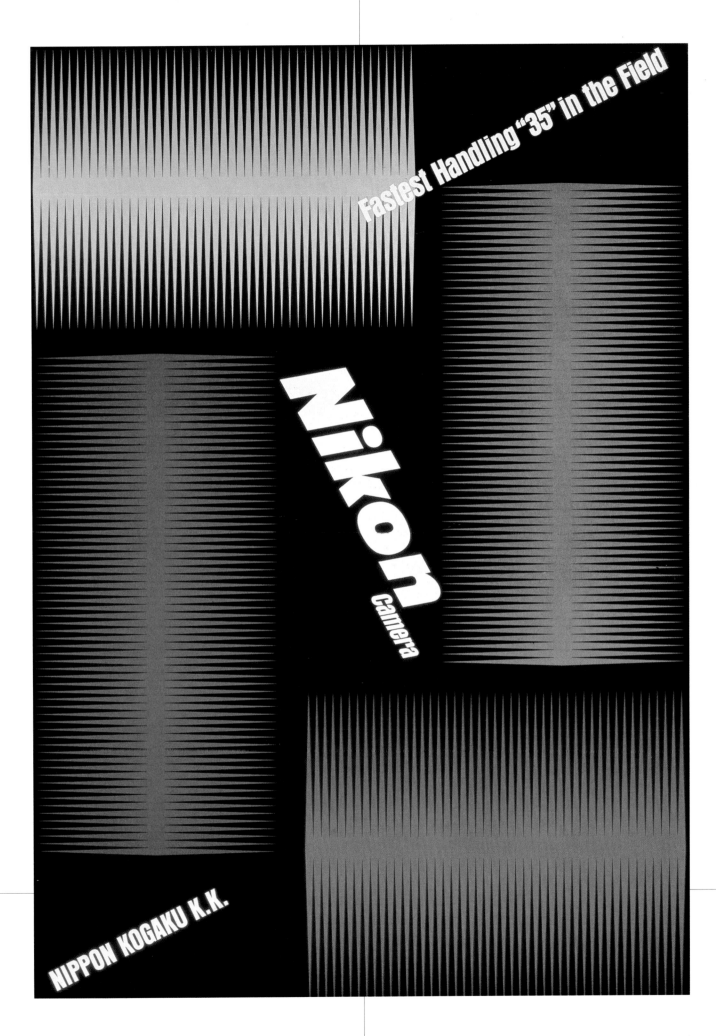

Trademarks and Symbols of the World (1965). He won his first award in 1953 for the Japanese Industrial Design Association symbol. His best designs are those based on abstract geometric forms, such as the Good Design or "G Mark" (see page 71) and the symbols for Yamagawa Electric and for Traditional Craft Products.

Many of Kamekura's internationally recognized posters in the Fifties emphasized geometric forms accented with bold, flat colours. His favourite colours were and still are grey-blue, chrome yellow, and a greyed orange with a grey or black background. He is recognized as one of the first designers to use geometric composition and trade traditional Japanese expressions for an internationally recognized use of image and concept. With neat simplicity, mixed with a little reverence for Japanese tradition, Kamekura quickly became the leader of the new generation of designers.

In the middle to late Fifties, he designed a series of geometrically based posters for Nippon Kogaku (Nikon Cameras), which he credits as his most significant work during his early years. The critic Masatuka Ogawa wrote of these Nikon posters in *The Works of Yusaku Kamekura* (1983): "His geometric shapes fit perfectly with the cool, sharp image of cameras and lenses and sent a refreshing breeze of new creativity into Japan's world of graphic design." Those posters produced between 1954 and 1960 have a Fifties look, with simple, flat, asymmetrical organization and sans serif type. They were important to Japan because they embraced the International Style and were devoid of traditional Japanese motifs.

While directing Nippon Design Center in the early Sixties, Kamekura received international recognition for his symbol design and posters for the 1964 Tokyo Olympics. The poster design, so simple and straightforward yet powerful in imagery, brought international credibility to Japan's design community. It is said that Kamekura was the first Japanese designer to collaborate with a professional photographer on a unified design concept.

He is equally at home in design for books, including their binding, which he does in the finest European tradition. Of all the design projects undertaken by Kamekura, generally his package designs seem less unified. They are too dependent on typography and in many cases show an unfamiliarity with Roman letter design. He has some expensive clients with extensive projects, such as packages for Nikon cameras and lenses and for Meiji chocolate bars. He has an unyielding

interest in excellence, combined with a youthful, competitive spirit. This is epitomized in a phrase he often uses: "Design lives for its freshness."

Kenji Itoh

The early career of Kenji Itoh parallels that of Kamekura, his friend and colleague. Both looked for international solutions to design problems and, after the war, both started their careers with the same company, Daido Worsted Mills. Born in Tokyo in 1915, Itoh graduated from Tokyo Industrial Art School, now the engineering section of Chiba University. One of Itoh's first posters for Daido Mills has a jumping ram with a body made from a photograph of fabrics with roughly sketched feet and head. After a successful series of posters for Canon cameras, he went on to become art director for the pharmaceutical magazine *Stethoscope*.

Itoh's approach to graphic design is as much in the mainstream as Hiromu Hara's. He has a twenty-year record of covers for *Stethoscope* magazine and a whole series of Kappa novels. He received several national awards in the Sixties for his spectacular lighted signs for Teijin and NEC, and for his highly inventive window displays for Wako Department Store. His sparse approach to window direction was highly influential for future displays in the West.

Tadashi Ohashi

Tadashi Ohashi is credited with establishing the public perception of the Kikkoman Soy Sauce Company. He has been the company's art director since 1950 when it and Meiji Confectionery became his first major clients after he had struggled to succeed as a freelance designer. Ohashi distinguishes his home town of Kyoto where he was born in 1918, with its history of fine fabrics and fashion, as an influence on his use of colour and attention to detail. During his study at Tokyo Industrial Art School, now Chiba University, he said he was introduced to the teachings of the Bauhaus workshops by Japanese professors who had researched the programme from translated publications. He also studied the works of Herbert Bayer who early on became his idol (when Bayer attended the World Design Conference in 1960, he gave Ohashi a signed inscription specially drawn on a Japanese square "shikishi" which still hangs in an honoured location in Ohashi's studio). Bayer's influences are combined with images of the traditional monsho in some of Ohashi's cultural

Kenji Itoh, poster for Canon cameras, 1954 (1025 x 730 mm). Itoh received considerable acclaim for his posters for Canon, for whom he created an international recognition device, using the "C" as a camera lens shutter.

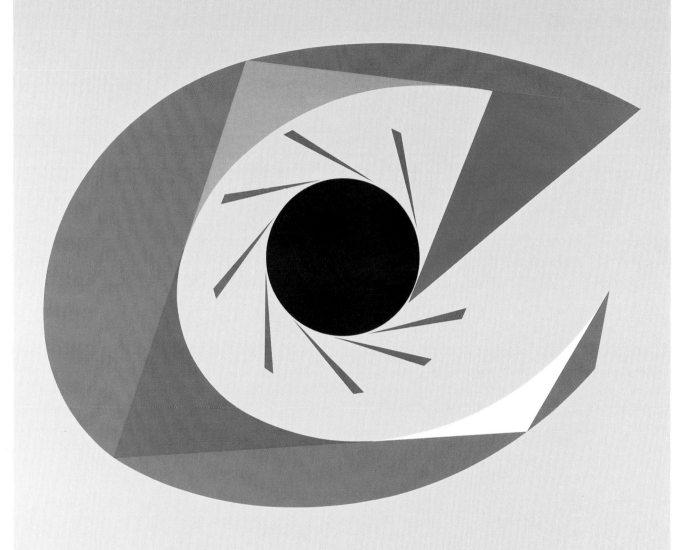

Canon
CAMERA

KEN.

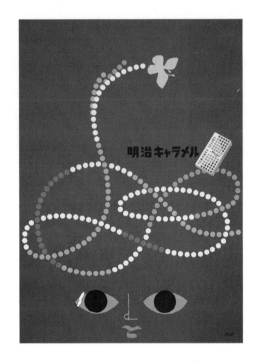

Tadashi Ohashi, poster for Meiji chocolate, 1953 (725 x 507 mm). In the case of chocolate, which originated in the West, there was a built-in excuse to use Western images. Here, a blue-eyed china doll with curly brown hair captures the attention; Western dolls were highly prized among Japanese children.

Tadashi Ohashi, magazine advertisement for Meiji caramels, 1956 (210 x 148 mm). Effective use of negative space and distinctive typographic treatment are characteristic strengths of Ohashi, who was influenced by the American designer Paul Rand.

Tadashi Ohashi, poster for Meiji caramels, 1957 (1053 x 752 mm). This poster was awarded the gold medal at the first annual exhibition of the Tokyo Art Directors Club.

symbol designs, such as his 1967 design for the Meiji centenary celebrations.

During World War II he began his career as a designer at Daimaru Department Store, then joined Dentsu Advertising Agency for a few years before opening his own office in 1944. After the war his big break came when a poster he designed for the national lottery received critical acclaim. He is best known for his technically perfect, carefully painted, icons of fish and vegetables reproduced on posters, magazine advertisements and calendars. These exquisite paintings, done in colourful transparent hues without the benefit of black, force us to re-examine in minute detail the surfaces of the foods they depict. Illustrations for Kikkoman Soy Sauce won Ohashi the Mainichi Design Award. In making the award, Masaru Katzumie said: "How elegant Ohashi is in serving as art director while doing illustrations, when there are so many American-type art directors who are like idea brokers."

Yoshio Hayakawa

While most of his contemporaries were doing their best not to use Asian images, Yoshio Hayakawa proudly crafted illustrations and designs that embodied the traditional spirit of Japan. He was born in 1917 and spent much of his life in the Kansai area, which stimulated a more traditional flavour in his work. He graduated in 1936 from Osaka Prefectural Industrial Arts School, majoring in wood and metal crafts. In the same year, he started work at Osaka's Mitsukoshi Department Store in its advertising and display section. During those early years he also worked at Kintetsu Department Store and the cultural section of the Osaka Municipal Office. By 1952 he had opened his own freelance business with an office in Osaka. Because of pressures to be active in Tokyo and a desire to be close to book publishing, he opened an office there in 1961, commuting back to Osaka until 1971, when he decided to move permanently to Tokyo.

His early work consisted of brush-stroke honesty that established his reputation: artists from the Kansai area or Naniwa (Osaka) are thought to have a brighter, more harmonious, approach towards colour than an Edokko (native of Tokyo). He claims to have been influenced more by Picasso than by any Japanese painters. His poster designs had great influence on the young designers living in Kansai. Ikko Tanaka, an Osaka resident, was one of his early enthusiastic fans. Yusaku Kamekura was also impressed enough to come from Tokyo to

see him and to encourage his participation in Tokyo design activities. In 1951 Hayakawa was western Japan's representative among the founders of the Japan Advertising Artist Club. He also participated as a panellist in the World Design Conference and as a member of the Tokyo Art Directors Club, and is credited with the development of a basic colour plan for Expo '70. He has won many awards for his designs and was the recipient of the Japanese Government Medal of Honour with Purple Ribbon in 1984.

Ryuichi Yamashiro

Another designer who migrated from Osaka to Tokyo in the Fifties is Ryuichi Yamashiro. He was born in 1920, graduated from the design course of Osaka City Technological School, and spent 15 years as a designer at Osaka Mitsukoshi and Hankyu Department Stores. During his early years he edited and laid out pamphlets and newspaper advertisements. By 1953 he had opened his own office in Osaka. He joined his friends Yusaku Kamekura and Hiromu Hara in 1959 to organize the Nippon Design Center, where he stayed for several years as one of the leaders. After leaving NDC, he concentrated more on producing experimental collages and illustrations, some for clients but many for personal enjoyment. Recently his impressionistic paintings of cats have been popular and are reprinted on many calendars.

This first generation of graphic designers began their careers independent of any design group or advertising agency. Their typical practice was to start with a company and, as soon as financially possible, open their own offices and hire a few assistants. Two major design organizations begun in the Fifties influenced the future direction of Japanese design and art direction. Light Publicity, organized as an advertising agency and currently with a staff of 80, maintains a more creative art department than the two oldest and largest agencies, Dentsu and Hokuhodo. It was organized by Tomio Nobuta, Jo Murakoshi and Hideo Mukai in 1951 to meet the design and advertising needs of corporations, and has employed some of the most talented art directors in Japan, such as Gan Hosoya, Sho Akiyama, Ikko Tanaka, Makoto Wada and Katsumi Asaba. The other influential organization was the Nippon Design Center, which made a pointed effort not to appear as an advertising agency, but simply as a gathering of Japan's best designers.

Above: Yoshio Hayakawa, poster for Japan Air Lines, 1958 (1032 x 730 mm). In this poster, produced as an uncommissioned design, Hayakawa displays ingenuity in the use of negative space, exemplifying the Japanese ability to place a few objects successfully in a large, open area.

Right: Ryuichi Yamashiro, *Trees*, poster designed for the Graphic '55 exhibition, 1955 (1052 x 740 mm). This poster received international attention and has since become regarded as one of the classics of Japanese graphic design. A visual exploration of the pictographic origins of Chinese calligraphy, it is based on the character *ki*, meaning tree. When two such characters are combined, the word becomes *hayashi*, wood; three together mean *mori*, forest. Few other Japanese words are so successful in their visual qualities; here, they give the impression of trees on a snow-covered hillside.

Ryuichi yamashiro

第五回　田村　楊貴妃　安宅　巴　天鼓　道成寺

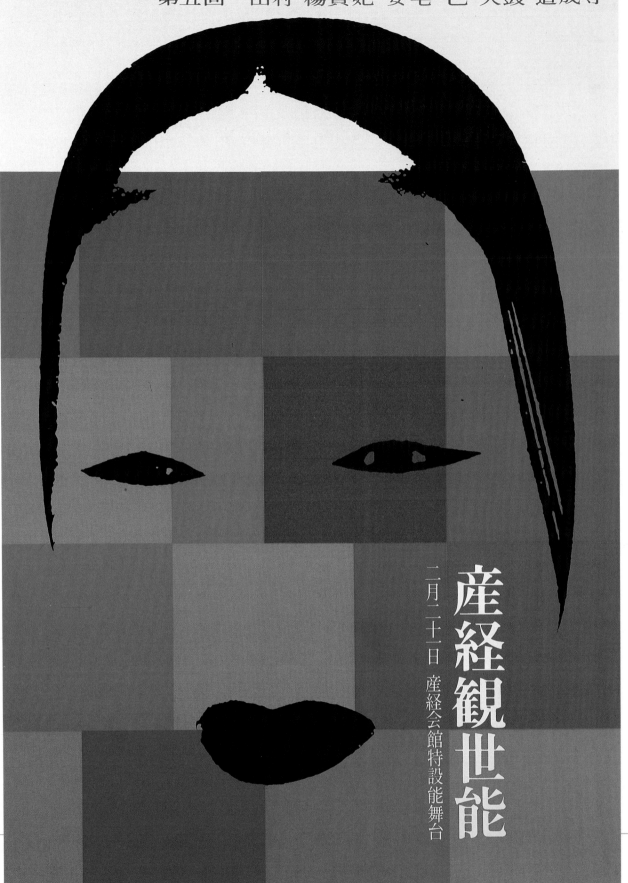

産経観世能

二月二十一日　産経会館特設能舞台

季刊誌●グラフィック・デザイン●九月創刊・発行所・芸美出版社

DESIGN BY IKKO TANAKA

'59/世界商業デザイン展
7月14日−19日 池袋三越6階 主催 共同通信社

Ikko Tanaka, poster for *The Fifth Sankei* at the Kanze Noh Theatre, 1958 (1033 x 730 mm). Tanaka's use of traditional Japanese motifs for many of his theatre posters made his work very popular with non-Japanese; it was a practice other designers avoided. Here, the noh mask is superimposed on traditional colours, with a splash of modern red.

Ikko Tanaka, poster for the World Graphic Design Exhibition, 1959 (728 x 515 mm). The artist regards this as one of his most important works, produced soon after he moved from Osaka to Tokyo; it is part of the permanent collection of the Museum of Modern Art in New York.

Nippon Design Center

In December 1959, when Japanese designers were trying to bring themselves closer to industry, eight leading companies with major advertising budgets teamed up with three top Japanese designers to form the Nippon Design Center. The companies were Asahi Breweries, Asahi Chemical, Daiwa Securities, Fuji Iron and Steel, Nippon Kogaku (Nikon Cameras), Nippon Kokan (Iron and Steel), Toshiba Electric and Toyota Motor Sales. They joined with designers Hiromu Hara, Ryuichi Yamashiro and Yusaku Kamekura. NDC began operation in March 1960 and operated much like an advertising agency, except that it did not buy media space like a typical agency. Industrialist Tamesaburo Yamamoto was the first President (the title was changed to Chairman) and Yusaku Kamekura was named Managing Director. When Kamekura resigned in 1962, Hiromu Hara took over and his title was changed to President. Initially, NDC had two important goals: to handle the design needs of their major corporate backers; and, more expansively, as expressed by the first President Yamamoto, "to be Japan's center of creative progress in advertising, design and commercial art."

These practical and nationalistic goals were met during its first year of operation, partly because Kamekura's name for the organization was so effective. As a Design Center it sounded as if its chief goal was the promotion of design – like, for example, the London Design Centre – and not advertising for a select group of clients. Nippon was chosen over Nihon because, according to Kamekura, it "had a more modern feeling." Nippon is also understood to be a more official name than Nihon; to list the organization as Nippon Design Center gave it an appearance of greater national responsibility. People outside Japan readily made all these assumptions, and Hara acknowledged in 1967 that it received mail from foreigners who assumed it was a government commission. The volume of mail was so great that someone who could write English had to be hired to respond to all the inquiries. In Japanese calligraphy the name uses kanji for Nippon and katakana for Design Center, indicating that the last two are foreign words which need phonetic spelling. Most frequently, however, Roman letters are used for all three words, or the abbreviation NDC (the translation Japan Design Center or JDC is almost never used, as it would confuse foreigners).

The three chief designers – Hara, Kamekura and Yamashiro – were joined by seven others who acted as art directors for

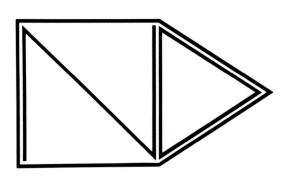

Kazumasa Nagai, logo for the Nippon Design Center, 1960. Nagai was one of the youngest of the NDC's original membership of art directors.

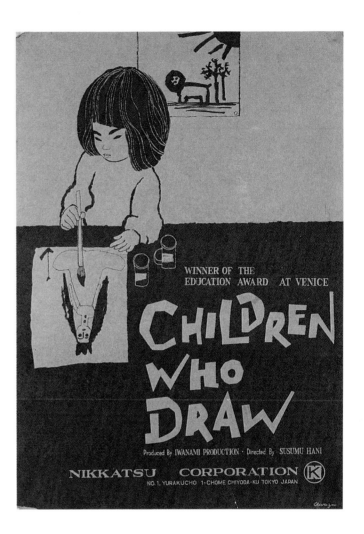

Shigeo Fukuda, trademark for a
children's clothes company, 1957.
The young Fukuda's simple form was
the precursor of the symbols used for
the 1964 Olympic Games and Expo
'70 (see page 99).

Kiyoshi Awazu, film poster, 1957
(1030 x 728 mm). This is an early
work by a designer who later earned
an international reputation; the
sensitive line drawing shows the
influence of the American illustrator
David Stone Martin.

major clients. The genesis of this group was a special club organized in the late Fifties called Niju-ichi (Twenty-one), gathered by Kamekura to discuss Bauhaus design theories. Concepts for the NDC were developed in these discussions but unfortunately the need for business goals was to bring commercial realities home to these idealistic designers. Kamekura stayed on as managing director until 1962 when he left the organization to form his own freelance design office, Kamekura Design Institute. Many of his friends found it hard to understand why he left such a successful organization, particularly since he was one of the founders.

Within the first three years of operation almost all of the "Seven Samurai," as the young art directors called themselves, had in fact left the organization; only Kazumasa Nagai stayed on. The reason for the exodus was said to be that the group's pure design goals were taking a secondary role to clients' commercial needs. This problem had been anticipated by two very popular and talented young designers, Kohei Sugiura and Kiyoshi Awazu, who came under considerable pressure from Kamekura and Yamashiro to join the group but had already adopted a policy of refusing commercial clients; they recognized that the NDC was dependent on major corporations for revenue.

But setting these commercial disputes aside, Nippon Design Center has a sterling history in design. An important side benefit is its role as a "graduate programme" for many young designers who receive their first training as assistants to one of the chief designers. Early assistants who have since established fame are Tadanori Yokoo, Akira Uno and, later, Keisuke Nagatomo, Masatoshi Toda and Makoto Saito. NDC's practice is to combine the talents of designers, illustrators and photographers with younger assistants acting in a master-apprentice arrangement. The NDC building in the centre of the Ginza area of Tokyo has been an important attraction for visiting foreign designers since it was established in 1967. Currently it houses about 160 designers.

Many of the current and past designers at NDC have exercised and continue to exercise considerable power in Japan's design establishment. They are the ones who hold responsible positions in organizations and design committees, such as JAAC, ADC, JAGDA and Olympic and Exposition design committees. Some younger designers who are not in positions of power have expressed the criticism that NDC seems to have an inside-track for leadership in these important groups.

新制作座公演

野盗、風の中を走る

プロローグと五幕十一場

作・演出　眞山美保

装置・松下朗　照明・原英一
音楽・木下忠司　効果・園田芳龍

9月26日―10月1日

開演6時、土・日・マチネー1時

読売ホール

¥350指定席・¥250一般席

Kiyoshi Awazu, film poster for *Bandits Running Through the Wind*, 1958 (746 x 1067 mm). The overlapping images of the warriors convey a flurry of activity; Awazu later became famous for the quality of his line drawings.

日本歌舞伎舞踊

Hiromu Hara, poster for kabuki dancers, 1957 (780 x 790 mm). In this uncommissioned poster, Hara creates a monsho-like image with a bold triple-edged box; the superimposed line illustration of the kabuki actor is reminiscent of Edo motifs. The border colours are those of the traditional kabuki theatre curtain, conveying the idea of a curtained stage.

Hiromu Hara, poster for a Japanese typography exhibition, 1959 (1028 x 730 mm). Four basic calligraphic strokes represent the features of a face, with an asterisk forming a spot above the lips - an example of Hara's skill with typography and its historical forms and his subtle wit.

日本タイポグラフィ展

4

world comes to Japan
1960-1970

The Fifties was a decade of conspicuous transformation for Japan. Memories of defeat in World War II were replaced by recognition from the rest of the world of their remarkable economic and social accomplishments. As a small island country with very few natural resources, Japan's only prospects for economic growth were to match the imperative for imports with an active production of exports. Following the Korean conflict, the automobile industry correctly predicted that a demand for small and medium-size vehicles would revive car production. Equally hasty expansion occurred in the chemical industry, pharmaceuticals, petro-chemicals and shipbuilding, with the major activity in manufacturing. By the end of the Fifties, 60 per cent of Japanese employment was in factories.

Design writer Stephen Bayley commented on this period in Japan's history in *The Conran Directory of Design* (1985): "At first [Japan's] ... emphasis was on cheap high-volume production, and manufacturers simply aped European and American rivals, but when the markets for these goods were saturated the Japanese began to explore higher-margin territory." He also pointed out that government regulations in the late Fifties forced major manufacturers to develop design policies. Swept up in this high economic growth of industries were designers who suddenly found their profession in demand. Their increased status gave considerable weight to the claim that an international design conference was needed, to focus on the social role of graphic designers, interior designers, fashion designers, industrial designers and architects, and on their importance to Japan's rising economy.

Tokyo World Design Conference, 1960

This was Japan's first collaboration between the different design professions, and her first international design conference. It was important not only for what was said, but in that it brought world attention to Japan's design activity. Influential designers from foreign countries were invited to experience the graciousness of the Japanese people and to see firsthand that they did not live in a feudal society with samurai roaming the countryside. For most it was their first visit to Japan and they were impressed with what they saw – a modern industrial society and exhibitions of the latest in Japanese design. Both provided a new perspective for the foreigners.

The Tokyo World Design Conference, known as WoDeCo, was held from 11-16 May 1960. It had 227 designers in attendance, 84 from 27 countries overseas and 143 from Japan.

Kohei Sugiura, poster advertising a concert of Stravinsky's music conducted by the composer, 1959 (1090 x 790 mm). This was Stravinsky's only visit to Japan, where his music was played by the Japanese NHK Symphony Orchestra. The wonderful blend of type, photography, engraving and drawing is one that Sugiura used again.

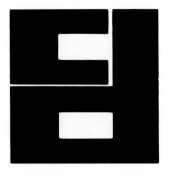

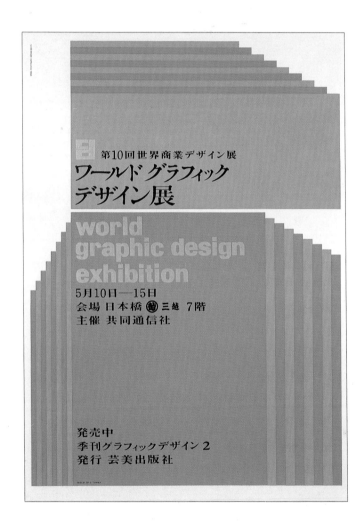

The Japan Design Committee organized the programme and it was sponsored by Dentsu Advertising Agency, with additional financial support from several corporations. The conference theme was: "What can the comprehensive image of the present century contribute to the future society of mankind?" or the shorter version: "Our Century: The Total Image." Chairman of the Executive Committee was Junzo Sakakura; participants from Japan included Yusaku Kamekura, Masaru Katzumie, Hideo Mukai, Kakeji Imaizumi, Seiichiro Arai, Hideyuki Oka and Kohei Sugiura. From Europe and America there were Max Huber, Otl Aicher, Thomas Maldonado, Bruno Munari, Joseph Muller-Brockman, Herbert Bayer, Herbert Pinzke, Saul Bass and Austrian industrialist Karl Oback.

Conferences generally leave little that is memorable; with this one the impact was in the event itself and not in the presentations. Masaru Katzumie made a thoughtful comment on the social responsibility of art directors when he reminded those attending that "beautiful advertisement and superior design are essential because advertising space is public space." Several Japanese who were present remember most the presentations made by Herbert Bayer and Saul Bass.

As most designers know, one benefit of a design conference is the publicity: the posters and the symbol used to promote it. The official symbol, designed by Takashi Kono, is a rather modest square shape with a block lower case "d" and "c" nestled together. Two posters for the event symbolize the state of Japanese design. The official poster, by Ikko Tanaka, was a 1960 Gold Medal winner at the Tokyo Art Directors Club annual exhibition. The other, by Kohei Sugiura, is considered to be one of the first Japanese posters to use constructivist concepts. It is filled with small geometric triangles and squares that correctly fit the description of a constructivist poster by the Swiss designer Joseph Muller-Brockman: as one "harmonious linking of surface and space, full of concentrated interest. There are linear and proportional correlations between all parts, each part integrated in the whole and the result is the optimum functional system of arrangement..."

Kohei Sugiura

Kohei Sugiura, born in 1932, has been mentioned earlier as being at the centre of several aspects of Japanese design and noted for his independence. He does not comfortably fit into any one group. In his early twenties he was a craftsman in producing graphic design based on the Russian Construc-

Top: Takashi Kono, symbol for the Tokyo World Design Conference, 1959. The modular letters seem devoid of any specific cultural identity.

Above: Ikko Tanaka, poster for the Tenth World Graphic Design Exhibition, held at Mitsukoshi Department Store, 1960 (728 x 515 mm). The predominantly geometric design uses unusual shades of green, which exemplify Tanaka's craft with colour and the use of space. The two different greens offer a play with depth and composition.

tivist concept. He approaches design with a scientific mind, examining the inner structure of space with mathematical precision. As his designs won acclaim from the establishment, he caught the attention of Masaru Katzumie who recommended that he be more involved in organizations. Yusaku Kamekura and Ryuichi Yamashiro urged him to join the Nippon Design Center at its formation and designers expected him to be part of this élite group. But he turned them down.

Sugiura had early aspirations to be an architect and developed also as a connoisseur of music. He graduated from Tokyo University of Art and Music in 1955 and spent two years in the mid-Sixties as a guest professor at the Hochschule für Gestaltung in Ulm, West Germany, in charge of visual communication and architecture. He never wanted to be identified as a commercial artist, but accepts the title of graphic designer. He concentrates his design activity on cultural posters and publications and thus avoids commercial clients. This independent direction also shows in his posters where he introduced new concepts and expressed his personal research activity into European constructivism. Because of his involvement in constructivist design in the Sixties and his influence on the introduction of religious imagery in the Seventies, Sugiura has been a major figure in Japan for thirty years.

In the last twenty years he has conducted research on the history of Japanese religion, travelling to India and other Far Eastern countries for study. He did little graphic design in the Eighties but, because of his past reputation, still continues his Tokyo design office and produces posters to represent himself in exhibitions. His structured/unstructured approach to publication design has been a major influence on Japanese editorial design. At first viewing, his work appears to be freely designed with no internal structure, but type, photography and art are carefully composed within an implied structure. His early emphasis on constructivism evolved into religious imagery, reflecting his studies, with depictions of mandalas or glowing images of Buddha and other Eastern religious symbols. Sugiura's current appearance with shaved head and Indian-style shirts projects the image of a devotee.

Many of the changes in Japanese design are the result of the accomplishments of individuals such as Sugiura. As corporations got on their feet in the early Sixties, individuals in their design departments also received attention. The cosmetics firm Shiseido continued its tradition of excellence of design under a new director.

Above: Kohei Sugiura, poster for WoDeCo, 1960 (1030 x 728 mm). This is considered to be one of the first Japanese posters to use constructivist concepts. A multitude of tiny squares and triangles achieves the illusion of depth. The poster was made in two different coloured versions.

Top: Kohei Sugiura, poster for a contemporary music festival concert, 1960. The concert of first performances featured both Western and Japanese composers. Sugiura repeats the constructivist concepts shown in his WoDeCo poster of the same year, with rhythmical geometric shapes resembling the internal structure of a piano.

次々に生まれる流行をいち早くとり入れる資生堂化粧品は、いつもフレッシュな感覚にみちています

Makoto Nakamura (art director) and Hideaki Murase (designer), poster for Shiseido, 1963; photograph by Noriaki Yokosuka. Nakamura masterminded Shiseido's change of emphasis from illustration to photography in its advertising.

Makoto Nakamura, poster for Shiseido, 1969 (1018 x 728 mm); photograph by Noriaki Yokosuka. Printed with silver lines to emphasise the soft effect, this won the silver award at the JAAC exhibition.

Shiseido, Part Two: Makoto Nakamura

When Ayao Yamana neared retirement age he was replaced in 1959 by an associate, Makoto Nakamura, as Chief of Advertising Division. Like his predecessor, Nakamura had been closely identified with the advertising success of Shiseido. Born in 1926, he graduated from Tokyo Art School's design course in 1948 and the following year joined Shiseido's advertising department. He remained there as a permanent designer until 1987 when his status was changed to consultant.

Nakamura recalls that at the time he replaced Yamana there was considerable pressure to continue the illustrative style Yamana had built up for Shiseido. Nakamura, not an illustrator, wanted to change to a photographic image. He was influenced by Man Ray's provocative photographs and had a desire to be a photographer himself. With the popularity of a new medium – television commercials – the public became accustomed to televised images and accepted Nakamura's introduction of photographs in Shiseido's print advertising. His first posters compromised by using photographs that resembled illustrations, and he admitted that these were only partly successful.

An influential trend Nakamura brought to modern Japanese graphic design and art direction was a renewed appreciation of the beauty of Japanese women. While most of his contemporaries used European and American models, Nakamura wanted to emulate the ukiyo-e artists who celebrated the beauty of the Japanese courtesan. It was a goal that went against the prevailing trends: in the Sixties, over 50 per cent of the photographed models in Japanese advertising were non-Asian. This practice changed in 1975, when Mokoto Nakamura met a model at a Paris showing of fashion designer Issey Miyake. Sayoko Yamaguchi had the look Nakamura wanted for Shiseido and he used her face almost exclusively on posters for the next twelve years, an unusually long time for a company to be associated with one model.

Working with Yamaguchi and his favourite photographer, Noriaki Yokosuka, Nakamura claims that he gets his best results at the end of a session, when the model is tired. He likes the model's skin to appear white, and insists that photographers produce light prints to achieve this. Japanese models' eyes and hair he regards as too dark, and he crops the finished prints to remove most of the hair. He does little retouching on the photograph, preferring to make changes with the printer and requesting three or four test prints, twice

Eiko Ishioka, poster for Shiseido, 1966 (730 x 515 mm); photograph by Noriaki Yokusuka. The double-image photograph is a sophisticated solution by the young Ishioka, working under the guidance of Nakamura. The model was Bibari Maeda, half-American and half-Japanese; a schoolgirl at the time, her career as a model and later pop singer was launched by this poster, as was Ishioka's success as an art director. Twenty years after the American occupation, "halfs," as they were known, were discriminated against in all other areas of Japanese life, but as models they were in demand.

the number required by most Japanese designers. Together with Ikko Tanaka and Tadanori Yokoo, he has been one of the leaders in improving Japanese printing quality since the early Sixties. He continues to pioneer new techniques to bring printing to the same level of excellence as was practised by the professionals who made Hokusai's woodblock prints during the Edo period.

Shiseido, as a large organization, offers the same kind of opportunities for young designers as Nippon Design Center, Light Publicity, Seibu Department Stores and Suntory Ltd by providing a training ground for recent graduates. Shiseido employs about fifty design assistants whose tenure is usually short (and many leave early because of low salaries). Designers who started with Shiseido who have achieved considerable success include Kuni Kizawa, Eiko Ishioka, Koichi Sato and Shin Matsunaga, all currently working as freelance designer-art directors employed by a variety of clients.

Tokyo Olympics, 1964

The Tokyo Olympic Games, held in 1964, offered the first opportunity following World War II for Japan to host thousands of visitors. The Design Committee was established in 1960 and included Hiromu Hara, Masaru Katzumie, Yusaku Kamekura, Seiichiro Arai and Masataka Ogawa. Their first project was a symbol that would combine the Olympic gold rings with a sign for Japan. In 1961 four designers were asked to submit proposals and Yusaku Kamekura's design was the unanimous first choice. The simple solution consists of five gold Olympic rings united with Japan's emblematic red sun from the Japanese flag. Kamekura's Olympic posters using Jo Murakoshi's photographs were the 1962 and 1963 Gold Medal winners of the Tokyo Art Directors Club. Ikko Tanaka described them as uniting the relationship between art director and photographer. Noting their success, he felt that designers and art directors should be more ambitious in their instructions to photographers.

An unusual aspect of the Tokyo Olympics was the appointment of Masaru Katzumie as supervisor of design. As usual, Katzumie approached his position magnanimously, expressing the need for Japan to show that it could "crawl up from the rock bottoms of the war defeat and devastation, to express itself." He saw it as a unique opportunity. "It is the expression of monumentality in an event like the Tokyo Olympic Games, and monumentality is not a matter of just build-

Yusaku Kamekura, symbol for the 1964 Tokyo Olympic Games, 1961. Kamekura designed the Olympic symbol while at NDC; it was a milestone in his career. The combination of the bold red sun of the Japanese flag, the linked Olympic rings and the very readable sans serif type was voted a unanimous first choice by the design review committee.

Yusaku Kamekura, poster for the Tokyo Olympics, 1962 (1030 x 728 mm); photograph by Jo Murakoshi. The symbol mark is used as a key design element, setting off the dramatically composed photograph.

Identifying pictograms for the events of the Tokyo Olympics, 1963. Designed by a group of graphic artists under Masaru Katzumie, their grid-based forms became the standard for future international events.

ings and sculpture." Katzumie recruited 30 relatively unknown young designers to design symbols for 20 sports and 34 facilities. They were unpaid. This unique set of simple, playful, integrated, unisex pictograms broke racial and language barriers, and provided a new visual vocabulary for international symbols that were easily recognizable.

The Tokyo Art Directors Club gave Katzumie a special award in 1965 for his art direction of the Tokyo Olympics. In acknowledging the award, he expressed his satisfaction with working alongside a team of young designers who transcended traditional borders of graphic, industrial and interior design. He predicted that this process "will doubtless greatly benefit the design movement in Japan in the future. The star system stage is now a thing of the past, and we are now entering the stage of teamwork." Katzumie's statement parallels the Japanese value of group acceptance over individual accomplishments. Unfortunately, however, the designer-art director star system in Japan is another of those contradictions too embedded in the profession to disappear so quickly.

Katzumie released the copyright on the Olympic symbols for future use at other international events. The pictograms were reworked with a special humorous appearance by Shigeo Fukuda for the 1970 World Exposition in Osaka. Otl Aicher, the German graphic designer and a friend of Katzumie, adopted the forms in his own unique expression for the Munich Olympics of 1972, to make a more harmonious collection. Aicher's mathematical skill produced a sharper, more precise structure for the various symbols; in Tokyo they were rounder and generally softer. History books have granted more attention to Aicher's work than to the original concepts by Katzumie and his young designers.

The success of the World Design Conference and Tokyo Olympics focused international attention on Japanese design, and in 1964 Yusaku Kamekura said that Japan was second only to the United States in its number of graphic designers. A major exhibition built on this number and popularity, "Persona," featured young designers who generally represent the second generation of Japanese graphic design.

Persona 1965, The Second Generation

Persona represented those graphic designers who are now best known among Americans and Europeans: a superb collection of personalities and talents that has formed Japan's graphic design image for the last twenty years. In the early Sixties, Ikko Tanaka and Kohei Sugiura felt that it was time for the younger generation of graphic designers to hold an exhibition with the same significance as Graphic '55. The event proved to be the pivotal exhibition in Japanese graphic design history, although Sugiura himself was not in the event on the list of participants.

Tanaka wanted to include himself and the other three members of an informal Osaka club who had stayed together for over ten years: Tsunehisa Kimura, Kazumasa Nagai and Toshihiro Katayama. Calling themselves the "a" club (the letter was set in lower case News Gothic), they were organized by Kimura in 1952 to share their interest in the teaching theories of the Bauhaus. They met regularly and in 1955 took the overnight train to Tokyo to see the Graphic '55 exhibition. Toshihiro Katayama remembers that the exhausting trip did not dampen their enthusiasm for the freshness of the printed pieces. All four were also impressed by the national impact this exhibition had on designers throughout Japan, an observation that set a goal for their own future.

Yusaku Kamekura recalls that when Sugiura and Tanaka presented a plan to him for an exhibition similar to Graphic '55, the young designers lacked enough prestige to obtain space and publicity. Kamekura, excited about their plans, was able to persuade Matsuya Department Store to hold a show in a large exhibition space in the Ginza store; Matsuya officials insisted that Kamekura's printed work also be included in the exhibition. In a 1987 interview, Tanaka characterized Kamekura as the "good father" who influenced the organization of the exhibition.

The "Exhibition of Graphic Design in Tokyo, 1965 Persona" identified the second generation of graphic designers. As Graphic '55 had had Paul Rand, Tanaka and Kamekura invited four non-Japanese – Paul Davis, Lou Dorfsman, Jan Lenica and Karl Gerstner – all of whom Tanaka had met on his travels in 1960 and 1965. The title "Persona" originated from Masaru Katzumie, who thought the exhibition would show the participants' real personalities or characters and not a "mask."

Tsunehisa Kimura

The recognized leader and theoretician of the "a" club, Tsunehisa Kimura has a reputation as a scholar of Bauhaus design concepts. Born in 1928, he was an early advocate of objective, abstract solutions and quickly established his tal-

Tsunehisa Kimura, poster for the Persona exhibition, 1966 (1030 x 728 mm). Described by the artist as a "crisis game escalation project," this uncommissioned piece foreshadows the design of illustrative newspaper charts that appeared during the Eighties.

図解・エスカレーション戦略(其の二)
《ケイレン的(理性を失った)戦争》

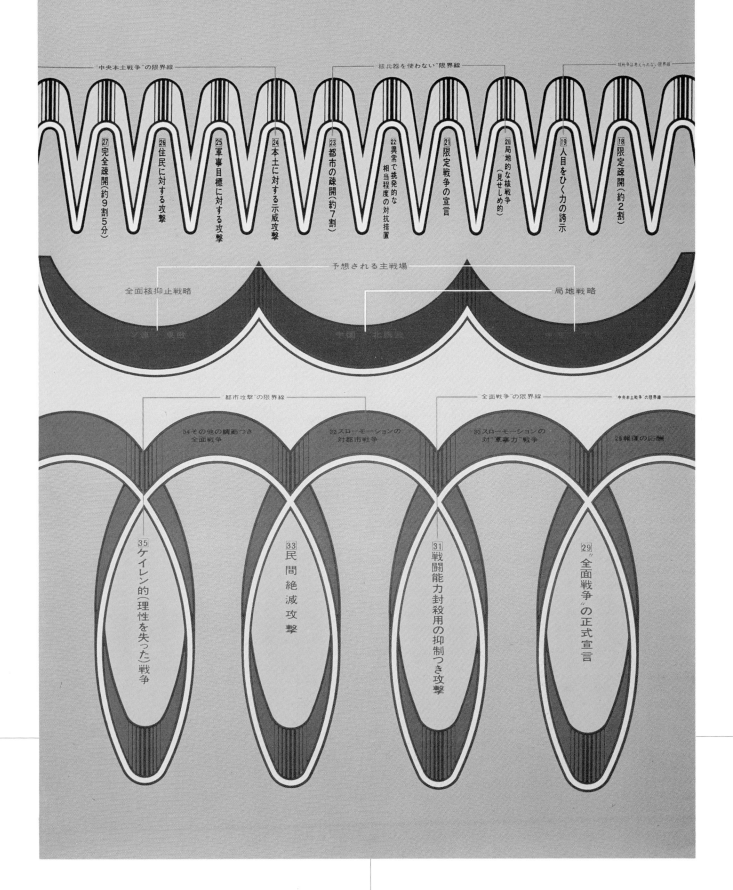

ents by winning the Idea Prize at the 1952 Design Contest run by the Mainichi newspaper (one of the most prestigious in Japan) and the Technical Prize at the JAAC exhibition in 1953. Early recognition in competitions and a scholarly approach to design caught the attention of the Nippon Design Center founders, who invited him to join them as an art director early in 1960. He stayed there only a few years before opening his own office. His contributions to Persona were typical of the designs he produced in the Sixties, based on repetitive geometric forms that resembled isometric drawings of undulating shapes.

By the late Sixties, Kimura's interest in Bauhaus became more focused on experiments with photomontage. He achieved marvels with the juxtaposition of seemingly unrelated images to create a different reality. In the past twenty years he has produced a wonderful series of discordant photomontage images. They combine both traditional and contemporary images to juxtapose the fantastic and the exotic, for example the illustration on pages 170-1 of New York combined with Niagara Falls.

Toshihiro Katayama

Unlike other members of the "a" club, Toshihiro Katayama changed his profession and moved to the USA where he now resides near Boston, Massachusetts. Born in 1928, he is a self-taught artist-designer who developed his interest in modern design theories in the "a" club. Katayama recalls the time the four spent together with considerable fondness, from the formation of the club through their continued association at the Nippon Design Center.

He remained at NDC for a little over three years and then left in disillusionment. In 1988 he claimed that he had destroyed all the design work he produced at NDC because he had not anticipated that the projects would be so commercial. Discovering that his personal interests were not being satisfied, Katayama left NDC to join the design group at Geigy Pharmaceutical in Basel, Switzerland, where he stayed until 1966. While at Geigy, he was invited to the United States to teach graphic design at Harvard University. Now Senior Lecturer at The Carpenter Center of Design at Harvard, in addition to his teaching duties he is an active painter and environmental artist with many significant architectural commissions in America and Japan; his media now range from paper to marble.

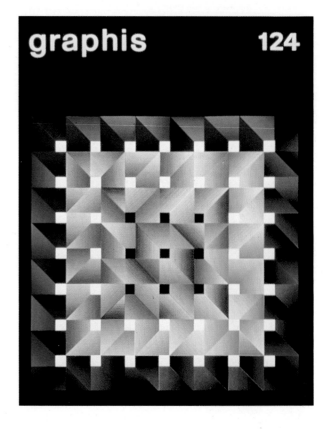

Toshihiro Katayama, cover for *Graphis* magazine, 1966 (300 x 240 mm). Katayama designed this cover while working for Geigy in Switzerland; it expresses his interest in the possibilities of movement and depth in geometric patterns. He has used the square as the basis for his design investigations for over twenty years.

Kazumasa Nagai

Kazumasa Nagai is equally adept at designing print advertisements or trademarks as well as posters. Another Naniwa designer who was born in 1929, Nagai attended Tokyo University of Fine Arts and Music in 1951, majoring in sculpture, then returned to Osaka as a graphic designer for Daiwa Spinning Company. Invited to participate in the establishment of the Nippon Design Center in 1960, he moved to Tokyo where he continues to live. When NDC president Harumu Hara became ill in the Seventies, Nagai was appointed president, and remained in that position until 1987.

Nagai's design style took a single path with few diversions: consistently abstract with limited motifs. His early experiments with constructivist compositions for a series of concerts show clear understanding of geometric form in space. These forms softened and grew more complex with increasing emphasis on lines to create depth and rhythm. Lines have been Nagai's chief source of inspiration. Occasionally they are used independently of other images, sometimes combined with photographs of clouds, sea, mountains, fields of flowers and sand dunes. These lines converge to imitate great depth, join others in circular forms, create flat grids, twist and form globes, or combine to become short, jagged shapes. Sometime the lines manipulate the viewers into chasms or propel them into great heights.

Since the Sixties, Nagai has continued his research on lines and has developed a remarkable series of works, with prints and drawings shown in solo exhibitions. These have become a source of inspiration to him for commercial projects. His abstract sensibilities are well suited to designs for trademarks that do not require realistic images, for companies such as banks, manufacturers and museums.

If there is any weakness in Kazumasa Nagai's designs it is repetition of concept. Each problem is handled with the same set of tools to create solutions that vary only with changes in the geometric configuration of lines and shapes. Examples include the many posters he designed during the Eighties for the Toyama Prefecture Museum of Art (one is shown on page 210). His solutions are superb compositions, with outstanding printing quality, but they offer little visual hint of the kind of exhibition or event that is being advertised. Nagai defends his solutions in a statement in *The Annual of Advertising Art in Japan 85-86*: "...instead of laying emphasis on one big work from among the many on exhibit, I try to express the

発売1年3億本 マイペースで飲もう アサヒスタイニー

Top: Kazumasa Nagai, trademark for the Suruga Bank, 1965. One of Nagai's many corporate symbols, this has an architectural structure which is organic in appearance.

Above: Kazumasa Nagai, poster for Asahi Stiny beer, 1965 (1030 x 730 mm); photograph by Muneo Maeda. The carefully arranged bottle caps - all bearing the symbol designed by Walter Landor in 1959 - commemorate the 300 million bottles sold in the previous year. The design of a completely photographic poster was unusual for Nagai.

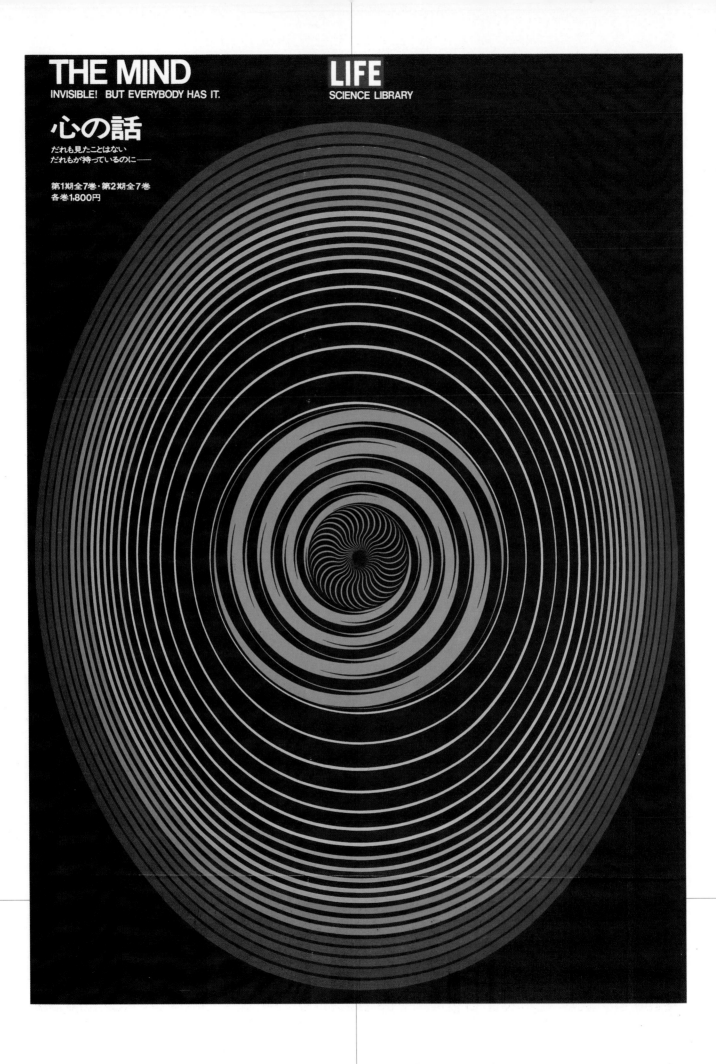

THE MIND

INVISIBLE! BUT EVERYBODY HAS IT.

LIFE

SCIENCE LIBRARY

心の話

だれも見たことはない
だれもが持っているのに——

第1期全7巻・第2期全7巻
各巻1,800円

THE MIND

INVISIBLE! BUT EVERYBODY HAS IT.

LIFE

SCIENCE LIBRARY

Kazumasa Nagai, poster advertising a *Life* Science Library book, 1966 (1024 x 740 mm). One of a series for *Life*, this silk-screened poster was an uncommissioned piece, with the pattern of lines being Nagai's recurring motif.

Kiyoshi Awazu, poster for a prints exhibition, 1964 (1030 x 728 mm). The traditional method of signature is Japan is a seal, made of ivory or wood, which stamps the identifying two or three characters of a family name. Awazu has used a collage of these on the central drawing.

中山悌一独唱会
ピアノ＝小林道夫
TEIICHI NAKAYAMA RECITAL

1 F・シューベルト　　"美しき水車小屋の乙女"より 何処へ　小川の子守唄 ／"冬の旅"より 菩提樹 溢るる涙

"白鳥の歌"より　わが宿 影法師 ／ 選歌　鱒 魔王

SCHUBERT

2 SchuMANN

R・シューマン　胡桃の樹／2人の擲弾兵

MAHLER **3**

G・マーラー　ラインのおとぎ話／鼓手／高い知性の讃辞

竪琴によす／旅あるき／眠れる幼子イエス／園丁　WOLF **4**　H・ヴォルフ

5 KILPINEN　　星は輝く／岸辺にて／夏の夜／君は何処に／高原の歌

Y・キルピネン

● 新会員募集中

入会のお申込は 神戸市葺合区御幸通り
国際会館4階／TEL.(22)8161・8361
神戸労音事務局へ　会費 150円・入会費 100円

神戸労音6月例会　主催 神戸勤労者音楽協議会

6月7日(火)6時半 国際会館

Ikko Tanaka, poster for a music recital, 1960 (728 x 515 mm). Tanaka is known for his mastery of type design; his mixture of Roman type styles in this striking poster predates by 25 years the letter-form arrangements associated with the Post-Modernists.

Ikko Tanaka, poster for a noh production, 1961 (1030 x 728 mm). One of Tanaka's specialities is his trademark design, born of his deep appreciation of the shapes and lines created by Japanese calligraphy. These kanji letters - silk-screened on a black field - are arranged in traditional fashion, reading top to bottom, right to left. The beauty of the letter forms is enhanced by the printing of different parts in distinct colours.

event itself. I believe that posters are independent of the art genre, that is, they play the role of visual prelude to an exhibition. And, in general, I believe the policy of the museum is to set a clear dividing line."

Kiyoshi Awazu

Much of the work of Kiyoshi Awazu (born in 1929) also focuses on lines as a design motif. However, he produces totally different results from those achieved by Nagai. He uses traditional tools to create a series of expressive lines drawn with contour-map regularity. His line quality and drawing construction have been directly influenced by the American artist Ben Shahn. His drawings are crude, resembling the tough quality found in much of Japan's folk art and, on the surface, have much of the same temperament as ukiyo-e woodblock prints. When compared to the technical constructions of most of his contemporaries, he is said to have a unique expressiveness that has been highly influential for the new generation of Japanese illustrators.

Avoiding commercial clients, Awazu prefers to limit his graphic design projects to cultural events and anti-war posters. He recalls that, while preparing documents and photographs on the atomic destruction of Hiroshima and Nagasaki, he became interested in editorial art as a political expression. He expanded his imagery beyond flat planes to include environmental design, and has taken on the role of art director of various important exhibitions, including The Great Japan Exhibition at the Royal Academy of Arts, London, in 1980. He is currently Professor at Kyoto Junior College of Art.

Ikko Tanaka

No other Japanese designer is recognized so well abroad as Ikko Tanaka, whose posters for Noh drama and design of popular books including *Japan Color* (1980) and a series for Mazda Motor Corporation, *The Wheel, The Hybrid Culture* and *The Compact Culture*, are familiar to many foreigners. A frequent visitor to the United States, his work has been shown at lectures in Washington DC, Honolulu, Dallas, New York City and at the Aspen Design Conference. He received considerable international attention for his design of the Japan Style exhibition at the Victoria and Albert Museum, London, in 1980 and its accompanying catalogue.

Born in Nara in 1930, he graduated from Kyoto City College of Fine Arts in 1950 and entered the Kanegafuchi Spin-

ning Company in Kyoto as a textile designer. He also worked on *Sankei Shimbun*, an Osaka newspaper, as a graphic designer from 1952 to 1958. He spent two years in Light Publicity, worked for Nippon Design Center from 1960 to 1963, then left to establish Tanaka Design Studio in Tokyo. When he began his career, European poster designer-illustrators Raymond Savignac and Herbert Leupin were at their peak. It was not their illustrative style that interested him, but their discipline in creating graphic images that communicate with little or no extraneous information. His knowledge of Bauhaus theories was developed in the Fifties and provided a foundation for the logical, mathematical structure of his work.

Tanaka's popularity in the United States and Europe can be attributed to his ability to provide Japanese graphic images most appreciated and expected by foreigners. His work is almost an exploitation of traditional Japanese images – masks, ukiyo-e prints, rimpa motifs, calligraphy and Japanese colour. He is recognized for his Kanze Noh Theatre posters, produced between 1953 and 1974, in which he mixes modern European design principles with traditional Japanese imagery. He walks a fine line in his Noh posters, carefully legitimizing Japanese souvenir-style visual clichés with a modern adaptation of colour, technical manipulation and focus.

In 1972 he was asked to design the annual report for Seibu Saison Group, which includes the fashionable Seibu Department Stores, Seiyu Food Stores, Parco and several other subsidiaries such as the Seibu Theatre and Seibu Museum of Art. In a friendly meeting with its President Seiji Tsutsumi, he was invited to do a few additional projects. This turned out to become an extensive association that lasted over twelve years and ranged, as he put it, from "large urban redevelopment projects to packaging for pickles."

Lou Dorfsman wrote in the introduction to *The World of Ikko Tanaka* (1975): "Ikko Tanaka is a modest, quiet man who forms a graphic bridge from Tokyo to San Francisco." When asked about this statement in 1987, Tanaka explained that colours in Southern Japan are brighter than in Tokyo; the soil, for example, is lighter near Osaka than in Tokyo. This light touch is characteristic of all Tanaka's work.

To update his 1975 book, Tanaka published *The Design World of Ikko Tanaka* in January 1987; it sold out in three months. He gives two important reasons for the popularity in Japan of books by designers about their own history: printing costs are lower than in the West, and there is a ready market

of young design students eager to purchase the books. Tanaka's latest book cost 15,000 yen, the equivalent at the time of about $75 or £65 – not cheap even for Japan's affluent youth.

Tanaka's skill in graphic design is so expansive that it is almost impossible to limit it to a medium where he is most successful. He is equally comfortable in type design, the creation of symbol marks, package design, environmental graphics, exterior and interior signs. His love of books provides a special touch in his book design.

Mitsuo Katsui

Sharing Ikko Tanaka's skill in design, Mitsuo Katsui is best known for his ability to manipulate the latest photograph and print technology. He was born in 1931 and graduated from Tokyo University of Education, where he studied both design and photography. He began employment at Aji-no-moto Company and worked there for a few years before he opened his own office in 1956. His first national recognition was in 1958 when he won the eighth Japanese Advertising Art Club Award. Long involved in education, he was an influential teacher at Tokyo University of Education and continues to teach at its successor, Tsukuba University. In a conversation in 1984, he talked about his experiences as a graphic designer in comparison with those of today's students, explaining that it had been hard for his generation to be involved in advertising because of the concept of pure design that had been formed by Western practitioners. Today, young students are more attracted to the excitement of advertising design and its potential for creative ideas.

Shigeo Fukuda

Known for his puckish approach to design imagery, Shigeo Fukuda has won more international poster prizes than any other Japanese graphic designer. His work is popular primarily for visual puns that are created by optical illusions and figure-ground reversals. Born in 1932, he graduated from Tokyo University of Fine Arts and Music with a degree in design in 1956 and, soon after, his participation in the Persona exhibition launched his career.

In 1966 Fukuda received the Encouragement Award at the Second Biennial of Graphic Design in Brno, Czecho-slovakia. The next year, his poster inviting artists to exhibit at Expo '70 was designated the official poster for the exhibition. One of Masaru Katzumie's team of designers who produced symbols

Ikko Tanaka, trademark for the Bank of Tokyo, 1967. Equally skilful with trademarks and logos as well as with posters, Tanaka expresses simple design and stability of form for this bank symbol.

もうひとつ
の顔を
よそおうのではありません

ねむっている
あなたの新しい魅力

をひきだすのです

MAX FACTOR

for the Tokyo Olympics, his experience led him to be commissioned to design pictograms and signs for both Expo '70 facilities and the Sapporo Winter Olympics. He was introduced to the United States with a popular exhibition of 1965, "Toys and Things Japanese," organized and staged by Paul Rand at the New York IBM Gallery.

Shigeo Fukuda's strength is his penetrating, satirical and often humorous graphic solutions. Influenced by Italian designer Bruno Munari's delightful visual illusions, his designs are effective more for their witty content than for any manipulation of visual elements, for example in the poster of himself apparently standing on a gallery wall. In his posters he frequently employs a single bold image, surrealistic in scale and with little concern for the principles of spatial composition. He described his approach to design in *The Annual of Advertising Art in Japan 85-86* as "30 per cent dignity, 20 per cent beauty, and 50 per cent absurdity." Paul Rand, in his introduction to *Shigeo Fukuda* (1979), wrote: "one can't help noticing that Fukuda's name begins with Fu as in fun and ends in da as in Dada, the art movement at the early part of this century that took pomposity out of art."

Akira Uno

Combining imagery of romantic women, similar to Yumeji Takehisa's of the Twenties, with the sexual liberation of the Sixties, Akira Uno provided a sensual stimulus for young people. He was born in 1934 and his career started in 1956 when he won a special prize at the Japan Advertising Artist Club annual exhibition. He entered Nippon Design Center in 1960 and left with Tadanori Yokoo and Tsundo Harada in 1964. They formed their own studio but stayed together for only one year when Uno started his Studio Re in 1965.

By the mid-Sixties he was art director for Japan's Max Factor cosmetics. His romantic, sensual drawings of European women in which he combined the qualities of Aubrey Beardsley with those of Takahisa did not quite fit the image of a corporate art director, but more of someone who wanted to be on the fringe of society.

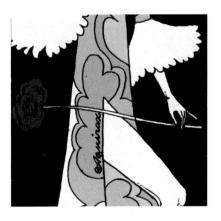

Gan Hosoya

Recognized more as an art director than a graphic designer, Gan Hosoya was one of the pioneers in the profession and the only participant in Persona who operated in the traditional style of an American art director. Many other partici-

Akira Uno, poster for Max Factor, 1965 (1091 x 793 mm). Uno's typically tall, thin figure with sorrowful eyes holds a branch of masks above her head. The copy reads: "We are trying to pretend with another face, but it is a test to awaken your sleeping charm." Uno was active as a designer in the late Sixties, but his work has remained relatively unpublicized.

Akira Uno, match box covers, 1967 (60 x 60 mm). In this series of designs, the woman's hand becomes the head of a bird and her foot is transformed into the head of a horned antelope. Match box covers were a popular promotion for designers and illustrators as well as for coffee houses.

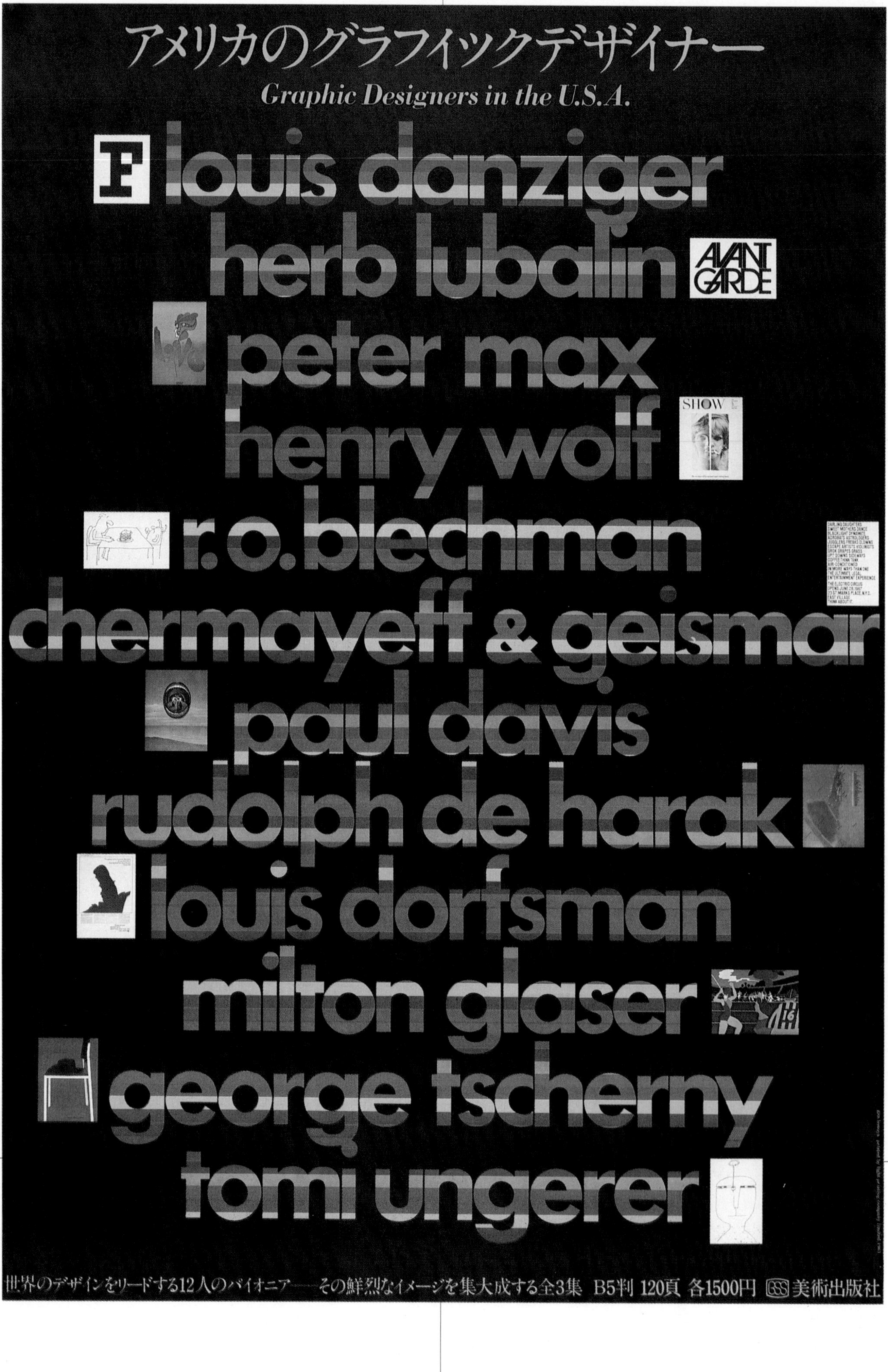

アメリカのグラフィックデザイナー
Graphic Designers in the U.S.A.
louis danziger
herb lubalin
AVANT GARDE
peter max
henry wolf
SHOW
r.o. blechman
chermayeff & geismar
paul davis
rudolph de harak
louis dorfsman
milton glaser
george tscherny
tomi ungerer
世界のデザインをリードする12人のパイオニア——その鮮烈なイメージを集大成する全3集 B5判 120頁 各1500円 美術出版社

pants, although listed as art directors and with membership of the Tokyo Art Directors Club, are effectively graphic designers. Hosoya was born in 1935 and, following his graduation in 1953 from the industrial design course at Kanagawa Prefectural Technical High School, joined Light Publicity where he continues today as an active art director.

Hosoya gives an insight into his philosophy as an art director in a statement included in the catalogue to a poster exhibition at Toyama Art Museum in 1982: "Looking around us, we realize that our daily life is filled with anxieties. We have become so accustomed to living with anxieties and have been immune to them for some time, we cannot imagine a life without them. I feel that expressing extreme anxiety, among other feelings, is part of my daily work – creating advertisements. In addition, I believe advertisements can succeed only when designers express these anxieties. There is nothing but boredom in work that has been produced from a stable life, and advertisements created 'on the edge of a cliff' are really valuable and will be rewarded."

Makoto Wada

Best known as an illustrator-cartoonist, Makoto Wada was included in Persona primarily because Ikko Tanaka had admired his work and energy and wanted him to receive recognition. Wada's early interest in cartoons was influenced by Saul Steinberg, Herbert Leupin, Raymond Savignac, and the emotional, earthly quality of Ben Shahn. Wada was born in 1936 and graduated from Tama University. He won the 1959 Japan Advertising Artist Club Grand Prix award and, in the same year, joined Light Publicity where he met Ikko Tanaka. Wada first gained recognition for a series of movie posters produced in the early Sixties. His bold style of illustration resembles expressive woodblock prints; it has become refined in recent years but is still dependent on flat colours filling black line illustrations.

Tadanori Yokoo

An enigma to his fellow designers, Tadanori Yokoo provided America with its first Japanese graphic design hero who designed and illustrated with such inventive passion that his influence was almost immediate. Crediting the Persona exhibition with providing his big break, Yokoo states that he owes Ikko Tanaka his thanks for providing respect and support during his difficult early years. Yokoo is one of the few fa-

Gan Hosoya, poster for a design book, 1964 (1030 x 725 mm). This Japanese publication promoted the work of American designers whose names would have been familiar to Japanese, but to assist in identification Hosoya incorporated samples of each designer's work.

Makoto Wada, poster for the 1956 King Vidor film of Tolstoy's *War and Peace* starring Audrey Hepburn, 1963 (728 x 515 mm). This is one of a series of silk-screened film posters which brought Wada a considerable reputation in the early Sixties. Each was illustrated with a single figure in one colour on a bright background.

mous Japanese graphic designers who did not go to one of the "right" universities; in fact, he had no formal art training other than a correspondence course during high school. Born in 1936, he worked first for a newspaper, *Kobe Shimbun*, and then for an advertising agency in Kobe where he felt that his work was naive and not of a high quality. His break came when he won a Japan Advertising Artist Club Award in 1957 for a Kobe concert poster at the age of 21. By the late Fifties, most good designers in Osaka and Kobe had left for Tokyo. Yokoo said he was so lonely in 1960 that he went to Tokyo to attend the World Design Conference, met Tanaka, and was invited to join Nippon Design Center.

Tanaka hired Yokoo on the basis of his 1957 award; Yokoo, however, still felt that he had to prove his talent. He stayed for four years, first working with Tanaka, then as an assistant for Kazumasa Nagai, involved more in illustration than design. Two posters, commissioned by Tanaka, were his best work at NDC. Both received awards from the Japan Advertising Artist Club annual exhibition. A poet friend, employed as a copywriter for NDC, introduced him to the seamy side of Tokyo's life, which became a major influence on his future life style. Yokoo left NDC in 1964 to work as an independent designer-illustrator.

During the Sixties the influential Katzumie was strongly critical in public about Yokoo for seeking commonplace Japanese motifs and ignoring intellectual constructivist theories. Instead of discouraging him, this inspired Yokoo to be even more vulgar and to scorn current international design directions. Yusaku Kamekura, on the other hand, had a great liking for Yokoo's work and always supported him, even though he considered him to be a trickster at that time. Yokoo described himself as a clown, who had more support from young people than major designers; the latter regarded him as an artist who brought "poison" to the design profession. His notoriety peaked when he rediscovered his Japanese heritage, which he flaunted to the delight of Americans and the bewilderment of his countrymen. It was precisely this arrogance in replicating Edo brashness that endeared him to foreigners, and liberated a new generation of Japanese designers and illustrators.

The Japanese design establishment has never quite known where to place Yokoo. Most designers regarded him as an illustrator, because of an emphasis on personal expression that was being consciously avoided by "modern" designers.

As his reputation grew in the eyes of young Japanese and an international following, he soon proved he was more than a graphic designer and had talents as an architect, movie star, photographer, writer, painter, occasional singer, printmaker and all-around celebrity. It seemed he was a success at everything he touched. By 1968 he was invited by the New York Museum of Modern Art to design the poster for their exhibition Word and Image.

Feeling restricted by his label as a graphic designer he broadened his interests to include a variety of areas: he joined with students to close down the Japan Advertising Artist Club, designed the Textile Pavilion for Expo '70, starred in his own television spy series, released a record album entitled *Opera – "From the Works of Tadanori Yokoo,"* won first prize at an international print show, published a 328-page book, *The Complete Tadanori Yokoo*, in 1971 with over a thousand illustrations, and organized a major exhibition of his work at the New York Museum of Modern Art in 1972.

The sheer number of pieces produced by Tadanori Yokoo from the mid-Sixties to the Seventies is astounding. There are very few areas of art and design he did not attempt. He brought Hokusai's "great wave" back into the Japanese lexicon, created typographic experiments predating post-modern clichés, introduced Marilyn Monroe as an icon, pictured American nude women promoting middle-class products, painted nudes so that their bodies appeared clothed, created art that satirized every convention, and used the poster as a collage that layered photographs, prints, paintings and English and Japanese type, all in brilliant colours. Ikko Tanaka once said with approbation: "Yokoo's loud colours and crude motifs shattered the conventions of refined taste."

During the late Sixties, as the Vietnam war threatened to expand into the Far East, Japanese students joined their comrades throughout the world in protest. In 1968, artists and designers participated in an "Anti-War and Liberation Exhibition" organized in Tokyo by 92 Japanese and American painters, sculptors and designers. By the end of the Sixties, it seemed that everyone's attention was on student strikes at the universities, anti-war movements, protests against the US Security Treaty (due for its ten-year ratification in 1970) and the eventual dissolution of JAAC. But these activities did not deter most Japanese designers from being involved in the first major international event of the next decade.

Tadanori Yokoo, poster for Persona, 1965 (1030 x 720 mm). Yokoo's poster pictures his life, stylistic death and rebirth. The climax referred to in the copy was the Persona exhibition itself. In order to rid himself of the burden of the success and failure of past work, the artist figuratively kills himself: he and his friends actually staged a mock funeral at a Tokyo cemetery, which was fully documented in his book, *The Posthumous Works of Tadanori Yokoo* (1968).

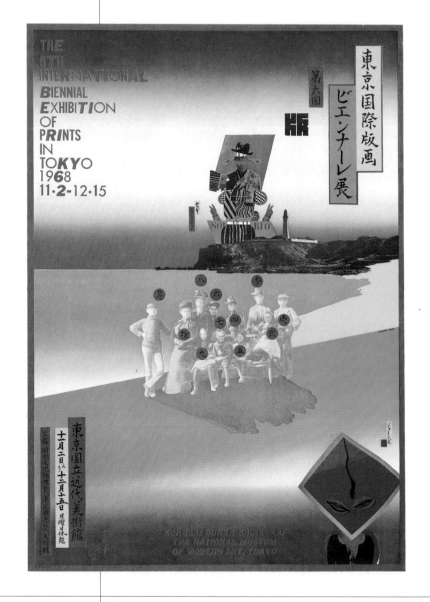

Tadanori Yokoo, poster for a poster exhibition at the Museum of Modern Art in New York, 1968. Surrounding the central eye is the symbol of the Imperial Japanese battle flag.

Tadanori Yokoo, poster for a prints exhibition at the Tokyo National Museum, 1968 (1042 x 740 mm). Mixing cultures and eras, Yokoo uses gradations of raw Pop-Art colours, collage techniques and type styles in a symmetrical design. The group is of a Western family.

Tadanori Yokoo, poster promoting an exhibition by the photographer Eiko Hosoe, "A Heartbreaking Tragicomedy," 1968 (1085 x 765 mm). The dancer squatting on a wooden frame used to dry bundles of straw is Tatsumi Hijikata, whose handprints are individually placed at the top of each poste

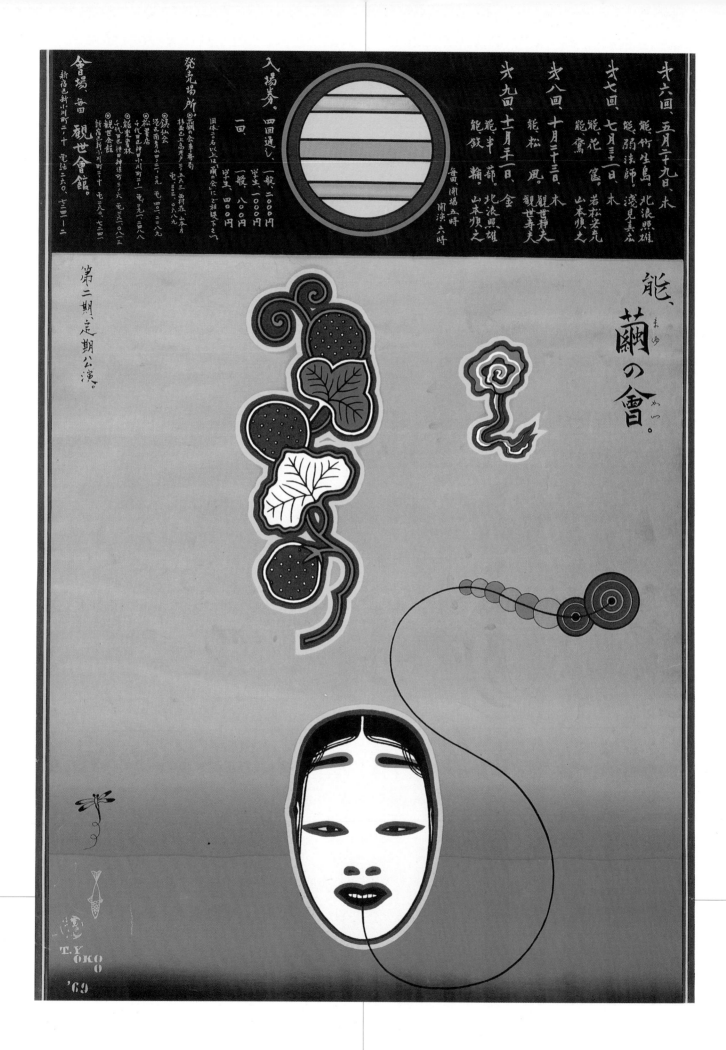

Expo '70, Japan's First World Exposition

Expo '70 was held outside Osaka for eight months. The Design Committee, consisting of Masaru Katzumie, Isamu Kenmochi, Takashi Kono, Hiromu Hara, Yoshio Hayakawa and seven others, held its first meeting in 1965. In 1966 they chose Takeshi Ohtaka's symbol mark, resembling a flower monsho.

The response of Japanese designers was very mixed. The preparations provided considerable activity: three years of lucrative employment in graphics, interiors and exteriors of pavilions, and site design. Favourable reviews of the results propelled some designers into even greater recognition, both with their countrymen and with the international community. But there were some problems. Ichiro Haryu in his article "World Expositions at the Crossroads" in *Graphic Design* magazine, wrote: "Expo '70 is the repository of the unfinished dreams of three generations of Japan's ruling strata. In the slogan, 'Asia's first World Exposition,' one senses the aspirations of Japanese monopoly capital, dreaming of restoring its political and economical harmony over Asia after the war in Vietnam. China, Asia's mightiest power, North Korea and North Vietnam did not even receive invitations."

It was clear from the beginning that the Fair would be as much of an education for Japanese as it would be for foreign visitors. For the millions of visitors it was a combination of architectural circus and coming-of-age experience. The futuristic pavilions with multimedia presentations provided such a barrage of information that most of it was probably absorbed without the viewers' knowledge or full understanding. For many country folk, this was their first experience with escalators. Some mistook outdoor sculpture for toilets: Shigeo Fukuda's carefully designed, cosmopolitan, international symbols for public conveniences were not clear to most Japanese and required hand-written signs taped underneath. The 76 foreign participants also provided many Japanese visitors from rural areas with their first experience of gaijin (non-Asians). Inside foreign pavilions, Japanese gained some experience of countries with histories different from their own, which created a curiosity about their own origins.

Expo '70 was a fitting way to close the decade. After ten years of foreign scrutiny, Japan was finally becoming recognized as a major economic power, with graphic designers who equalled those found anywhere in the world.

Site map for Expo '70, 1969;
coordinated by Masaru Katzumie. In
the tradition of illustrated European
city maps, this was the first time an
isometric map was used in Japan.

Eiko Ishioka, poster for Expo '70,
1968 (1015 x 730 mm). More
enigmatic than Kamekura's poster,
this has a red sun emblematic of
Japan on which the Expo '70 symbol
is subtly projected.

人類の進歩と調和 / 昭和45年3月15日—9月13日:大阪

Above: Keisuke Nagatomo, poster for the sports clothes manufacturer Jantzen, 1965 (1090 x 760 mm). Nagatomo was a young designer at NDC when he won a Japan Advertising Art Club award for this uncommissioned poster with a silk-screened blue-grey colour over fluorescent paper. By the end of the Sixties Nagatomo had left NDC to form K2 with his friend the illustrator Sietaro Kuroda.

Tadashi Ohashi, symbol to celebrate the centenary of the Meiji Restoration, 1967. The artist took the chrysanthemum monsho that represents the Imperial family and turned it on its side.

Tadahito Nadamoto, poster for a visiting troupe of actors performing traditional Chinese songs and dances, 1965. The figure jumping above the cloud is wearing traditional Chinese costume.

全国労音招聘

大阪労音ＡＢＣ選択例会

中国の歌と踊り

民族楽器オーケストラ

● 九月二十八日㊏二時三十分
　　二十九日㊐二時三十分　六時三十分
● 十月三日㊍六時三十分
　　四日㊎六時三十分

● フェスティバルホール
　特別会費四〇〇円

十一月Ａ例会予告　帰ってきたイベット・ジロー

Left: Keichi Tanaami, poster advertising a book of the artist's illustrations, 1968 (1030 x 728 mm). In this self-promotional silk-screened poster, the artist uses just enough sex to provoke interest. Tanaami (born in 1936) went on to become art director of Japan's *Playboy* magazine for many years.

Above: Katsumi Asaba, poster promoting Neptune whiskey, 1969 (1030 x 728 mm); photograph by Yoshihiro Tatsuki. This Sixties version of a bijin-ga picture uses a Euro-Asian model to provide a refreshing metaphor for the product.

Ryuichi Yamashiro, poster for an exhibition of the artist's collages, 1969 (1030 x 662 mm). At this period Yamashiro was experimenting with collages, using old postage stamps and envelopes.

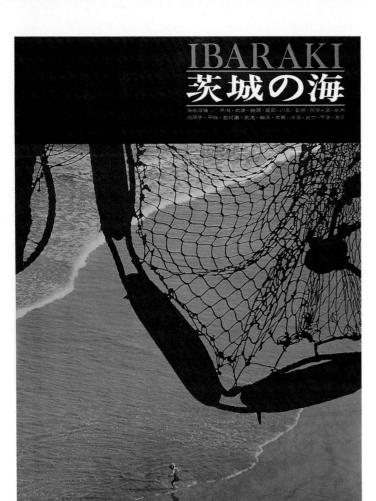

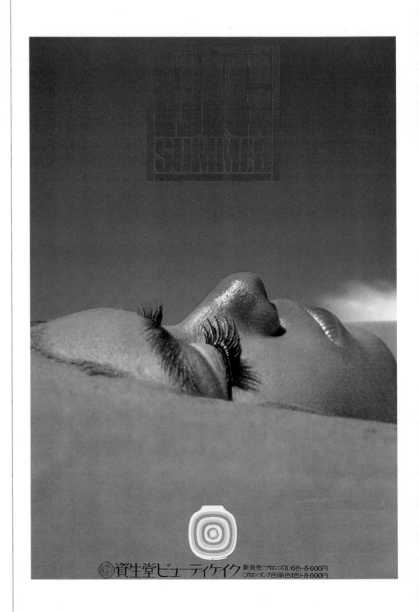

Tadashi Masuda, travel poster
advertising the Ibaraki district near
Tokyo, 1969 (1030 x 728 mm);
photograph by Mitsuo Doki. This was
one of a series of popular travel
posters.

Shin Matsunaga, poster for Shiseido
thick dark make-up, 1970 (1018 x
730 mm); photograph by Noriaki
Yokusuka. This was one of a series by
Shiseido; the photograph effectively
conveys the idea of sand, sun and
sweat.

Makoto Nakamura, poster for Shiseido, 1970 (1018 x 728 mm); photograph by Noriaki Yokusuka. In the late Sixties English words made a popular accompaniment to photographs of Euro-Asian models. Phrases such as "Lip Art," "Pink Pow-Wow" and "Pink Pop" were blazoned on posters; here the punchline is in the heavily shadowed type favoured at the time. Notice that the model facing the camera does not have a left ear; Nakamura had the photograph retouched because he felt that the ear detracted from the other model's features.

Yuzo Yamashita, poster encouraging travel to New Zealand, 1970 (1030 x 728 mm). The UNESCO village in a suburb of Tokyo features exhibits of daily life in different countries; this poster accompanied a special exhibition on New Zealand.

Kiyoshi Awazu, poster for an avant-garde theatre group, 1970 (728 x 515 mm). The shocking image is typical of those designed at the time, and bears comparison with work by Tadanori Yokoo and Keichi Tanaami.

5

Back to the origins
1971-1979

In many ways, the Sixties was an exhausting decade for Japanese graphic designers. It was an era of such radical change and growth that it took several years to realize its long-term effects. Designers reached an international audience with many individual and group successes – in competitions and exhibitions in Japan and abroad, in a cover story in *Communication Arts* magazine in 1968, and in double-issue coverage in *Graphis* magazine (Numbers 168 and 169) the same year. It seemed that their quest for recognition was over. But as with so many goals, once success was achieved it was greeted with apprehension and question.

As Japan entered the Seventies, a change in graphic design was inevitable. It is interesting to look for early harbingers. One appeared in Ikko Tanaka's article in the 1968 *Graphis* double issue, "Japanese Younger Generation of Designers." He led with this observation: "There are no longer any Oriental features unique to Japan's younger generation of graphic designers. With the rapid development of transportation facilities and mass communication media, Japan's graphic designers now share new trends with their counterparts abroad." Tanaka continued on recent influences of decorative design and Art Nouveau and a "resistance by young Japanese graphic designers against highly rational design. This phenomenon shows that Japan's graphic designers are now moving out of the era of imitating foreign cultures into a new era of 'sharing' new trends with their colleagues in other countries."

Another indication of change was the impact of Expo '70. During the early Seventies, tantalized by what they had seen in the foreign pavilions, many Japanese travelled abroad and reflected on their impressions of foreign culture and society. Intellectuals were also stimulated to re-examine their country's religious and cultural origins found in China, India and Korea. With the reopening of diplomatic relations with the People's Republic of China in 1972, and with opportunities for more personal contacts in China, there were new interests in tracing the sources of Japanese art, architecture, crafts and social structure. The late Edwin O. Reischauer, in his important study *The Japanese* (1977), confirmed this quest: "The early '70s books and journal articles appeared asking what it meant to be a Japanese and what was Japan's distinctive role in the world. The Japanese called it the Nihonjin-ron, which might be translated as 'the debate over being Japanese.'"

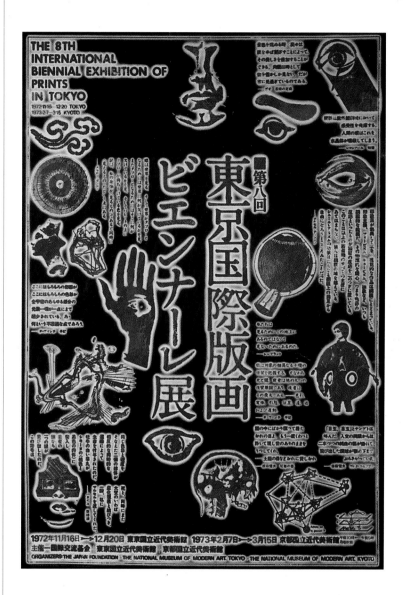

Kohei Sugiura, poster promoting a prints exhibition, 1972 (942 x 681 mm). Similar in spirit to his 1959 Stravinsky poster (see page 93), this contains a mixture of English and Japanese, reading both left to right and right to left.

This review of their Asian heritage contributed to a significant shift in the direction of Japanese designers, who developed a strong sense of pride in their work and questioned the need to establish identity by following international directions and joining the various fads occurring in America and Europe. The change in emphasis did not occur suddenly in an organized fashion, nor was it promoted by any of the various influential design organizations. It appeared in a more evolutionary form, over a period of six to eight years, through research and designs produced by some influential designers, such as Tadanori Yokoo, Kazumasa Nagai and Kohei Sugiura.

The search for roots was promoted by a poster campaign by Japan National Railway in 1973, to encourage families to rediscover their heritage. The series of outstanding transport posters called "Discover Japan" won top awards in the Tokyo Art Directors Club Annual in 1974. Designed by Yoshi Hasegawa (born in 1947), the posters were placed in the extensive urban train and subway system that covers almost every area of Tokyo, Osaka and Kyoto. The success of this campaign greatly promoted the use of posters in trains and subways as an advertising medium.

Nakazuri: Transport Posters

Transport posters have been around for a hundred years, providing an increasing visual impact on the population. *Naka* means centre and *zuri* means hanging: nakazuri posters hang in the centre of trains and subways, always in constant view from any standing or seated location, even during the rush hour when people are packed in by station attendants to fill all available space. They are only one form of advertising found in transport systems; just about every surface of the car is used – windows, doors, and even hanging straps have advertisements attached. In addition to posters in the centre of cars, there are posters along the side and above windows. One subway car can display 24 to 26 posters; trains have space for 28. They are small in size, 14¾ inches deep and 20¼ inches wide (36.5 x 51.5 cm). Each car displays two side by side, back to back, down the length of the centre of the interior. During rush hour they provide 8 to 10 inches clearance above most Japanese heads. In the summer months, open windows and electric fans hung from the ceiling keep them in constant agitation.

These posters first appeared in 1885 in private rail coaches and, soon after in 1891, they were hung in national rail cars.

Nakazuri posters hanging in the centre of the cars on the Yamata line that encircles Tokyo. They are usually hung for just a few days before being replaced; most promote magazines or department store sales.

Poster promoting *Young Lady*, a weekly magazine for young women, 1984 (365 x 515 mm). Many posters advertising magazines are derivative of the Twenties and Thirties, with complex typographic designs, interspersed with small photographs and illustrations. They usually give the contents and the type reads from almost every direction.

Their use continued during the Meiji era but for some reason they were discontinued during most of the Taisho period (1912-26). The first exhibition of "Outstanding Train Posters" was held in 1956, sponsored by Orikomi, a leading advertising agency. Many nakazuri posters are not of the same quality as the "Discover Japan" series, but still far exceed what is seen in most Western countries. Those that win awards in annual competitions are usually smaller, re-designed versions of posters found in the Tokyo Art Directors Annuals.

The value of nakazuri as a medium is its selectivity in terms of its audience. By choosing a particular train line that originates in a suburb, advertisers can determine the audience to be housewives, office workers, professional people, students or any combination. Or they can concentrate on inner-city riders who travel from one urban village to another. Surveys show that these posters are remembered. In a 1980 survey taken by Orikomi Advertising Agency and reported by Hisayoshi Nakayama in his article "Transit Advertising," 43 per cent of the riders could remember a particular poster, suggesting that nakazuri will become one of the top advertising media in Japan, competing with magazines, newspapers, television and radio.

Its unique characteristic of low-cost production in proportion to the size of its audience makes nakazuri the ultimate medium for disposable designs. The high quality of the design and printing is remarkable in a medium where the posters are seen for only two or three days and then taken down and destroyed. Magazine and book publishers are the largest sponsors, followed by manufacturers of electronic goods, food stores, department stores and retailers. There are even a number of small organizations that take advantage of the low unit cost – schools, entertainment groups, wedding organizers and tourism promoters. Major advertisers who seem to be natural candidates for this medium are the publishers of comic books, the most popular reading material in Japan.

Manga: Japanese Comic Books

One of the many apparent contradictions in Japan is a 99.9 per cent literacy rate in a population addicted to reading comic books. But these comics are not just for pre-teenagers who seek discovery of their possible future or retreats into fantasy, but for Japanese people of all age levels, male and female, blue collar and white collar. Japanese comics are of a size that rival Manhattan phone books, with 300 to 500 pages.

2月25日号本日発売
毎月10日・25日発売／定価2

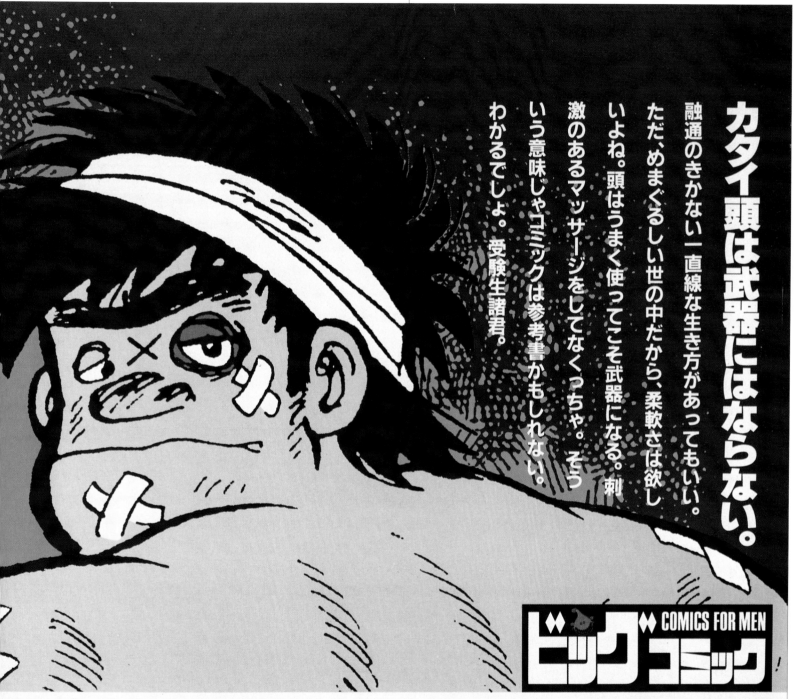

Tsunekazu Seiki, comic poster, 1981 (365 x 515 mm). Adult comics are enormously popular in Japan; this one, a successful fortnightly called *Big Comic*, is aimed at young men. A train car full of such posters provides foreigners with a good opportunity to observe the latest social trends, revealed in popular articles and magazine stories.

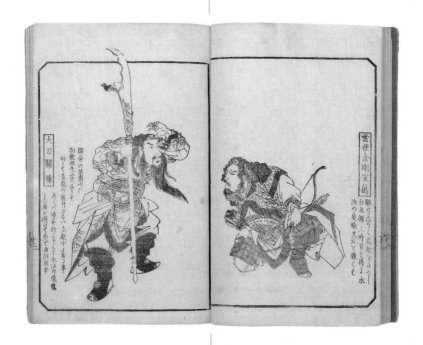

Top: Kunisada, spread from a manga based on an ancient Chinese story, about 1860 (220 x 150 mm). Nineteenth-century manga consisted of separate woodblock prints, bound together into a book.

Above: Keiko Takemiya, page from the comic book *Passé Composé*, published by Shinshindo Shuppan, 1979 (300 x 210 mm); the story is of a country girl trying to be sophisticated in the city. Modern manga appear first in bulky volumes printed on cheap paper. When an illustrator becomes popular, like Takemiya, comics are reprinted on glossy stock, cased, with special full-colour sections on the life style and travels of the artist.

Many appear weekly and are readily available at train station magazine stands and bookshops on just about every corner in towns and cities.

The nineteenth-century ukiyo-e artist Hokusai used the word *manga* to try to describe some rough, whimsical sketches for popular woodblock prints of fantasy and everyday life that were printed from the eleventh to the nineteenth centuries. Early forms of manga were organized on scrolls, with stories that continued while they were unrolled. During the Edo period, artists produced sewn, bound books of woodblock prints with illustrations accompanied by extensive writing. Once European and American culture was brought to Japan in the late nineteenth century comics took on a Western organization, with story panels. Even with these modernizations, the word manga is still used for contemporary Japanese comic books.

In all initial appearances, other than black-and-white instead of colour printing inside, manga resemble Western comics. The illustrations range from basic human caricatures to carefully drawn sequences providing as much detail and drama as could be found in a Kurosawa film. With closer scrutiny, however, differences abound. One comic book contains several stories, each with their own distinctive drawing styles and printed on different coloured, recycled paper. Adult comics make no attempt to conceal violent acts, including all sorts of killing and maiming. Sex is open, but still carefully controlled by censorship. Manga must be read following traditional Japanese directions – from the top right-hand side of the page, down columns sequentially, top to bottom across the gutter to the left-hand page, continuing to the bottom left. The copy, however, may follow vertical, right-to-left movements, or it may be written horizontally, left to right. Action within frames continues a directional play by controlling different viewing sequences. All of this should cause considerable eye fatigue.

Story lines in manga vary considerably. In Frederik L. Schodt's comprehensive book, *Manga! Manga! The World of Japanese Comics* (1983), he wrote: "The huge boys' comic magazines carefully balance suspense with humor: dramatic stories of sports, adventure, ghosts, science fiction, and school life are interspliced with outrageous gag and pun strips. Girls' comic magazines also strive for balance but are distinguished by their emphasis on tales of idealized love, featuring stylized heroes and heroines, many of whom look Caucasian. Adult

Top: Junko Murata, cover of *Asuka Comics*, published by Kadokawa Shoten, 1989 (180 x 115 mm). Comics come in many forms; one popular format for young teenagers is the small, soft-bound book. The young artist Junko Murata, who draws bright-eyed young people of international ethnic origins, has a growing following.

Above: Katuhiro Otomo, page from *Akira, Part 1*, published in paperback by Kodansha, 1982 (260 x 180 mm). Otomo is famous for his action-packed stories which contain very little dialogue; he is a master-draftsman who loves showing every gory detail. This story first appeared in *Young Magazine*.

magazines have themes which range from the religious to the risqué, mostly emphasizing the latter, and teem with warriors, gamblers, and gigolos."

Very few comic artists cross over to graphic design; Tadanori Yokoo, who dabbled as a cartoonist in his early years, is an exception. The popularity of manga encouraged illustrators to experiment with a range of styles, themes and expressions. And, as photography in advertising waned in the Sixties, illustrators gained new popularity in the Seventies.

Illustration

There is a long tradition of Japanese illustration based on the stylistic representation of everyday life found in ukiyo-e. Only after European influences were felt did Japanese artists discover the magic of realistic presentations in the exquisite bijin-ga pictures of beautiful women in the first half of the twentieth century. During the Sixties, influenced by an extraordinary variety of Western illustrative styles, Japanese artists were encouraged to undertake further experimentation. Illustrators in the Fifties and early Sixties, such as Yoshio Hayakawa and Tadashi Ohashi, joined with Western artists Paul Davis, Milton Glaser and Jan Lenica, to encourage younger artists to try new expressions. During the Sixties, initial leaders of the younger generation were Makoto Wada, Akira Uno, Harumi Matsumoto, Tadonori Yokoo and Kiyoshi Awazu; all were involved in organizing the Tokyo Illustrators Club in 1964. Within two years they published their first *Annual of Illustration*.

Tadahito Nadamoto

Many of the early illustrators combined their talents to include both graphic design and illustration. One of these is Tadahito Nadamoto, who has considerable talents in poster design as well as in illustration. Nadamoto, who was born in 1927, set up his own studio in Tokyo in 1967 after six years assisting Yoshio Hayakawa as chief designer in Hayakawa's Tokyo office. In the early Sixties, he won several awards for exceptionally crafted posters that contain his expressive illustrations of women, a popular subject for him. He describes his illustrations of women as having no particular nationality and as his way of adding emotion and feeling to his work. Nadamoto also likes to add English words to some of his illustrations, not for their meaning but for their visual texture and implied international identification.

Tadashi Ohashi, calendar illustration for the Moon Star rubber company, 1967 (250 x 250 mm). Ohashi blends technical skill with a sharp imagination in his treatment of natural objects such as flower buds.

グラフィック デザイン＋ 1973/74 WINTER 52

Tadahito Nadamoto, cover for the
magazine *Graphic Design* +, 1974
(300 x 260 mm), one of a series of
covers by different illustrators
invited to contribute by the
magazine's editor Masaru Katzumie.

Makoto Wada, poster for Edward's men's boutique, 1973; art director Keisuke Nagatomo. Wada is an astute follower of cultural and political trends; his caricatures of celebrated film stars, politicians and other notables, both Western and Japanese, have been very popular in Japan. The illustrations for this menswear poster showing stars of silent comedy films were so popular that they were merchandized on teeshirts and stationery. His black-outlined figures, filled with flat colour, express a disarming simplicity in capturing a personality.

Yutaka Sugita, poster for the Bologna Children's Book Fair, 1979 (675 x 480 mm). Sugita is one of Japan's best known children's book illustrators; for this poster his original watercolour was enlarged in the printing to emphasise the texture of the paper and smudged paint.

Yoshitaro Isaka

Another illustrator who joined his art direction skills with the illustrative sensitivities of Taisho artists and old European stylizations was Yoshitaro Isaka (1928-1970), affectionately called "Pero." He had a loyal following with illustrations of romantic realism similar to those usually found in the work of artists of the Thirties. In 1957 he joined Light Publicity where he won many awards, including admission into the Tokyo Art Directors Club in 1969.

Harumi Yamaguchi

It is easier for women to be successful as illustrators than as art directors or designers in Japan. One of the most successful is Harumi Yamaguchi who was born in 1936 and had her start as an illustrator for Seibu Department Store. Her former husband, Tatsu Matsumoto, a successful art director at Seibu, collaborated with his wife on several advertisements and posters that received awards from the Tokyo Art Directors Club during the early and mid-Sixties. These initial illustrations, credited to Harumi Matsumoto, were rather naive drawings of Caucasian women promoting the latest fashions, using black outline filled in with colours or shading.

By the early Seventies, Yamaguchi had discovered the airbrush and quickly became a master. Beginning with the 1974 ADC Annual, her airbrush paintings of sensual Western women were frequent award winners. Several of her airbrush illustrations were reproduced as note cards by Paper Moon Graphics in Los Angeles. Parco published a large-format poster book entitled *Harumi Gals* in the early Eighties, featuring some of her more popular illustrations.

Teruhiko Yumura

One illustrator who prides himself on his American Pop satire is Teruhiko Yumura, recognized as one of a group of artists who avoid any semblance of control. Yumura is attracted to American genres of the late Sixties and early Seventies, such as the movie *American Graffiti*, American "love" comics, from which he frequently borrows images, and English, French or Spanish phrases to communicate a Western image. In contrast to his traditionally based childhood centred on his father's employment in a Kabuki theatre, he says his illustrations stress an immature style. Born in 1947, he studied with Ayao Yamana as a design major at Tama University but has been more influenced by the style of his mentor, Tadanori Yokoo. After

 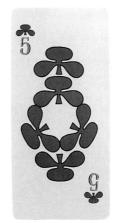 

Yoshitaro Isaka, pack of playing cards, 1970 (120 x 57 mm each), elegantly illustrated with provocative figures to entertain the players.

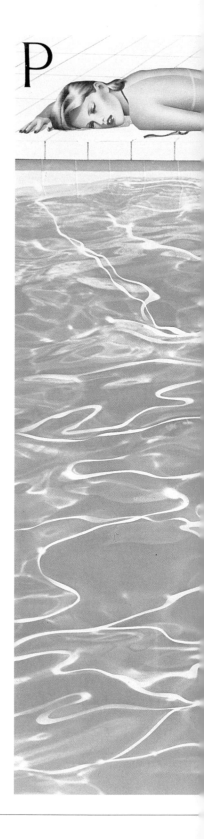

Harumi Yamaguchi, poster for Parco,
1969 (1035 x 727 mm). Yamaguchi
worked in a commercial vein, as in
this poster for the opening of a new
branch in Tokyo of Parco, a
subsidiary of Seibu Department
Stores. Her early illustrative style
drew on simple black lines and flat
colour; she avoided illustrating Asian
women.

Harumi Yamaguchi, poster for Parco, 1977; art director Yoshio Hasegawa. By the mid-Seventies Yamaguchi was a master with the tools and composition of airbrush illustration. The art director developed the concept for this poster after a trip to Okinawa.

several abortive associations with other illustrators he formed Original Flamingo Studio in 1975. As his reputation grew, he published two soft-bound books in 1981 of his drawings and paintings: *Terry's Hitparade* and *Terry 100%*, published by Parco Views.

Independent Art Directors

As international attention turned towards Japan, graphic designers were uncomfortable, recognizing that they had no clear direction. The accomplishments of the Sixties and the recognition of Japanese design only fuelled this period of uncertainty. But one group of professionals, the independent art directors, were finding new freedoms in their images and providing a new sense of pride for Japan. They were catalysts in changing the direction of Japanese advertising concepts.

During the early formation of graphic design and advertising organizations, Japan looked to Europe and the United States for examples. These Western countries endeavoured to maintain clear distinctions between those who were involved in advertising and those whose emphasis was on basic communication designed to promote cultural events or provide essential information for corporations. The distinction between advertising art/commercial art and graphic design/visual communication appeared on the surface to be clear, but it was difficult to articulate. The Western world had successful heroes as models for each group, each with a philosophy to match; the camps were clear and there were few defections. The Bauhaus model provided even further delineation between duties and added a corporate element with scientific theories as a back-up. Graphic design existed first to assist corporation in defining its image, and only secondarily to sell the product.

Japanese viewed these two professions through the same filtered lens as they viewed everything from foreign countries. When the time came for their own definitions, adjustments had to be made. Japan's major problem was a lack of professionals to make an adequate division of the responsibilities; art directors sometimes had to work as graphic designers and sometimes as illustrators. Those first generation graphic designers were the same first generation art directors. Yusaku Kamekura, who brought the name graphic designer to Japan, was a founder of JAAC and ADC and was president of both organizations. The current two leading design organizations, Japan Graphic Designers Association and Tokyo Art Directors Club, still share the same individuals as leaders. Masaru Katzumie, the champion of a rational, universal approach to visual communication, promoted designers and art directors equally in *Graphic Design* and was adviser for both groups until his death in 1983.

This blurring of professions is not evident to casual followers of Japanese graphic design, and a review of the written material from Japan implies more differences than actually exist. In 1968, Yusaku Kamekura, in his article "Advertising Art Today" for *Graphis* 168/169, wrote: "there are two types of designers. Some designers undertake advertising projects with a positive, constructive attitude, while others prefer to preclude advertisements from their scope. It is noteworthy that a number of designers in the JAAC belong to the latter category." Kamekura carefully compliments both groups. Today, almost every member of the Tokyo Art Directors Club also holds membership in the Japan Graphic Design Association (formerly JAAC), giving credit to their dual roles.

One particular phenomenon in Japan is the tradition of the independent art director, who handles design for a few major companies yet maintains independent status. Yusaku Kamekura, as an independent, handled accounts for Nikon cameras and Meiji chocolates; Tadashi Ohashi is art director for Kikkoman; Ikko Tanaka provided a variety of design activities for Seibu Department Stores – yet all three have their own independent design studios. In 1987, of the 72 members of the Tokyo Art Directors Club, 42 were independent art directors; the others included fifteen from Nippon Design Center, nine from Light Publicity, two from Hokuhodo, two from Dentsu and several from Shiseido.

Advertising organizations such as Nippon Design Center and Light Publicity perpetuate fuzzy distinctions. They both act as advertising agencies in creating advertisements, but they refuse to buy space. Existing agencies such as Dentsu, Hakuhodo and Orikomi have large staffs of art directors but only a few individuals have design duties; most art directors coordinate activities and produce television commercials. Dentsu, recognized as one of the largest advertising agencies in the world, with an annual billing in excess of $3 billion, has a staff of about 450 art directors, photographers, copywriters, television producers, etc. As one of two members of Tokyo Art Directors Club from Dentsu, with whom he has had over twenty years' association, Jun Tabohashi is a director of one of the four creative divisions. In an issue of *Communication*

Teruhiko Yumura, poster for a concert by a Japanese blues singer, 1984 (1030 x 728 mm). Teruhiko, who has named his office Flamingo Studio and likes to be known as "Flamingo Terry," realised his style in the Seventies and has hardly changed it since.

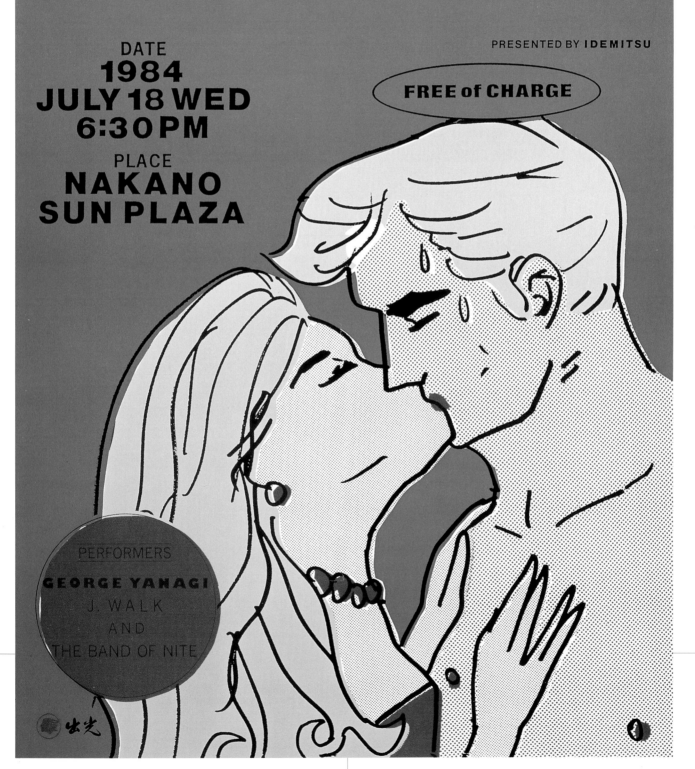

Arts magazine in 1983, Ko Noda and Mill Roseman relate how Tabohashi differentiates between the role of an advertising agency art director and an independent art director. Agencies maintain 95 per cent control of placements in broadcasting and much print advertising, with their art directors concentrating more on broadcasting. In contrast, independent art directors work more as practitioners of the fine arts, with an emphasis on self-expression.

Major corporations such as Shiseido and Suntory, and large department stores such as Seibu, Tokyu and Matsuya, have their own design staff and also hire independent art directors. Much of the success of independents is due to a recognition by the industry that there is a need for self-expression to establish identity. Independents have the freedom to combine talents with equally independent copywriters, photographers and illustrators, creating a unique mixture of creative skills.

Designer-art director Masuteru Aoba, a leader in ADC, estimated in 1987 that there were at least twenty thousand independent art directors in Tokyo, but only about sixty to a hundred were well known. Most operate in studios of five to ten people, with annual turnovers of up to $2 million. They work about twelve hours a day for five days a week, but of course, when deadlines are tight, there are all-nighters and seven-day-a-week schedules.

One independent art director who would like more separation between art direction and graphic design is Tsuyoshi Fukuda. He feels that graphic designers have a definite edge in competitions over art directors. Judges for design annuals are drawn from the same group of people who decide the contents of the Tokyo Art Directors Annual, and the criteria for judging graphic design are better defined than those for advertising.

The freedom of expression allowed to the independent art director has contributed to increased recognition for individual Japanese graphic designers in the Seventies. At the annual joint exhibition of the Tokyo Art Directors Club and the New York Art Directors Club held in December 1972, Kazumasa Nagai characterized the feelings of most Japanese designers. In the past, he observed, exchanges indicated that Japanese designers were lagging behind Americans, with a difference equal to that which might be expected "between teacher and students." But after reviewing the 1972 exhibition Nagai said proudly, "this current exhibition proves the Japanese are no longer students."

Contributing to this pride is a new group of designers and art directors who are sometimes referred to as the "third generation." With such a small group of professionals, Japanese designers continually speculate on the number of generations. If the rough rule of thirty years between generations is used, grouping would be easy, but generations are usually determined more by attitude than age. Using this perspective, it is clear that Takashi Kono and Yusaku Kamekura belong to the first generation and Kazumasa Nagai and Ikko Tanaka, though only 15 years younger, are the second generation. Masatoshi Toda and Makoto Saito, two of the youngest in this survey, are 16 to 20 years younger than Tanaka and are more appropriately called the third generation. This places another group of successful art directors somewhere "in between".

The In-Between Generation

Many in this new group gained notoriety in 1969 when a number of young designers – Masuteru Aoba, Takahisa Kamijyo, Keisuke Nagatomo and 15 others of the same generation calling themselves "Silencer" – formed around members of a Tokyo gallery. They published a collection of their works in 1974 under the title *Sandwich Silencer*. In the mid-Seventies, Yusaku Kamekura wanted to provide recognition for these designers and organize another major exhibition, also entitled "Silencer", with the idea that it would have the same national impact as Graphic '55 and Persona in 1965. Kamekura exercised his usual power with people and companies but, due to several complications, the exhibition was delayed until 1981. By this time the group composition had changed and included several who would be considered in the third generation.

Most of these in-between generation designer-art directors began working in the Sixties and had established their reputations by the late Sixties and early Seventies. What is distinctive about them is that they were the first group whose primary activity was art direction. All were independent art directors in Tokyo and members of the Tokyo Art Directors Club. Each of them stressed the importance of individual expression over basic information, and each was a harbinger for a new direction in Japanese advertising design. Another link in common is their reliance on photography to communicate their unique imagery.

Kuni Kizawa

A student activist in the Sixties, Kuni Kizawa, who was born in 1937, first used his talents to design a house magazine for the students' anti-war movement. After graduating from high school he joined the establishment and designed for Fuji Bank and the Tokyu Department Store. By the end of the Sixties Kizawa was employed at Shiseido where he spent eleven years as an editorial designer, and art director of their magazine *Hanatsubaki*, which is known for its inventive layout and free-spirited covers. He left in 1981 to establish his own studio in Tokyo.

While at Shiseido, Kizawa promoted Japanese models over the popular trend of photographing Caucasian models for advertising. He continues to hold this nationalistic philosophy as expressed in a statement in *Graphics Japan* (1987): "I want to behold Japanese culture, based on its traditions. I want to see art, religion, nature, food, clothing, play, laughter as they are and as they derive from my own roots." Currently he designs magazine editorial pages and covers with photographs that emphasize the moment. Much of his work presents casual, animated models, who are not afraid to show emotion and express a personality.

Eiko Ishioka

Eiko Ishioka, a Tokyoite born in 1938 and educated at Tokyo University of Fine Arts and Music, experienced a school system organized by the American occupation forces which promoted equal values for men and women. It is her generation of women in Japan who are effective leaders in a male-dominated society. Her educational philosophy, combined with a degree from the prestigious Geidai, has given her an edge over other female Japanese graphic designers. Following graduation she joined Shiseido's advertising department in the early Sixties, where she was recognized for her outstanding skills through awards from the Tokyo Art Directors Club.

During the early Seventies Ishioka became art director for Parco, a series of fashionable boutiques housed in a large building and part of the Seibu conglomerate. Instead of promoting individual shops, Ishioka concentrated on a corporate identity based on her own aesthetic to establish Parco's image. In the Eighties she expanded beyond graphic design, and was production designer for the film *Mishima*, and set and costume designer for the Broadway production of David Henry Hwang's play *M. Butterfly*.

Kuni Kizawa, cover for Shiseido's magazine *Hanatsubaki*, 1979. Kizawa designed over fifty covers for this magazine; all are photographic.

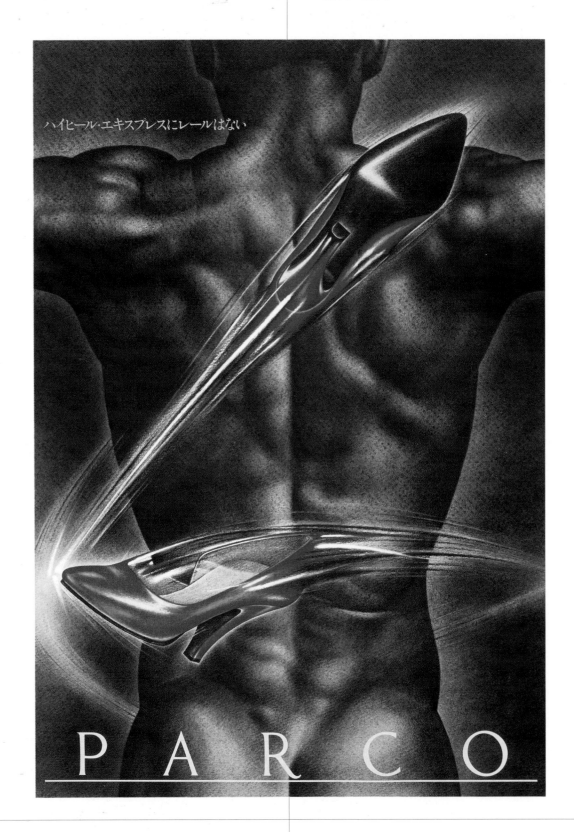

ハイヒール・エキスプレスにレールはない

PARCO

Eiko Ishioka, poster for Parco, 1977; illustrator Katsu Yoshido. The copy reads: "There are no rails on the high heel express; you can go anywhere." The Parco image has been largely established by Ishioka's work in the early Seventies.

Eiko Ishioka, poster of a Kenyan woman from a series for Parco, 1978 (1030 x 730 mm); photograph by Shinya Fujiwara. Several of Ishioka's Parco posters have become classics, including her series from 1977 to 1980 of posters and books of photographs featuring African and Indian women.

わが心のスーパースター

PARCO

Ishioka is admired by her fellow art directors not only for her exceptional design skills but as an art director willing to take risks. Ikko Tanaka wrote of her in 1968 as "playing a leading role today among Japan's younger generation of graphic designers" – quite a compliment from an established professional to a young designer, and a most unusual comment about a woman. In *Graphics Japan* (1987) she states her design philosophy: "Within my own inner world, my production design for a film or a corporate logo-type design hold the same importance, as one influences the other. In design, a true expressive method cannot be achieved without a strong statement from the designer himself. If it isn't there, design is nothing more than beautiful trash."

Masuteru Aoba

A designer much quoted for his observations on Japanese art direction, Masuteru Aoba is a leader in the Tokyo Art Directors Club and on the Board of Directors for Japan Graphic Designers Association. Aoba was born in Tokyo in 1939 and studied design at Kuwazawa Design Institute, where Ikko Tanaka was an early influence. After graduation he joined Orikomi Advertising Agency and created posters for the Tokyo Metropolitan Government Office. Eight years later he became an independent art director and graphic designer. A recent client has been Seiyu Food Stores; he is also art director for *Idea, Asahi Journal* and *Design Age* magazines, and has worked on *Graphic Design* magazine.

Greatly influenced by social issues confronting Japan and the world, Aoba strives to keep problems of pollution and potential nuclear war in the forefront of designers' consciousness. He devotes considerable personal time and money to producing posters on these issues, many of them effective in their straightforward design with simple forms, such as doves and guns, portrayed with photographic manipulation. He explained his social philosophy in the *Annual of Advertising Art in Japan 85-86*: "I believe there is much room for a graphic designer to work not only for profit but also with service to the community in mind. With the power of visual language, one can deal with the theme of racial discrimination, peace, food problems, pollution, etc. I spend my Sundays and my free time in making posters with the above in mind. I would like to have as many people as possible from all over the world see my posters, not sad posters but peaceful and happy posters, not those which would arouse the dark past but those

looking forward to the future." Recently he suggested that the United Nations needs a good art director who could serve as a guide for international mass communication.

Keisuke Nagatomo and Sietaro Kuroda

These two creative artists, both born in 1939, joined forces in 1969 to set up K2, a Japanese version of New York's Push Pen Studio. Nagatomo had worked at Nippon Design Center where he won a JAAC Award for a Jansen poster, silk screened with grey over a fluorescent colour paper. He left after three years to join Kuroda who was then assisting Yoshio Hayakawa. They chose the name K2 because, they explained, "names don't count." Both brought an uninhibited approach to problem-solving and their open Kansai colour sense: colours used in this southern area of Japan are brighter and more vivid than those often used by Tokyo designers. Kuroda's early recognition was as a disc jockey on radio and a host on television; his influence on the team is evident in his distinctive, slashing illustrations that express strong individual characteristics.

The two captured attention in the early Seventies with their extensive campaign for the Heiwa Sogo Bank. Instead of using conservative images befitting a staid financial organization, K2 produced calendars and nakazuri posters that featured nude women romping in the woods or on the beach. It was one of the few times they used photography except in their editorial design. Nagatomo continues his interest in the sensuous image as art director for *Goro*, a men's magazine that features provocative photographs of women, and *Ryuko Tsushin*, a monthly style magazine, where he is able to use his skills in geometric compositions. He favours the cluttered design look, layering shapes and textures with experimental type arrangements.

Ryohei Kojima

Designer-illustrator Ryohei Kojima, who was born in 1939, graduated from Musashino Art University and started employment at Ginza San-ai Co. He moved on to Light Publicity where he stayed for twelve years, leaving to establish his own office in 1974. In the mid-Sixties, when he was in his twenties, he illustrated Kodansha's well known Encyclopedia with precise medical illustrations done in bold, flat colours – a style that he continues today for posters and publication covers. He credits influence from Western designers Herbert Bayer,

Keisuke Nagatomo and Sietaro Kuroda (K2), poster for Edward's menswear shops, 1969 (1030 x 728 mm), a "pop" image designed to appeal to young consumers.

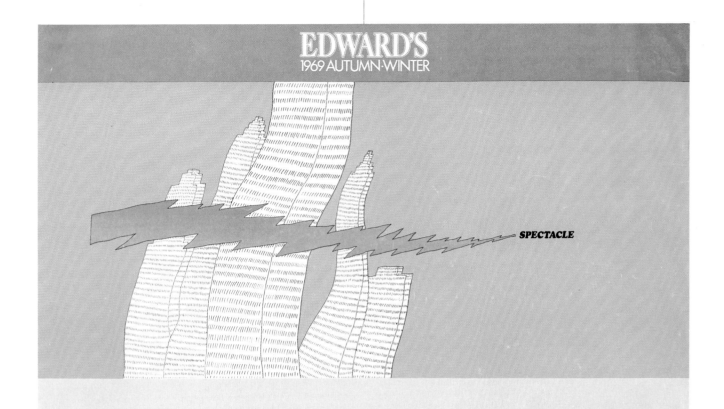

戦闘機乗りは真昼の星を見た。

いい視力いつまでも。

Ivan Chemayeff and Thomas Geismar. As an independent art director his current clients include Japan Broadcasting Corporation, IBM Japan and *Design News* magazine for which he designs covers.

Katsumi Asaba

One of Japan's more inventive art directors of his generation is Katsumi Asaba. Born in1940, he graduated from Kanagawa High School, then worked in a Yokohama department store while studying at Kuwazawa Design Institute. He then worked for a typographer before joining Light Publicity where he remained for nine years. Asaba now has two independent studios – Katsumi Asaba Design Room and ASA 1,000 Company – where he produces graphic design, advertising design and photography. He is best known for his free-thinking concepts with a photographic content based on his own aesthetic. His skills are equally competent in his designs for several logos and television commercials.

Shin Matsunaga

Born in 1940, son of a famous calligrapher, and a graduate of Tokyo University of Fine Arts and Music in 1964, Shin Matsunaga was influenced by his father's appreciation of letterforms. This knowledge is evident in his skill with the design of logos and packaging where he provides careful attention to alphabetical forms in structured compositions. He began his career with Shiseido for a few years before he opened his own office in Tokyo. In 1982 he designed a book on the Japanese constitution that made it both visually pleasant as well as enjoyable to read. Recently he has won several awards for his packaging design.

Takahisa Kamijyo

Another designer receiving encouragement from a father who was a prominent painter, Takahisa Kamijyo had early acknowledgement for his outstanding drawing skills. He was born in 1940 and graduated from Tokyo University of Fine Arts and Music in their craft courses. In 1964 he joined Takashimaya Department Store's advertising department. After employment at some small advertising studios, by 1972 he had opened his own office.

Ryohei Kojima, poster for the All Japan Optical Chain, 1978. This unusual information poster, encouraging eye care, adopts the approach of an encyclopedia in its design and illustration.

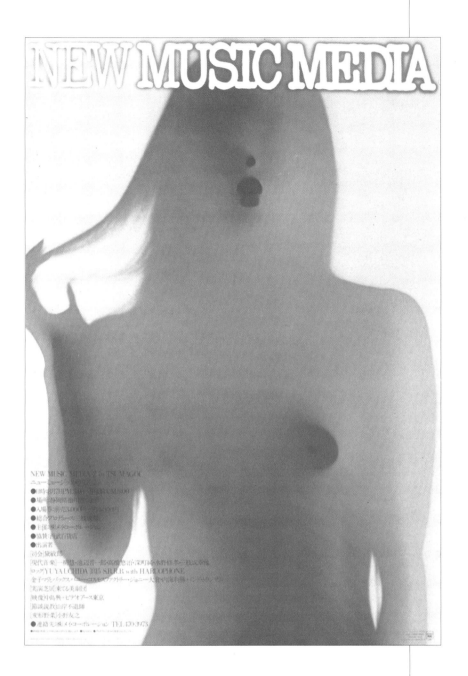

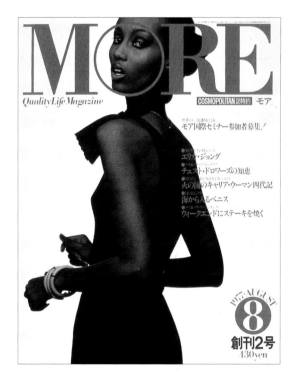

Shin Matsunaga, poster for a concert sponsored by Seibu, 1976 (1030 x 728 mm). In the tradition of early bijin-ga, the cool blue, sensual image of a woman need have nothing to do with the concert.

Shin Matsunaga, cover of *More* (the Japanese edition of *Cosmopolitan*), 1977. Many magazines in Japan promote an international look.

大キッチのおみくじ。やたらとツイてる。

Katsumi Asaba, spread from a fashion magazine, 1978.
Asaba art directed this extraordinary photograph of a
stuntman dressed as a typical businessman flying through a
burning hoop, not quite fast enough to prevent his coat
catching fire. He is followed by a flying white pig dressed in
a pink bow. One wonders how many takes were needed -
and who was responsible for catching the pig.

スキヤンダル・パンプス。

婦人靴・銀座
Diana

Katsumi Asaba, poster for Diana
shoes, 1978. The simplicity of the
composition draws attention to the
sexuality of the figure: the copy
reads "Scandal pumps," and the
gauze screen is reminiscent of the
device used to censor nudity and sex
scenes out of imported Western
films.

Packaging Design

Japanese packaging serves several purposes: to protect the goods, to provide the proper attraction to consumers, to reflect appropriately the personality of the giver and to give pleasure to the recipient. With centuries of highly structured, formalized procedures, gifts are big business in Japan, where the normal course of social and business events includes their frequent exchange. Kazumasa Nagai wrote in "Packaging Design in Japan" (*Graphis*, 1968): "The [package] has to embody certain personal and spiritual values, and not only to serve a material purpose. This attitude is related to the spirit of the tea ceremony or of Zen Buddhism. Perhaps as a result, many traditional Japanese packages display a simple and sober charm rather than being gay or decorative. However expensive the contents may be, they avoid any superficial luxury and seek their beauty in a modest restraint." Modern Japanese packaging design seems to have few restrictions and few references to traditional motifs.

Keiko Hirohashi

One of the few women packaging designers, Keiko Hirohashi, born in 1931, graduated from Tokyo National University and was first employed by the Morinaga candy company. In 1962 she opened her own office and won her first packaging award in 1965. A member of Tokyo Designers Space in 1977, she began to receive national attention for her unusual constructions with wood and surface designs for paper: She approaches wrapping paper, for example, as if it were fabric for a kimono. She wrote in *Package Design in Japan* (1988): "The functional beauty found in the unique style of clothing and cloth wrappers of Japan has the wisdom of the Japanese wrapped up inside it."

Katsu Kimura

Recognized as a master of modern packaging design, Katsu Kimura, who was born in 1934, has considerable respect for the complicated traditions of Japanese gift packages. As he explained in 1984, the packaging is as important as the value of the gift. If it is an expensive gift, its wrapping must be suitably elegant. Each gift occasion requires its own colours, knots and folding configurations. All folds must be sharp, surfaces clean and wrinkle-free and decorated appropriately. Important colours include red or gold and white for happy events, and black or blue and white for sad events.

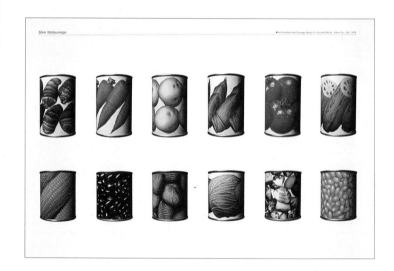

Top: Takenobu Igarashi, can label for Summit Foods, 1978. As a young designer, Igarashi was given the assignment to design Summit's corporate identity programme; the project included the trademark and a series of labels. The large katakana letters here sound out the words "tomato juice."

Above: Shin Matsunaga, labels for canned vegetables for Kibun Sozai, 1977; illustrator Yoshuke Onishi, photographs by Kiyofusa Nozu. The realistic depictions give the effect of looking through a transparent container at the contents themselves; all copy was kept to the other side of the label.

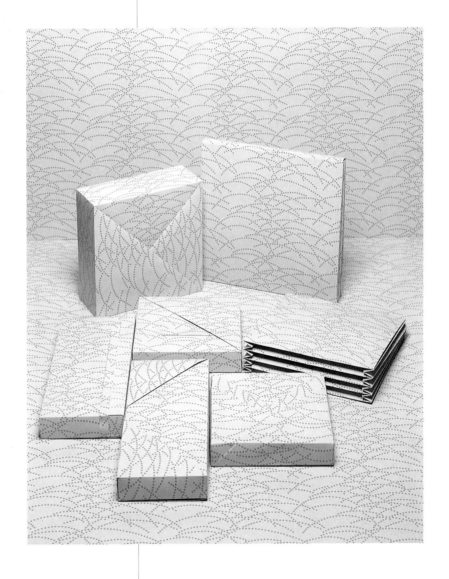

Kazumasa Nagai, bottle for "Jun," a
new liqueur from Takara Shuzo,
1977. The simple line and type
design emphasises the clarity of the
liquid; the word *jun* means pure.

Keiko Hirohashi, gift boxes, 1981.
Gift packaging is of great social
importance in Japan, and Hirohashi is
one of the few successful female
packaging designers working in
Tokyo. Here the allover pattern of
the paper is treated in the same way
as a designer would treat fabric.

Katsu Kimura, containers for
Masamune class 1 sake, 1967. Black
brush calligraphy and kanji characters
printed in soft colours make a perfect
blend of tradition and modern
design.

Kimura has designed an assortment of packages that express both traditional forms and contemporary inventive imagery. Some of his early designs in the Sixties were for sealed sake packages; designed to look traditional at first, on closer examination his arrangement of calligraphic letters showed a special skill in controlled contrast and balance. It is a skill similar to that of his friend Ikko Tanaka. Kimura's packaging forms may look traditional in concept, but their construction and materials are inventive and quite contemporary. His work was first exhibited in 1972 and again in 1979. Recently he published his style book, *Package Direction of Katsu Kimura*, with the slipcase in the form of a famous cigarette package, greatly enlarged.

Advertising Photography

The dominance of the photographic image in advertising began in the Sixties and waned somewhat in the early Seventies as art directors favoured the personal expression of illustration. The magic of photographic images, in providing both fantasy and authenticity, reinstated its popularity in the Seventies and it has steadily increased. As with all other special interest groups in Japan, a few nationally prominent advertising photographers formed their own group in 1958 – the Japan Advertising Photographers Association – which is still an active organization, with an impressive annual.

In an article in *Graphis* 168/169, Shigene Kanamaru, who was on the faculty at Nihon University until his death in 1977, suggested that advertising photography first appeared in Japan about 1927. (Others cite the 1922 sepia photograph shown on page 43 as the first advertising photograph.) It was at this time that the photographic works of Moholy Nagy, the German design association DWB, Herbert Bayer and the photomontages of the Russian Constructivists received widespread attention at a series of exhibitions in Tokyo.

Kanamaru lists three important stages in the development of advertising photography. The first occurred when advertising revenues were reduced during the depression of the early Thirties; Japan's newspapers sponsored a series of photography contests featuring specific commercial products. There were over three thousand entries, but most were of such amateur quality that few, if any, were used. But the contest increased interest in the use of photographs in advertising, although photographers were still not considered to have professional status.

Kanamaru's second stage occurred after World War II when art directors, attracted by the techniques and style of American photographers Irving Penn and Richard Avedon, demanded similar results from Japanese photographers. But because of small budgets for small-scale projects completed with unsatisfactory printing techniques photographers received little recognition and came under the complete creative control of art directors. Their low status resulted in low photographers' fees and little incentive for creative people to join the field.

By the mid-Sixties professional fees had not significantly increased but the quality of photography and improved printing techniques moved photographers into the third stage as photography became a dominant tool. Kanamaru also points out other contributing factors: the increased demand for quality colour photographs used on calendars; improved quality of transport posters; more attention to photography in magazine advertisements, and the popularity of posters. Advertising photographers of note in the Sixties and Seventies are: Yutaka Takanashi, who worked with Kazumasa Nagai at Nippon Design Center, Mitsuo Doki, who collaborated with Tadashi Masuda on several travel posters; Noriaki Yokosuka, whose long career spans over twenty years with art director Makoto Nakamura at Shiseido Cosmetics, and Kishin Shinoyama, a famous photographer of women in traditional settings.

Today's advertising photographers are more likely to have independent studios or be part of large advertising agencies such as Dentsu, Orikomi and Hakuhodo. Suntory employs several photographers who have received recognition. Almost all are men, working in Tokyo. Examples of some of the new breed of photographers are Shigeru Akimoto, noted for his fashion photography; Yuichi Eguchi, who favours photographing cars and motor cycles; Shintaro Shiratori at Hakuhodo, who has won several awards for photographs that concentrate on a single person, and Senji Urushibata, employed at Suntory and a past colleague of Masatoshi Toda, who prefers photographs with an enigmatic content.

In reviewing recent editions of *Advertising Photography in Japan*, the Association's annual, there is an overwhelming impression of open spaces. Most photographs centre on one or two objects or persons, open landscapes, with an emphasis on the uncluttered look; many are taken at locations outside Japan. This atmosphere would not be so striking and unusual without the realization that the image is directed at a society that, on a daily basis, confronts crowded subways,

清らかな香りほど妖しい。 資生堂香水 [禅]
9,000円

grid-locked streets and tiny rabbit-hutch-like apartments. A possible reason for this persistent photographic fantasy can be found in a quotation from Robert Christopher's book *The Japanese Mind* (1983): "While Americans dream of making lots of money, a young Japanese dreams of acquiring space – just plain room."

Another observation from the annuals is the predominance of Western models: the ratio is two to one over Asians, a trend started in the Fifties as Japan joined an international approach to advertising. The early bijin-ga beauty poster concept was still popular, but kimono-clad women were replaced by fashionably dressed (or often undressed) American and European models. Seeing them in Japanese advertising and as department store mannequins has always been a disconcerting experience for most Western visitors to Japan. Many feel it is inconsistent to see blonde, blue-eyed models selling to consumers in a country where 99 per cent have black hair and dark eyes. The reasons most frequently heard from Japanese for this phenomenom are that the product's identity is Western and that Japanese women do not have the same "beautiful proportions" as Western women. In their fashion-conscious country they claim it is difficult to promote French and Italian styles on an Asian figure.

But the physical differences are only part of the reason. Underlying the practice is Japan's preoccupation with an international appearance. A small island nation, surrounded by Third World countries with economical and political instability, Japan's question is with whom should she identify? Photographs of Japanese women in advertising perpetuate a provincial image of a small country with limited markets, whereas Western models tie the country's image to the industrially wealthy America and Europe. This not only influences the thinking of the Japanese people but is also persuasive for international visitors doing business in Japan.

By the late Eighties, Japanese advertising photography had become even more multi-racial, with photographs of Africans, Hispanics, Pacific Islanders and other Asians occurring frequently. Using the exotic features of foreign models was not a moralistic campaign promoting ethnic diversity but more a question of novelty.

Most advertising photography annuals are not true indicators of the more commonly printed material that is locally distributed as flyers, handbills and promotional posters. Such everyday printed ephemera is more likely to have Japanese

Makoto Nakamura, poster for Shiseido perfume, 1978; photograph by Noriaki Yokusuka. The image of the model, Sayoko Yamaguchi, is closely cropped to present a striking effect. The perfume box in the top left corner is in black and gold to imitate lacquerwork.

Kazumasa Nagai, poster for Expo '75 held in Okinawa, 1974 (1038 x 728 mm); photograph by Toshio Innami. To promote this Ocean Exposition, Nagai matched the image of a calm sea with an Edo-style wave pattern, with the photograph providing both texture and colour.

EXPO'75

INTERNATIONAL OCEAN EXPOSITION
OKINAWA, JAPAN, 1975
MARCH—AUGUST

models to promote household products, new apartment complexes or small shops. Typical printed material aimed at a national audience can be seen in the *Annual of Advertising Production in Japan*, where about 150 small design firms each reproduce their best work – a mixture of quality design and throw-away trash. Nippon Design Center buys the first four pages to establish an anchor.

Award-winning photographs in *Advertising Photography in Japan* are generally recognized as promotional material for big budget companies seeking to sell an international image rather than product information. It is in these projects that creative Japanese advertising photographers have established international recognition.

Japan Graphic Designers Association

In an effort to reorganize graphic designers after the demise of the Japan Advertising Artist Club, the Japan Designers Union Preparatory Committee was established in 1974 and joined the Tokyo Commercial Artists Association as the parent body. They, in turn, joined Nippon Advertising Artists Club and its president, art director Susumu Sakane, as a nucleus. Its aim was to replace the dissolved JAAC with a national group that would provide professional status for Japanese graphic designers and have a global perspective. It is surprising that designers should have waited four years before organizing a replacement for the popular JAAC. After considerable activity, the new group – called the Japan Graphic Designers Association and known as JAGDA – was formed in 1978 with 705 members who also held membership in almost all the major visual design organizations including graphics, advertising, typography, display and packaging. The number quickly grew to 1,200 members, of whom 45 per cent work in the Tokyo metropolitan area. According to its director, Tatsuo Nagai: "Our objective is to establish a professional status stable enough for all graphic designers to go about their work with peace of mind." He predicted an eventual membership of 3,000, but by 1987 it had levelled off at just over 1,500.

In 1982 the members decided that JAGDA needed better organization and invited the "boss" Yasaku Kamekura to exert his power and leadership. He reorganized it and added members of the Japanese graphic design establishment – including Ikko Tanaka, Kazumasa Nagai and Shigeo Fukuda – as cabinet leaders for various committees. Masaru Katzumie was named as adviser. The purpose was not to promote "stars"

Okinawan Kazuo Kishimoto, symbol for Japan Graphic Designers Association, 1977. Kishimoto describes the central tilted "G" as a letter that "does not return to the same circle but keeps expanding forever like a spiral."

or place power in the hands of a few members, claimed Kamekura, but to emphasise professionalism.

Since 1981, JAGDA has published its own annual, entitled *Graphic Design in Japan*. Its large format, with about one thousand colour reproductions of the best work from Japan, is a favourite of American designers. Designs submitted for publication are reviewed by a selection committee of about twenty members, including representatives from all three "generations". Since it covers all of Japan, it is broader than the Tokyo Art Directors Club annual, which has more emphasis on advertising.

Design Events in the Seventies
In addition to the accomplishments of individuals and organizations, several events were held in Japan during the Seventies that drew attention to progress made in graphic design. They reflected a series of social concerns born with the decade: restructured communication that centred more on human sincerity; nostalgia for the handwork of past artisans; an awakening to problems with our fragile natural environment; and a recognition of the limitations of world resources brought on by the oil crisis in 1973-74.

Contributing to an examination of past design influences, a special exhibition celebrating the fiftieth anniversary of the Bauhaus was held at Tokyo National Museum of Modern Art in 1971. It contained over 1,500 items collected from Weimar, Dessau and Berlin periods as well as New Bauhaus and the Hochschule für Gestaltung in Ulm. Following this major comprehensive exhibition, one would think that graphic designers would have continued the study begun in the Thirties on the Bauhaus principles of type and design developed by the first generation graphic designers. In fact, no noticeable influences during the Seventies resulted from it.

During the early Seventies some designers were busy preparing for the 1972 Winter Olympic Games to be held in Sapporo. Masaru Katzumie, Chairman of the Design Committee, coordinated its symbol mark, designed by Kazumasa Nagai, and the information symbols, which were essentially the same ones Shigeo Fukuda designed for Expo '70. Takashi Kono designed the official poster, and a design manual was published in 1971 under Katzumie's editorial supervision.

A more major event for many graphic, industrial and interior designers was the World Industrial Design Conference, called ICSID Design Forum '73, held in Kyoto with the theme

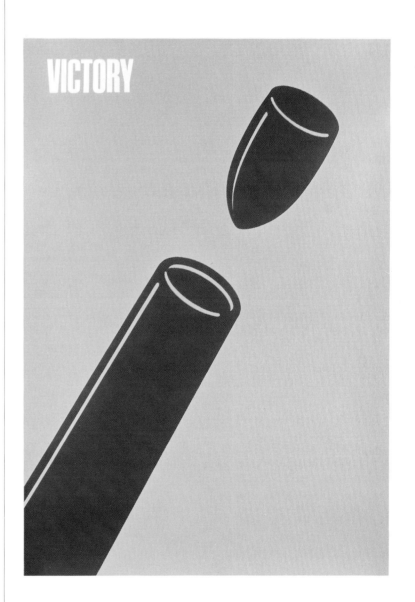

Shigeo Fukuda, Victory peace poster, 1976 (1030 x 728 mm). One of a series promoting peace, this shows a gun barrel with the bullet going back in. Fukuda is at his best with a single dominant image done in bold line art.

Takashi Kono, official poster for the
1972 Winter Olympics at Sapporo,
1972 (1035 x 78 mm). The simple
geometric shapes in a blue field
convey the cold Hokkaido location.
The official symbol in the top half of
the poster was designed by Kazumasa
Nagai, adapting Kamekura's 1964
Tokyo Olympics design by adding a
blue snowflake.

"Soul and Material Things." The Seventies was an influential decade for industrial designers because of exposure to major European design, such as Braun products. As with European design in the past, Japanese designers surpassed these stylistic features and introduced solutions that the Germans would never attempt. Stephen Bayley's observation in *The Conran Directory of Design* (1985) that "nevertheless, Japanese product design remained, and still is, deficient in ergonomics, and emphatic in expression and in emotive appeals to consumer psychology" is equally true today.

Another world exposition was scheduled in Japan that would provide recognition for a series of islands recently returned to the Japanese people. During World War II, Okinawa and the Ryukyu Islands were occupied by Americans, who retained them until 1972. Partially in recognition of the islands' return, and riding on the success of Expo '70, Japan organized an Ocean Exposition in Okinawa (Expo '75) with the theme "The Sea We Would Like to See" as part of their recognition of environmental problems. Kazumasa Nagai designed the symbol, selected by a screening committee chaired by Masaru Katzumie; the committee invited designers from Okinawa to produce several promotional posters.

Throughout the Seventies, several exhibitions of Japanese graphic design were featured in major foreign countries: an exhibition of traditional packaging toured the United States in 1975; an illustration show toured Paris and London in 1977 and, the same year, a poster exhibition was held in São Paulo, Brazil; and in 1979 a poster exhibition, "Edo and Tokyo," opened in Paris and toured Europe.

A significant event for Japan was held in the United States in 1979 at the 29th International Design Conference in Aspen, Colorado, entitled "Japan in Aspen." The conference, co-chaired by Lou Dorfsman and Kisho Kurokawa, was the first to concentrate on one country. Over one hundred Japanese designers joined 1,600 others in what was said to be the best-attended conference in history.

The theme, "Japan and Japanese – Synthesis of Contradictions," had several secondary messages, with Japanese words such as *ke* (atmosphere) and *ne* (sound) that were far too difficult for discussion in Japanese, let alone translation into English. The Japanese participants found that they were expected to portray Edo era craftsmen and not modern philosophers and designers: once again, Westerners showed that they preferred souvenir-style Japonica over modern Japan.

Top: Yusaku Kamekura, symbol for the Association for the Promotion of Traditional Crafts, 1975. The design is equally effective whether displayed as a large sign outside the Aoyama Street showroom or used as a tag for various products.

Above: Yusaku Kamekura, poster for the ICSID design forum of 1973 held in Kyoto, 1973 (730 x 515 mm). This shows one of several different versions of the ICSID symbol, initials on a cube disappearing into the centre of concentric circles. The effect is three-dimensional, with a strong relationship to monsho design.

Toshihiro Katayama, poster promoting an exhibition of his own
work at Harvard University, 1971 (785 x 616 mm). This is one
of a series of posters, each based on a mathematical division
of a square to emphasise the structural qualities of three-
dimensional form. The silk-screening conveys brilliant colours
that enhance a lineal play with figure and ground. Katayama
claims to be greatly influenced by Max Bill and Karl Gerstner.

Kazumasa Nagai, logo for the Tokyo
Central Museum, 1971. Nagai has
designed very many corporate
symbols; this soft "T" with the hole
in the centre is one of his most
effective.

Kazumasa Nagai, poster for Adonis
Printing Company, 1976 (1038 x 728
mm). Over a photograph of the sea, a
pattern of red lines cover the sky to
form a geometric "A." The logo of
the printers is deliberately kept very
low-key.

Tadanori Yokoo, poster featuring the actress Ruriko
Asaoka, 1971 (1037 x 728 mm). Yokoo caused
considerable controversy with this unauthorized poster
featuring his favourite actress in the nude. The small strips
of copy above her body give her measurements, while
above her neck is written "I like Ruriko," and next to the
photograph of Charlton Heston "I like Charlton Heston."
Asaoko was deeply offended; Yokoo's form of public
apology was to produce another poster showing himself in
the nude.

Tadanori Yokoo, self-promotional
poster, 1972 (1038 x 728 mm).
Yokoo's emerging interest in Oriental
religion is shown in this composition,
in which he combines mystical images
of Buddha, and Christian and Hindu
icons.

音が氾濫している世の中だから、

Gan Hosoya, poster for Pioneer
Electronics hi-fi equipment, 1979;
photomontage by Tsunehisa Kimura.
The Niagara Falls are superimposed
on the New York skyline, while the
copy declares: "Sound is flooding our
world."

美女はすぐ退屈するから困る。 ── マスカラの深いきらめき

資生堂シフォネット

Kazuhiko Ota, magazine advertisement for Shiseido mascara, 1973. This prize-winning advertisement appeared early in the career of the young art director. The copy calmly states: "A beautiful woman is easily bored."

Ryuichi Yamashiro, poster for Seibu Department Store's Christmas sale, 1973 (1029 x 730 mm). Elaborate English Gothic calligraphy is printed sideways to create a column of textures; in typical Japanese fashion, its use is not to inform but to decorate. The gold frame recalls the appearance of an English Christmas card, and the copy raises the issue of how many presents the customer has to buy by asking: "How many people on earth do you love?"

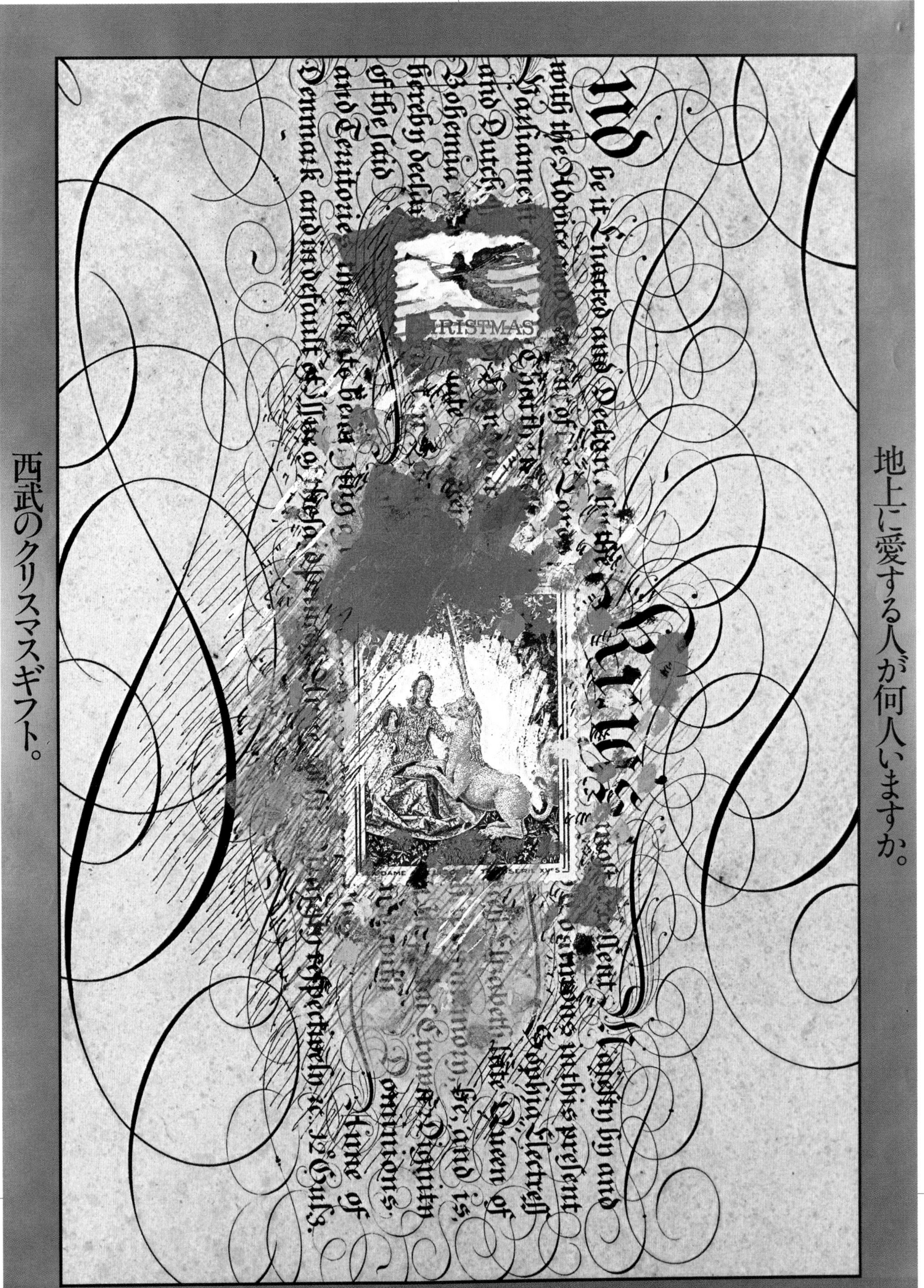

地上に愛する人が何人いますか。

西武のクリスマスギフト。

SEIBU

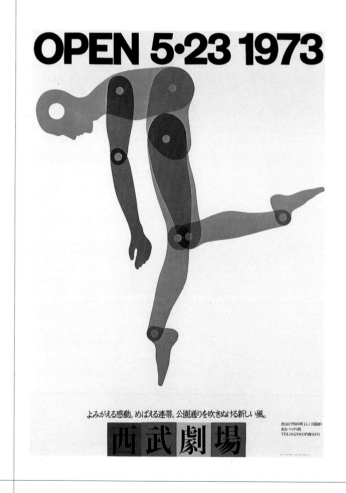

Ikko Tanaka, spread from a book for
Shiseido on the fashion designer
Issey Miyake, 1978 (364 x 250 mm);
photographs by Noriaki Yokusuka
and others. Tanaka himself joined in
as a model while working on the
book. His ability to control the use of
space is outstanding.

Ikko Tanaka, poster for the opening
of a new Seibu theatre, 1973 (1030 x
728 mm); illustration by Takahisa
Kamijyo. Information is given in the
direct, simple style for which Tanaka
is famous.

Ikko Tanaka, poster for the annual
Music Today concert at the Seibu
Theatre, 1974 (1030 x 728 mm).
Bright colours and play with the
figure and ground contribute to the
success of this poster.

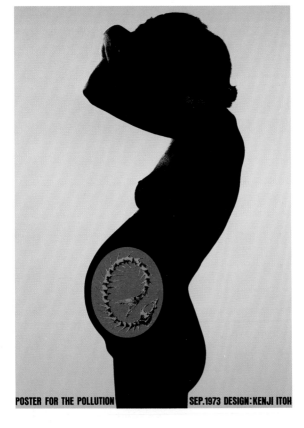

POSTER FOR THE POLLUTION   SEP.1973 DESIGN:KENJI ITOH

Tsuyoshi Fukuda, magazine
advertisement for Miss Pancaldi
shoes, 1978. Fukuda shows his sense
of humour and his interest in testing
the permissiveness of the Japanese
advertising code. The cool setting
with the warm flesh tones is more
European in appearance than
Japanese. The copy reads: "Hello
sister! Is your marriage going well?"

Kenji Itoh, poster drawing attention
to atmospheric pollution, 1973 (1030
x 730 mm). Itoh, one of the first
designers to use photographs as
illustration in Japan, had extensive
experience in designing covers for the
medical magazine *Stethoscope*. The
curled fish skeleton, superimposed on
the pregnant woman's womb, is an X-
ray photograph.

道中見聞録

奥州街道。平泉の落日は大きい。
一ノ関は上野から5時間。
特急やまびこ号、はつかり号、みちのく号など
毎日たくさん出発します。国鉄

DISCOVER))) JAPAN

Yoshi Hasegawa, nakazuri poster in the "Discover Japan"
series, 1973 (364 x 515 mm); photograph by Katsumi Otami.
Hasegawa's award-winning series captured the look of old
Japan, with evocations of small villages, Edo architecture and
non-urban scenes; this one shows an inn in the north of the
country. Using tightly cropped images to keep out all
references to the twentieth century such as telephone lines or
cars, the designer clipped the corners to make the posters
suggest ukiyo-e prints.

6

The eighties

Japan's recent economic history is as familiar to Western-ers as well designed "Made in Japan" Sonys, Hitachis, Hondas and Nikons. With the West's insatiable appetite for Japanese products, it is no surprise that by the end of the Seventies Japan was second in the world for industrial production. This increased production was primarily for export, because the buying habits of Japanese are so different from the Western world's. They are limited in how they can spend money, with large, expensive items, such as cars and housing, impractical or economically impossible. Japan's excellent mass transpor-tation system makes cars unnecessary; petrol is expensive and before Tokyo residents are allowed to purchase a car, they must show that they have a place to park. Single family dwellings are rarely built, except for those far from commut-ing distances to major cities; most people's only choice for housing is in apartment blocks, affectionately called "rabbit hutches." Flats are so small that there is no room for many possessions – such as large kitchen appliances or overstuffed sofas – or for entertaining groups of friends and family. This life style has promoted certain characteristics of Japanese commodities that have made them famous – compactness, miniaturization and adaptability. With attention on fewer items, more consideration is given to good design and quality workmanship.

In the late Seventies and early Eighties Japanese industrial designers were influenced by the new functionalism of Italian designers such as Giorgio Giugiaro, who was hired by Seiko and Nikon to redesign watches and cameras with ergonomi-cally determined control positions. Japanese furniture de-signer Shiro Kuramata, who designed interiors for Issey Miyake, worked with the radical Italian group Memphis. Fashion de-signers also brought international recognition to Japan in the Eighties. The first to achieve celebrity status was Hanae Mori, closely followed by Kenzo Takada and Issey Miyake, who studied graphic design at Tama. Younger innovators in the mid-Eighties were Yohiji Yamamoto and Rei Kawakubo.

Tadanori Yokoo regards fashion as today's major influ-ence on Japanese life: people want to express their individu-ality or personality in order to separate themselves in a crowded society. It is hard for Japanese to show personal taste in tiny apartments, and very few people have cars. The only thing left for self-expression is one's life style, characterized by fashion – one's costumes – which can be changed to suit individual characteristics.

Yukimasa Okumura, poster promoting the musician Haruomi Hosono, 1984 (1030 x 728 mm). Okumura describes this computer-aided poster: "The base is comprised of Mr Hosono's portrait and an illustration of a female face (goddess). These two portraits were made to look like Tokyo's urban sights by increasing the number of chips. It is not a collage but a photoprint, the result of numerous exposures. Some seventy photoprints were made and these were selected at random to be used for LP jackets, magazine advertisements and posters."

There are two groups of consumers for whom fashion is most important, and both are major targets for advertising. One group – teenagers – have had money from their parents to spend on fashion since the Sixties. The difference now is even greater wealth. But as the young gain wealth, their interest in the renowned Japanese work ethic of their parents is being challenged. Parents now complain that teenagers lack direction, are obsessed with material goods, and spend all their time visiting coffee houses. Design professor Shinichi Watanabe wrote in a 1984 issue of *Idea* magazine: "For quite some time, young people have been described as suffering from Three-No-isms (no energy, no interest, and no responsibility). A recent newspaper article reports that it is now come to Thirteen-No-isms." Fortunately Watanabe did not list them.

The other, new, market for fashion are young and middle-aged wives, who are also challenging their traditional position in the family. More and more continue working after marriage and are therefore able to afford fashionable clothes. Middle-aged women who are not working and whose children are at school occupy subways and trains after the morning rush hour to meet each other at fashionable Ginza restaurants, to shop in Harajuku boutiques and to work out in their sports clubs. Since wives do not participate in their husbands' business or social events, they dress up for their own daytime social life.

Today's graphic designers are part of these challenges to the family and the work ethic. They enjoy the rewards of high economic growth, but many find their life is pulled in a direction that is no longer desired. Family life has become more important as they tire of modern urban problems. Young Tokyo designer Michio Nadamoto expressed his appreciation for the casual and open American life style adopted by most urban Japanese, but he does not want to lose his identity as a Japanese. He said that all the Western appearances visible in Tokyo are only on the surface.

In the Eighties, foreign exposure to Japanese graphic design continued at the same level of activity as in the Seventies. Notable events included the ambitious exhibition "Japan Style" at London's Victoria and Albert Museum in 1980; the UCLA-Japanese Classical Performing Arts Festival and Travelling Poster Exhibition coordinated by Masaru Katzumie in 1981; joint exhibitions by Japan Typographers Association and New York Art Directors Club in 1982; "Tradition et Nouvelles Techniques – 12 Graphistes Japonais" in Paris and an exhibi-

Kiyoshi Awazu, UCLA festival poster, 1981 (1030 x 728 mm). The traditional female noh mask is shown in negative within a field of colourful lines. Awazu borrows early motifs and successfully makes them modern.

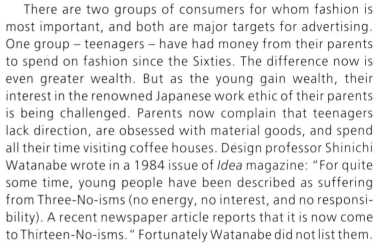

Takahisa Kamijyo, UCLA festival poster, 1981 (1030 x 728 mm). The Korean model is in traditional Buddhist festival dress for the theme *gagaku*, ancient music from the Imperial Japanese Court. The combination of photographs with illustration is a marvel of technical and production skill.

Nihon Buyo

UCLA
Asian Performing Arts
Institute 1981

Los Angeles
Washington, D.C.
New York

Ikko Tanaka, UCLA festival poster, 1981 (1030 x 728 mm). The face of a geisha, drawn in the ukiyo-e style, is reduced to a few basic geometric shapes. Variations of this abstraction were later used by Tanaka in other graphic design projects.

tion of Japanese design in Moscow, both in 1984; a 1985 exhibition, "Japan, Future of Avant-Garde," in Italy, and the 1986 travelling exhibition "Tokyo: Form and Spirit" organized by the Walker Art Center.

In 1989 there were two important events. The first was an exhibition in Brussels, "Modern Posters of Japan," which included work by most of the established Japanese designers. The second was the Design Exposition held in Nagoya from mid 1989 until almost the end of the year. The major intentions were for corporations to promote their goods and to draw national attention to the city of Nagoya, always overlooked in favour of Tokyo, Osaka and Kyoto. But there were several events focused on design, including a historical exhibition of Japanese posters that showed work going back a hundred years, much of it exhibited for the first time. An extensive book resulted from the exhibition, *Posters/Japan, 1800–1980s*, published by the Bank of Nagoya with the cooperation of the Institute of Contemporary Arts. It illustrated over 740 posters and handbills, crowded into 258 pages.

Contemporary Graphic Design

For most foreigners, the attraction of Japanese graphic design is its mystical spirit, initially enjoyed for the surface treatment of space, colour and technique, and for its Asian content. Three basic characteristics remain evident in most work being currently produced: emotional content rather than objective information; copy that has a tenuous relationship to the product or service promoted by the client; and imagery that is often ambiguous and sometimes evocative, yet still possesses all the beautiful traditional Japanese qualities – attention to detail and colour, emphasis on space, technical virtuosity and the abstract.

Emotion

During the Seventies, with interest in their historical origins and an increased sense of confidence, Japanese designers discarded the International Style. Philip Meggs in his book *A History of Graphic Design* (1983) defined this design style: "Personal expressions and eccentric solutions are rejected in favour of a more universal and scientific approach to design problem-solving." Although the International Style was a goal for most Japanese graphic designers in the Fifties and early Sixties, it is no longer desired. Instead of rejecting personal solutions, Japanese art directors and designers promote individual expression and eccentric resolutions to establish their own clarity and order. This is particularly evident in recent personal statements made by designers about their work, where the word "expression" is frequently used.

Emotion and personal expression have a long history in Japan. Edwin O. Reischauer, in *The United States and Japan* (1965) noted: "The peoples of East Asia have consistently given a greater place in their higher culture to direct emotive response to outside stimuli and have shown far less interest than we in systems of logic. . . Emotional expression in art or poetry is more their forte than a reasoned analysis."

Kazumasa Nagai also explained this Japanese characteristic in *Graphis* in 1968: "Although I admire the absolute beauty of. . . functional designs, I often feel that something is missing in them. I find them too rigid to allow the free play of space and form, to permit the enjoyment of what we call *ma* in Japanese, which might be translated as 'fluidity.' This peculiar sense of *ma*, which is not accessible to rationalistic thinking, has come down to us through the ages in various fields of our culture, such as music, painting and architecture." American or European daily lives are based on rationalism; Japanese people can operate with more freedom and not be restricted by functional principles imposed by content. Nagai claims that the Japanese are weak in analytical thinking and that their society recognizes that a sensitive approach may have just as much justification as a rational one.

The most prevalent example of emotion in Japanese graphic design and art direction is the sensual image. The Japanese male-dominated society exploits women to sell and promote just about everything. There is also humour, particularly with expressive illustrations that mimic a range of styles found in comic books. Sombre, moody photographic images are used to set an emotional tone with their expressive content and colour. Even violence is sometimes evident in illustrative solutions. Generally, there is a predominance of content-filled images over flat design and typographic solutions.

Copy

The Eighties was the decade when the copywriter came into prominence, surpassing the position of art director. Many copywriters operate like independent art directors as freelances with no ties to an advertising agency or corporate public relations department. Frequently copywriters provide the intellect for some prize-winning campaigns and exert influence

Masatoshi Toda, poster for Parco, 1983 (1030 x 728 mm); airbrush illustration by Harumi Yamaguchi. The original illustrations were quite bright, but Toda toned them down to create this misty image, with the copy: "The skin of a woman sounds like the blues." Yamaguchi is inspired by the beauty of the female body and denies any sexual exploitation.

Masatoshi Toda, poster for Vivre 21 boutique, 1987 (728 x 1030 mm); photograph by Sachiko Kuru. The model in this poster, one of a pair, is wearing the devil make-up from noh drama. The photograph was then rephotographed with an ant resting on it; the copy reads "Bulb." On the other poster is a shell, and the copy reads "Liquid." The copy, by Masayasu Okabe, is intended to provide a thoughtful dimension to the poster.

on many design concepts. Clients generally trust art directors and mistakenly think they will know current trends in society. But it is more typical for copywriters to be better educated and have more research experience to provide a broad base for conceiving new approaches in communication. Their experience with words enables them to exploit the Japanese fondness for puns and inventive use of complicated kanji letterforms. Some of the copywriters who are currently popular are Shigesato Itoi, Takeo Nagasawa, Takashi Nakahata and Yoshinari Nishimura.

One reason for more freedom in copy is the Japanese reluctance to produce comparative advertising; Japanese manners do not condone the practice of one company degrading the products of another. Their art directors and copywriters are free from using comparative words such as "bigger," "better," "brighter" and "faster," providing them with opportunities to develop far more creative concepts.

The Japanese have centuries of practice with haiku poetry, which has patterns of five, seven and five syllables; and the longer tanka poems, with their lines of five, seven, five, seven and seven syllables. Both poetic forms provide a unique synthesis of language and meaning based in a culture noted for reductions and refinement. In this background it is natural for copywriters to approach advertising copy as poetry.

Imagery
American advertising executives call it "image advertising," where photographs, illustrations and copy say almost nothing but leave the viewer feeling good about the product. The trend started in Japan with television commercials in the Seventies when the product received only brief mention at the end of a thirty-second anecdote. This unrelatedness in Japanese graphic design was discussed in an article, "The New Generation of Japanese Graphic Designers," in a 1984 issue of *Print* magazine: "There is no direct relationship between the concept and the advertised product. Even the copy does not necessarily bridge the gap." At about the same time, New York art director Barry Day labelled this advertising approach as "ambiguity" in an article for *Ads* magazine in October 1984. He identified it as a "marked move in the direction of . . . open-ended communication in Japanese advertising" which he attributed to their growing self-confidence. Two years later, Lou Dorfsman repeated this theme in his article "Lessons from the Japanese" in *Adweek Portfolio of Graphic*

Makoto Nakamura, poster for Shiseido perfume, 1982; photograph by Noriaki Yokusuka. In the late Sixties, Shiseido chose English words to accompany Eurasian models; once Nakamura discovered the beauty of model Sayoko Yamaguchi, he turned to Japanese headlines written in the style of haiku poetry. Here, the copy "White autumn image" accompanies an evocative photograph of Yamaguchi caressing a kimono textile. The poster promotes a perfume called "Koto," the name of the traditional Japanese harp which emits melancholy sounds.

脈。

VIVRE21

物

Design, where he referred to Japanese magazine advertising that deals almost exclusively with images. "Beautiful images. Provocative images. Gentle images. But images that have no apparent connection to the product being promoted. There is little or none of our concern with a tight concept and a true unity of headline, copy and visual elements."

Dorfsman went on to say that what works for Japan will not necessarily work in America. Robert Christopher in *The Japanese Mind* (1984) agrees: "Image creation and skilful appeals to consumer emotions and fantasies work better in Japan than they do in the United States – a fact that may be explained by the psychic pressures imposed upon the average Japanese by high productivity standards, crowded living quarters and the demands of a conformist social order." A casual review of current American print and television commercials, however, reveals a growing trend towards this kind of unrelated imagery.

The New Generation

Those who best express this allegorical, unrelated advertising are the new generation of Japanese graphic designers: the "third" generation, who have established prominence in Japan and are beginning to achieve recognition abroad. They were born either in the last years of World War II or the few years following, the first of the post-war generation of graphic designers. As residents of Tokyo they can also be identified as the "New Edokko," who are replicating the elegance of old Edo. Included here are a few to represent the new spirit in Japanese graphic design.

Tsuyoshi Fukuda

Art director Tsuyoshi Fukuda predicts there will be even more changes in the future for Japanese art direction. As the younger generation takes hold of the graphic design establishment they will not carry the same power as did the first generation. Born in 1943 and a graduate of Nihon University in 1969, he worked briefly at J. Walter Thompson, Japan, before he opened his office, Chameleon, in the Harajuku section of Tokyo in 1972. He has attracted considerable attention by his European style of art direction for such fashion clients as Charles Jourdan, Miss Pancaldi and Mary Quant Cosmetics. Recently he has won awards for his television commercials.

Top: Masatoshi Toda, poster for Vivre 21 boutique, 1986 (728 x 1030 mm); photograph by Sachiko Kuru. The woman in white hair is inspired by a scene from Akira Kurosawa's film *Ran* of an old man with flowing white hair which was both exquisite and grotesque, and projected a strong and compelling mood. This is one of a pair of posters: in the other, the woman's hair, instead of hanging straight down, is fashioned as a messed-up geisha wig. The copy, by Atsuko Iizuka, reads "Pulse" on this poster and on the other, by Masayasu Okabe, "Peach."

Above left: Koji Mizutani, magazine advertisement for Mitsui real estate agency, 1988 (297 x 430 mm). The stark, sharp kanji character, contrasting with the mysterious unfocused image of the chairs, reads simply, "Things." The client's identity is restricted to a tiny line at the bottom of the image, out of the frame.

Tsuyoshi Fukuda, poster for the telecommunications company NTT, 1988 (1030 x 1456 mm); photograph by Katsuo Hanzawa. The picture and copy tell the story of the last sturgeon fisherman in New York State's Hudson River, likening him to the hero of Ernest Hemingway's *Old Man and the Sea*. The text raises the issue of communication, with a headline reading, "The day I talk to the fish."

Takenobu Igarashi

With an extended Californian experience, Takenobu Igarashi is as comfortable in America as he is in his home country. Born in the northern island of Hokkaido in 1944, he graduated from Tama University in 1968 and, in an unusual move, received a Master of Arts degree from the University of California, Los Angeles, in 1969. When he returned to Japan he had difficulty being accepted by design firms because of his time abroad but, ignoring rejection, he opened his own Tokyo office in 1970 where he continues a successful business, operating more as a graphic designer than an art director. He has maintained close ties with friends in California, returning to UCLA in 1975 to teach for one year. During the mid-Seventies Igarashi experimented with isometric drawings of alphabetical forms. His experiments began to explode the structure, creating an illusionary three-dimensional playground that appeared to be more European than Japanese.

Igarashi leases a small but well designed studio building in the Minami-Aoyama area of Tokyo where he employs a staff of 14. Their production includes work for both cultural and corporate clients, and is split roughly equally between graphics and product design, the latter being a natural direction for him to take because of his interest in sculpture.

Koichi Sato

A philosophical designer with a delicate touch in the finest tradition of a rimpa artist, Koichi Sato has had a meteoric rise in reputation in the last few years. He was born in 1944 and, after graduating from Tokyo University of Art and Music, began his career with Shiseido in 1968. After two years, he became an independent designer in Tokyo. His identity has been firmly established by his delicate motifs of rimpa half-moons and a glowing aura surrounding simple shapes.

In preparing for a project he sometimes starts with a rough sketch, which he finds is less likely to be misunderstood than verbal explanations, but he would rather show clients finished examples of past projects; a rough does not have the same feeling and technical completeness as a printed work. A few years ago clients favoured American West Coast design solutions, but now he says they are looking for more traditional Japanese symbols. Sato likes to use Edo motifs to create an international Japanese feeling, as international as Mount Fuji and as appreciated as ukiyo-e. In *Graphics Japan* (1987), which he helped edit and organize, he wrote: "As Pop art was

Takenobu Igarashi, official poster for Expo '85, 1982 (1030 x 728 mm). One of several early posters by Igarashi that played with alphabetical forms, this one makes the letters themselves become a structural study - appropriate for a scientific world exhibition.

Above: Takenobu Igarashi, redesign of the symbol for Mitsui Bank, 1984. The three lines are the first part of the name *mi*.

Top: Takenobu Igarashi, sign for Parco Part 3 Department Store in Shibuya, 1981. It was a natural evolution for Igarashi's isometric drawings to be transformed into sculptural forms which he calls his "Architectural Alphabet."

Above: Takenobu Igarashi, carrier bag for The Museum of Modern Art, New York, 1985. The cool, corporate image of the museum is expertly conveyed by this geometrically designed monochrome pattern.

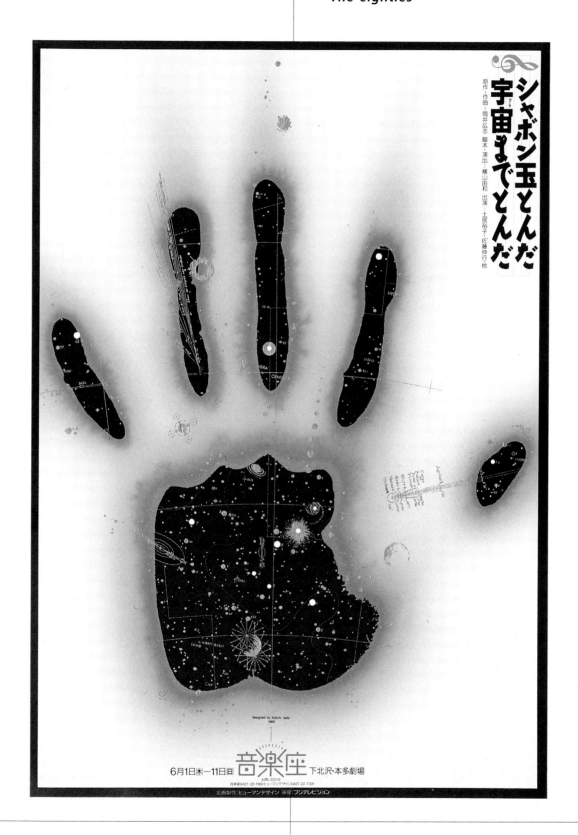

Shigeo Fukuda, poster promoting the work of twelve artists, 1984 (1030 x 728 mm). It shows Fukuda himself standing on the gallery wall to have a closer look at his own poster. This version of Leonardo Da Vinci's *Mona Lisa* was one of a series of works in which Fukuda used tiny reproductions of different national flags to represent colour and value.

Koichi Sato, poster for a musical, 1989 (1030 x 728 mm). The musical is based on an old Japanese nursery rhyme about soap bubbles flying into the air; here, a hand print suggests that the bubbles are flying into space. Sato wants to entice the viewer into his designs and to provide several levels of experience to elicit a variety of feelings. He thinks people should find their own meaning when they view his works and enjoy them as they would enjoy music: the more one hears, the more one enjoys and is moved by it.

ニューヨークからきたモデル・スクール
John Casablancas
470-3452

モデルも結局、松竹梅。

Ryoko Ishioka, poster for the John Casablancas Modelling Agency, 1986; photograph by Kazumi Kurigami. The copy, by Jun Maki, almost defies translation: it is a play on classifications to convey the idea that this agency makes first-class models. The three last characters represent top, medium and low classifications as well as bearing the literal meanings of pine tree, bamboo and plum.

the expression of an original American culture, I should like to create a form of visual communication which is uniquely Japanese. Although there is such a tradition in Japan, like most Japanese, I don't care for things simply because they are old. Through new technology I want to discover the mental mechanism of the Japanese, who always likes things new."

Sato's poster prints are exquisite, as fine and perfect as art prints. When he was a child, he was thought of as a "little inventor," and continues inventing new printing techniques to reproduce his work. He prides himself on knowing as much as printers and likes to approach printing problems as an engineer, influenced by his father, who is an electronics engineer. His studio is a remodelled apartment located in north central Tokyo, at the other end of town from the expensive section of Aoyama. It is neatly carpeted and has cabinets covered with grey plastic surfaces, an environment as clean and sparse as his graphic imagery.

Ryoko Ishioka

Attempting to step outside the shadow of her famous older sister Eiko, Ryoko Ishioka first received recognition with her enigmatic interior displays at a department store. She was born in 1945 and graduated from Tama University. After winning two Tokyo Art Directors Club awards, she was first employed in 1982 at the Nippon Design Center. By 1984 she had opened her own design office in Tokyo where she is art director for publishers, record and fashion companies.

Kazuhiko Ota

Favouring photographs that demonstrate openness, even empty space, Kazuhiko Ota's images have a wonderful feeling for space, colour and narrative. Born in Beijing in 1946 and a graduate of Tokyo University of Education, his first major position was as art director in the advertising production department of Shiseido Cosmetics. In the late Eighties he resigned from Shiseido and opened his own company, Amazon Design Office (in naming design offices, art directors use the same free-wheeler thinking as when creating advertising concepts for products). In *Graphics Japan* (1987) Ota typifies his fellow art directors' obsession with expressive communication: "I always try to keep bold imaginations and elegant, emotional work in my mind. I have devoted myself to photographic expression. From now I would like to expand the area of expression."

Ryoko Ishioka, interior display for Seibu Department Store, 1984. A life-size figure of a woman dressed in scuba-diving gear climbing out of a sardine can, this was placed at the end of an escalator. It was one of several outrageous yet realistic displays that brought Ishioka considerable attention.

松任谷由実にゴロニャンの方は、レコード屋さんへニャンニャンして下さい。 ニューアルバム「パール・ピアス」発売中
LP:ETP-90175 ¥2,800 CASSETTE ZH28-1200 ¥2,800 EXPRESS

グッドモーニング。女らしさキラッキラの発香体。今日もまぶしいね。 資生堂香水 琴
shiseido koto perfume

Top: Kazuhiko Ota, poster promoting a new album, "Sepia Pearl," by the singer Yumi Matsutoya, 1981; photograph by Minsei Tominaga. A kitten flies across an empty room with the music score floating in the centre and an image of the singer on a television set to one side. This poster is reminiscent of Katzumi Asaba's flying pig (see page 154).

Above: Kazuhito Ota, magazine advertisement for Shiseido perfume, 1987; photograph by Minsei Tominaga. In a series of elegant yet curious advertisements for "Koto" perfume, Ota gives a new look to content. A figure appears to be getting out of bed, and the copy reads, "Good morning."

Tsuguya Inoue

Born in 1947, Tsuguya Inoue is recognized by his contemporaries as one of the more creative art directors. He established his own office, Beans Co. Ltd, in 1978 and his list of clients includes major companies such as Parco, Seiko and Suntory. It is hard to identify his particular touch in art direction. He favours photographic solutions that express the texture and surfaces of objects that are completely unrelated to the client's product.

Yukimasa Okumura

Yukimasa Okumura is more likely to experiment with combined graphic imagery. Born in 1947 and a graduate from Kuwazawa Design School in 1969, he founded his own studio in 1979 and by 1982 was winning ADC awards for his designs for the rock group Yellow Magic Orchestra. His images combine design elements, photography and typography with a little Eastern religious mysticism.

Masatoshi Toda

One of the most popular younger generation designers is Masatoshi Toda, whose approach is as much intellectual as it is artistic and emotional. He was born in 1948 and had three years of advanced study at Meguro Seminar in Tokyo before he was employed at Takashimaya Department Store at the age of 22. After three years he entered Nippon Design Center, staying there for another three years before opening his own office. He works very closely with photographers in shooting sessions and maintains complete control as art director in choosing shots. Several of the photographs in his finished posters have a smoky, grainy effect, which he achieves by reshooting the photographic print. He prefers photographs to illustrations because he is better able to express his personality through them, and they are easy to change through alteration of the print or during the plate-making and printing processes.

In a conversation in 1987 he discussed his sources for inspiration, particularly for the Suntory advertisements based on the writings of the French poet Arthur Rimbaud. He said he does not read much because he does not like to look at printed characters. He does like watching Western and Japanese movies, which encourages his real ambition to be a movie director. Many of Toda's photographic solutions are beautifully staged with careful attention to every detail. He

Top: Tsuguya Inoue, poster for Parco, 1981. This is one of a series of advertisements, posters and a television commercial for Parco featuring rock-and-roll musician Chuck Berry. A simple, direct approach draws attention to the emotion of the singer expressed in his posture.

Above: Tsuguya Inoue, poster for a new album "Rouge Magic" by the rock singer Ryuichi Sakamoto, 1982; photograph by Bishin Jumonji. Two musicians, dressed in ragged Edo-style clothing, have their tunics stuffed with money. The copy, by Takashi Nakahata, reads: "His mother says to him, 'I'll never forgive you.'"

Top: Masatoshi Toda, newspaper advertisement for fashion designer Yohji Yamamoto at Setan Department Store, 1988; photograph by Kazumi Kurigami. A striking composition of contrasting tones, this impressive advertisement carries the copy line, "There is no copy."

Above: Masatoshi Toda, poster for the Olympus XA2 camera, 1983. This curious vignette has a blonde Western woman wearing a low-cut Korean-style underdress of a type popular during the Taisho period sitting back-to-back with a man wearing a traditional Japanese loincloth. They seem to be completely uninterested in each other, despite the copy line: "Let's do a photograph together." Toda did not want to tell a story, he explained, but to express softness and hardness. In the bottom right corner is the Olympus A-11, accompanied by the "G" Mark for good design.

likes classical music, particularly that of Mahler, and traditional Japanese music, Noh theatre, John Lennon and the artist Jasper Johns.

Koji Mizutani

Another art director who favours photography, Koji Mizutani was born in 1951 and graduated in engineering from Chubu University in 1973. He joined Nippon Design Center in 1977 where he produced Wacoal and Parco posters. In 1984 he established his independent studio. Mizutani likes to use dramatic photographs, sometimes rephotographed or with flat saturated colours and featuring one dominant image.

Makoto Saito

One of the youngest and currently brightest stars in Japan is art director Makoto Saito, who was born in 1952. He has a casual disdain for his clients, from whom he insists on complete freedom; he has the same attitude to many of his designer colleagues. He cares little about design and art direction awards because he says he is the best judge of his own work. From his studio in the popular Minami-Aoyama area in Tokyo, 90 per cent of his work is designing posters – mostly for fashion houses, and 10 per cent is producing television commercials for Parco Department Stores. Generally his posters use photographic images of Western models.

Saito had little formal art education other than training in silk screen printing. He is critical of Japanese teachers who try to make all students identical and do not allow individual recognition. After graduating from high school he worked in a department store art department for only six months, freelanced for another six months, joined a design office for another six months, and freelanced again before joining Nippon Design Center for five and a half years. While at NDC he was Masatoshi Toda's assistant for eight months. He and Toda are still friendly rivals and they constantly follow each other's progress. When asked to compare competing art directors he boldly said he was not aware of any who share his talents. He would admit that the best are Toda, Tsuguya Inoue and himself; and he plans to stay "on top" for at least ten years.

Unlike their predecessors of the Fifties, there is very little group identity with these younger generation designers. Alliances are generally based more on interests than age. Occasionally some are brought together for special exhibitions,

Koji Mizutani, fashion advertisement, 1987 (728 x 1030 mm). This intriguing composition is difficult to decipher until the woman's eye and nose is located in relation to the soft, off-centred image of the hat. Fashion advertisements can provide the greatest flexibility in imagery.

Masatoshi Toda, poster for Suntory whiskey, 1983 (1030 x 1456 mm). One of a series depicting a circus fire-eater and a midget woman with wings, the Fellini-type imagery is made the more provocative by the tearing out and repositioning of one of the figures. Toda claims the torn piece is meant to emphasise the nihilistic theme of the campaign. The copy, written by Takeo Nagasawa, reads: "Rimbaud, an exceptional person." The design is inspired by the work of the French poet Arthur Rimbaud, precursor of the Symbolists, which is noted for its hallucinatory, dream-like quality.

ランボオ
あんな男、
ちょっといない。

Top: Makoto Saito, poster for Garo boutiques, 1984. This is one of a pair of posters featuring a bilious green tie on a man's cast shadow; the other has a yellow tie. The large embroidered hiragana character expresses the sound "oh"; the other poster has the sound "nh" (the copywriter was Masayasa Okabe). The first and last kana syllables, they have no independent meaning: the idea is that the posters are hung together on a wall and "people can fill in their own story between them." According to Saito, there is no need to show fashionable clothes on posters, providing they are intriguing enough.

Above: Makoto Saito, poster for Garo boutiques, 1983 (1030 x 728 mm). The greatest freedom in concept is possible with promotional material for boutiques. A rough papier-mâché saddle shoe sets off the hand-stamped typography which translates: "You came here, didn't you?"

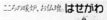

私は先祖の未来です。

Makoto Saito, poster for a manufacturer of domestic Buddhist altars, 1985 (1030 x 1456 mm). One of a pair (the other showed a pelvic bone), this stark image of a carefully painted humerus bone astounded Saito's design colleagues. The copy, by Masayase Okabe, reads: "I am the ancestor of the future," and the character on the left reads "life," but it is upside down. Saito explained: "It came to my mind instinctively that bones would be the only suitable subject for a Buddhist altar … I wanted to transmit their beauty…" The two won the Tokyo ADC Gold Medal Awards for 1985.

such as when Yusaku Kamekura asked Makoto Saito and Masatoshi Toda to organize a group of their generation for the exhibition Blood Six, held in August 1987. As it was with Persona in 1965, the younger designers did not have enough power to reserve space in a large department store, so Kamekura went to Matsuya Department Store and reached an agreement provided that some more established names would join the younger designers. Blood Six included work by young designers and a selection of posters from the show "Four Graphic Designers: Kamekura, Nagai, Tanaka and Fukuda," exhibited at Toyama Art Museum early in 1987. This exhibition provided a thorough review of these designers' work: much of it was familiar, and impressive.

The younger generation designers share with the older designers an emphasis on the importance of education. Almost all of the designers discussed in this book continued their education beyond secondary schools into the many art and design schools and universities that are available in Japan. Many designers credit the success of their careers to the quality of their education and the reputation of a particular school, pointing out the value that education plays in the Japanese society.

Graphic Design Education

Emphasis on design education "boomed" in 1967, when Japanese journalists estimated that there were a thousand new designers entering the field each year, the majority graduates from leading design schools in Tokyo and Osaka. It was prompted by the national attention given to designers during the World Design Conference, increased recognition accorded to popular designers through exhibitions such as Persona, and the growing popularity of decorative posters. As designers achieved celebrity status it followed that design education was the route for young people who wanted to gain the same attention and reap the financial rewards.

Advanced education came to Japan during the early years of the Meiji Restoration, the late nineteenth century. By 1953 Japan had its first design graduates, who called themselves "graphic designers." National universities offering art programmes after World War II were: Tokyo University of Art and Music; Chiba University; Tokyo University of Education (Tokyo Kyoiku, which moved to the north and was renamed Tsukuba University in 1973), and Kyoto National University. Osaka University of Fine Arts and Music was founded in 1964

凛として女、

Harumi Yamaguchi, poster for Parco, 1980 (1030 x 728 mm); art director Masatoshi Toda. The fish in this airbrush composition adds to the unrelatedness of the copy, which reads: "Woman as a proud spirit."

Harumi Yamaguchi, poster for Parco, 1989. Yamaguchi shows a new direction in her painting style in this poster celebrating the dancer Isadora Duncan.

イサドラ・ダンカンのように

Isadora Duncan 1877~1927

サンフランシスコの裕福な家庭に生まれる。芸術的環境の中でダンスに目
ざめるが、父が事業に失敗、貧困生活を味わう。それでも、彼女のダンスへ
の情熱は消えることはなかった。古いモラルや、窮屈な衣装に反発、ギリ
シャ時代のやわらかな布と素足で踊る自由なダンスを目指すが、アメリカ
では受け入れられず、ヨーロッパに渡る。1920年パリで"素足のイサドラ"
と評判をとると共に恋の花も開くのであった。演出家ゴードン・クレイグと
の激しい恋、出産、別離、そして何よりもダンス。イサドラは自由に生きた。
やがてイサドラはダンス学校の設立に意欲を燃やすがその間、二人の子
供を事故で失う。そして18才年下のセルゲイ・エセーニンとアメリカに戻る
が、アメリカは二人を拒否した。1927年首にまいたスカーフが車に巻きこ
まれそのまま帰えらぬ人となる。あまりにも劇的な50年の人生ではある。

PARCO

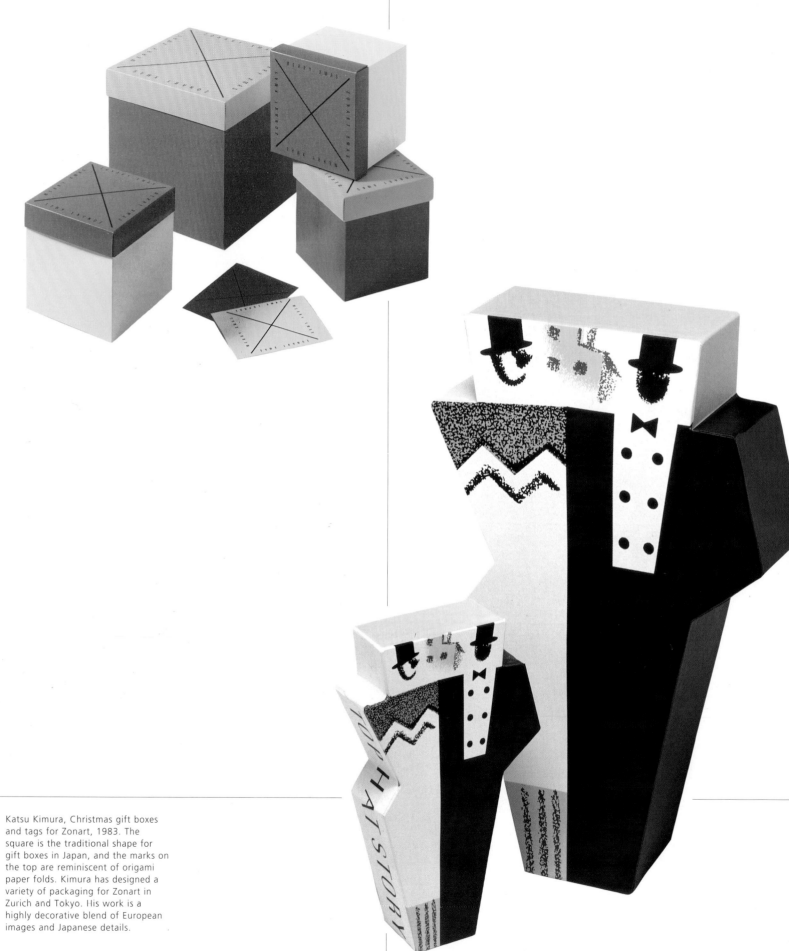

Katsu Kimura, Christmas gift boxes
and tags for Zonart, 1983. The
square is the traditional shape for
gift boxes in Japan, and the marks on
the top are reminiscent of origami
paper folds. Kimura has designed a
variety of packaging for Zonart in
Zurich and Tokyo. His work is a
highly decorative blend of European
images and Japanese details.

and Nagoya University of Arts introduced a design programme only in 1983. Recently, several prefecture (state) schools, such as Kanazawa College of Arts and Aichi Prefecture University of Arts, have added design programmes and offer a commendable curriculum.

Public institutions, funded through taxes, are inexpensive and hugely popular. Generally they have excellent reputations and the demand far exceeds the available space for new students, so up to 80 per cent of Japanese students are forced to attend the larger, and more expensive, private universities. Several of these have outstanding design programmes, including: Women's University of Fine Arts in Tokyo, established in 1900; Nihon University in Tokyo, established in 1922; Imperial Art School, established in 1929 and reorganized as Musashino Art University in 1962; Tama Art School, opened in 1935, which also has ties with the Art Center College of Design in Pasadena; Kuwazawa Art School, established in 1954, and Tokyo Zokei University, opened in 1966 with Masaru Katzumie as Director of Design. All institutions with four-year courses, public and private, are requested by the Ministry of Education to provide 40 per cent of courses in general studies and 60 per cent in art and design for the baccalaureate.

Admission to all schools requires passing an extensive examination that emphasizes traditional Japanese literature, grammar and composition, a foreign language – usually English – science, social science and a performance test in drawing and design. Because of the popularity of art and design education, prestigious schools are filled to capacity. More than two-thirds of the applicants are rejected and have to wait one or two years before they can make a reapplication. These students, called ronin, after the ancient wandering samurai who had no lord to protect, crowd into prep schools with one- or two-year programmes, and continue their study for future examinations while they wait.

Of all schools, Tokyo University is reportedly the most difficult for admission and still ranks as the top Japanese university. Shigeo Fukuda wrote in *Idea* magazine that competition in its 1984 design programme was the highest in history. This exclusive reputation is based not on an outstanding design programme but more on a history of educating Japan's future leaders. There is a definite show of respect for those designers who have a degree from "Geidai," as it is called, and their success with corporations is more assured. Some young designers complain that alumni favour other

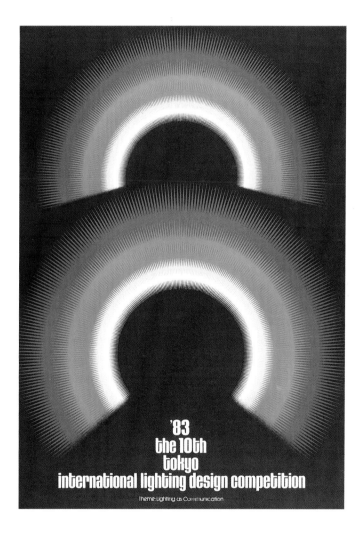

Katsu Kimura, gift box design, 1986 (395 x 250 x 90 mm). In the tradition of Japanese gift giving, the package becomes more important than the gift inside.

Top: Yusaku Kamekura, symbol for Nippon Telephone and Telegraph Company, 1987. The symbol for this huge Japanese company is based on the mathematical mark for infinity.

Above: Yusaka Kamekura, poster for a lighting design competition, 1983 (1030 x 728 mm). The spiked linear pattern is reminiscent of those created by Nagai in the Seventies, who in turn borrowed the idea from Kamekura's posters for Nikon in the Fifties.

Yusaka Kamekura, poster for the annual Hiroshima Appeals, 1983 (1030 x 728 mm); illustration by Akira Yokoyama. This moving image of burning butterflies is a rare exception for Kamekura, whose work usually avoids emotion. This was the first poster chosen for the Hiroshima Appeals, at which a poster competition is now an annual event.

Yusaku Kamekura, poster for Design Expo '89, 1987 (1030 x 728 mm). A stark landscape of white geometric forms on a flat, dark plane, with long shadows emphasising the austere design, is typical of Kamekura's recent work.

植物は眠らせるチカラがある。

キューピーマヨネーズ
FRESH KOMPE MAYONNAISE
野菜をもっとたべましょう。

Top: Gan Hosoya, poster for the
magazine *Omni*, 1982 (1030 x 728
mm). Hosoya is art editor of *Omni*,
and clearly has had fun with this
Magritte-type piece of trick
photomontage.

Above: Gan Hosoya, poster for Kewpie
mayonnaise, 1983 (1030 x 1456 mm);
photograph by Tetsu Nakagawa. One
of a series of photographic
advertisements, it is typical of product
advertising in the Eighties in its image
of a strange object in an unusual
location, preferably outside Tokyo - in
this case the mushrooms were
photographed in New York City.

alumni in hiring practices, particularly those who have degrees from Geidai, Tama and Musashino.

Once students are finally admitted to a university programme they have little reason to leave, keeping the drop-out rate quite low – between 3 and 7 per cent. Competition between students in classes is kept to a minimum and differences in ability are underplayed. Actually, school faculties rarely fail any students and they let them coast through their four years as a reward for passing the entrance examination. This has led to problems with class attendance, but recently students have been improving.

The increased interest in graphic design education has prompted some schools to improve their facilities. In the late Sixties many of the studio facilities were in deplorable condition, particularly at Tokyo University. Buildings at several schools were constructed in post-war concrete "factory" architecture – grey, bleak structures that were bitterly cold in the winter. Inside, furniture was old and there was little attention given to the latest technology. Since that time there has been a major renaissance in construction in many schools. Concrete is still favoured, but with more attention to providing personal warmth, both visually and physically.

Another major difference between Japanese design schools and Western schools in the late Sixties was the small percentage of female students majoring in art and design; approximately 6 per cent in 1968. This imbalance underlined Japanese society's lack of acceptance of women as professionals. The percentage has radically changed since then: in the Eighties four-year art and design programmes were about 50 per cent women, and two-year programmes had 80 per cent. However, women still have little hope of making it as designers or art directors in Japan. In a recent conversation, art director Tsuyoshi Fukuda talked about his search for a young assistant to join his firm, Chameleon. After interviewing several applicants, he decided not to hire anyone: the only applicants were women, and he would not hire a woman. Pressed for reasons, he said women were not strong enough to be good art directors and those who are strong are usually too aggressive for his clients. Women use a different form of language, which is more polite and honorific than men's. Conversations between art director and client are expected to be at a masculine level. But women who refuse to follow the feminine mode are usually not accepted by men in business discussions.

Undergraduate and graduate degrees in art and design from American schools have recently become popular and acceptable for Japanese. There was a time when students who studied in America were not readily hired when they returned because firms felt that the young designers would have lost their feeling for Japanese procedures. Designer Takenobu Igarashi finished his graduate degree from the University of California, Los Angeles, in 1969 and had difficulty finding employment when he returned to Japan. His solution was to organize his own studio in Tokyo, where today he is very successful, with an impressive client list of established corporations. Graduate education in Japan is about as unpopular for Japanese graphic designers as it is in the United States, where few students continue studies instead of seeking employment. Professor Shinichi Watanabe at Nihon University reports that they receive many requests for graduate admission from foreign students – Taiwan, the People's Republic of China and Korea – who plan to return to their home country to teach graphic design at the upper levels.

For several years *Idea* magazine has had an annual summer article on the graduation works from sixteen to twenty of the larger design schools. Several pages are filled with reproductions, many in colour, of student work accompanied by the graduation "charge" from one of the leading professors. Tokyo University of Art and Music is given the honour of leading the section with one or two pages, followed by other major schools. The design work is all quite lively, with colourful, highly professional examples of typography, illustration, photography, packaging, advertising design and some recent application of computer graphics.

Many of the examples are experimental poster designs not unlike the final projects of young graphic designers anywhere in the world. The poster as a design project holds a special significance. Its large size and emphasis on a dominant image makes it an ideal representation of the potential talents of an aspiring designer. But few countries produce as many posters or regard them with such honour as Japan.

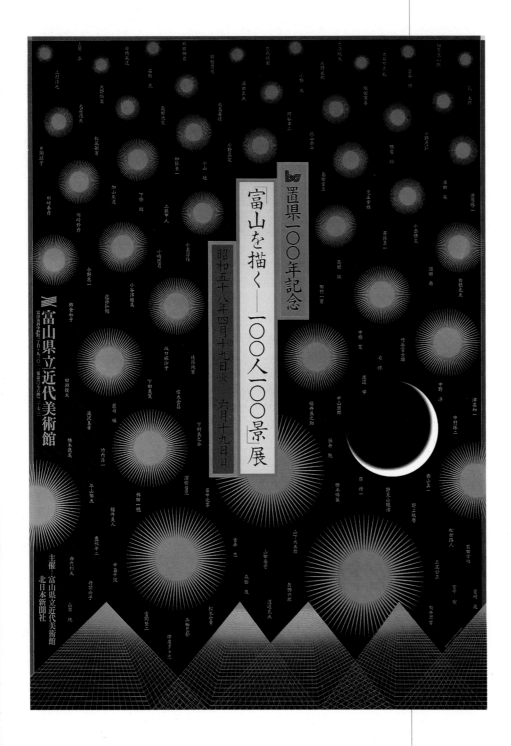

Above: Kazumasa Nagai, poster for an exhibition at the Museum of Modern Art in Toyama, 1983. Nagai designed several posters for this museum which show marked similarities. This one, for the exhibition *100 Paintings of Toyama by 100 Artists*, is done in his familiar play with spiked forms and lines depicting the mountains and snowflakes north west of Tokyo.

Above right: Kazumasa Nagai, symbol for Minami Nippon Broadcasting Company, 1983. Here again are the spiked lines so often employed by both Nagai and Yusaka Kamekura.

Right: Teruhiko Yumura, film poster, 1984 (730 x 515 mm). Yumura's illustrations range from crude comic-book line drawings filled with primary colours to those that resemble scribbled doodles by children preoccupied with bodily functions. Other illustrators express themselves bewildered with Yumura's style. Wada claims that he is "not a skilful drawer," but then goes on to say, "his work is beyond the concept of 'skilful' or 'unskilful'." Yumura himself claims: "My hobby is illustration. So I will keep on drawing 'hetaumi' (drawn both poorly and well) illustration."

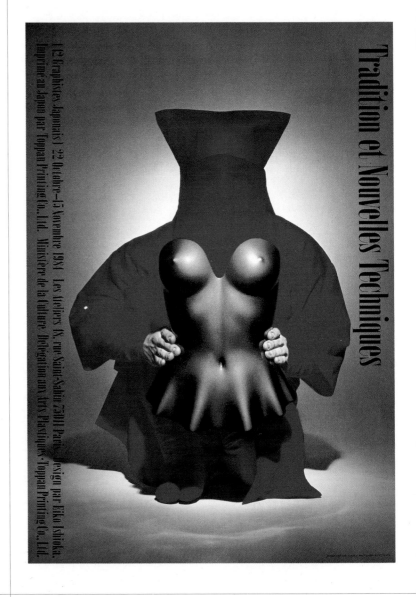

Kohei Sugiura, cover for *Ginka* magazine, 1983 (260 x 185 mm). *Ginka* is a magazine devoted to art and culture; traditional New Year decorations are shown in this special issue devoted to the Japanese use of colour. Sugiura, one of Japan's leading editorial designers, takes full advantage of the character of Japanese calligraphy.

Eiko Ishioka, poster for "Tradition et Nouvelles Techniques," 1984 (1030 x 728 mm). Ishioka's Paris exhibition poster shows a traditional *bunraku* (puppet) handler with a new torso fashioned by Issey Miyake.
Traditional *bunraku* handlers are dressed in black so that they are not visible; Ishioka uses red to draw the attention.

Right: Kiyoshi Awazu, poster for the Hiroshima Appeals, 1984 (1028 x 700 mm). Radiantly coloured doves fill the poster, with the smaller ones at the bottom, seemingly carrying the load. Awazu has progressed from careful line work to more expressive crayon drawings with colour and texture, loosely drawn and brilliantly composed.

LOVE HIROSHIMA APPEALS 1984 PEACE

design / illustration : kiyoshi awazu   printing : toppan printing co., ltd.   sponsors : hiroshima international cultural foundation, inc., jagda (japan graphic designers association inc.)

明石

ああ、絶景かな。格調の名書体。

沼島
淡路島
大毛島
島田島
小豆島
男鹿島
上島
坊勢島
松島
家島
鹿久居島
西島
伊島
粟島
佐柳島
真鍋島
六島
大飛島
女木島
直島
男木島
屋島
本島
北木島
広島
高見島
白石島
宇治島
高島
手島
犬島
井島
豊島
前島
長島
因島
江ノ島
向島
魚島
能美島
倉橋島
大島
大黒神島
伊吹島
仙酔島
大島
走島
田島
小水無瀬島
大水無瀬島
睦月島
野忽那島
豊島
似島
中島
大崎上島
厳島
浮島
四阪島
上蒲刈島
下蒲刈島
高根島
大崎下島
佐木島
高井神島
黒髪島
江田島
阿多田島
柱島
屋代島
牛島
長島
由利島
平郡島
生口島
興居島
大三島
鹿島
怒和島
野島
青島
前島
津和地島
二神島
八島
姫島
久居島
祝島
戸島
祝島
向島
人津島

モリサワ
大阪本社=大阪市阿波座南通2-6-25 〒550 TEL.06-543-2731
東京支社=東京都新宿区下宮比町1-5 〒162 TEL.03-262-1231
札幌・仙台・名古屋・京都・神戸・広島・松山・福岡・鹿児島・沖縄

Left: Ikko Tanaka, poster promoting a new typeface for the Morisawa Typesetting Company, 1985 (1030 x 728 mm). For a typeface called Akashi, the name of a famous and beautiful resort in Kansai Prefecture, Tanaka has illustrated the Seto inland sea, using characters giving the names of all the islands, in their correct positions and in an appropriate size.

Top: Ikko Tanaka, symbol for the Ginza Graphic Gallery, run by the Dai Nippon printing company, 1986.

Above left: Ikko Tanaka, logo for an exhibition about the Silk Road held in Nara, 1986. The Roman letter "S" takes on a monsho effect, with a leaf added to suggest the route of a tree-lined road.

Above: Ikko Tanaka, poster announcing the opening of the Ginza Saison Theatre with the first performance of Peter Brooks' *Carmen*, 1986 (1030 x 728 mm); photograph by Eikoh Hosoe. This theatre has also hosted the *Mahabharata* and performances of contemporary music.

Keisuke Nagatomo, play poster for *Mosquito on the Tenth Floor*, 1982; illustration by Sietaro Kuroda. The Imperial battle flag and Japan's red sun appear in the top corners, while the lines through the figure's eyes and mouth provoke an emotional response typical of Kuroda's work.

Keisuke Nagatomo, play poster, 1986 (1030 x 728 mm); illustration by Seitaro Kuroda. The play, by Kenji Nakagami, has a title in dialect from the south west of Japan and is taken from the story of a best-selling Japanese novel.

Right: Makoto Wada, play poster, 1985. Wada uses images of dreams from a play about the subject of sleep to illustrate the poster. The monochrome composition is accented with a splash of colour in the headline

WALTZ

GC CIRCLE

Top: Shin Matsunaga, logo for a shopping centre, 1986. In this design, in which the English word "Waltz" emphasises feeling over logic in the true Japanese fashion, computer pixels are combined with Post-Modern stair step shapes.

Centre: Tsuyoshi Kindaichi, book title design for *GC Circle*, 1987. When Japanese typographic designers approach Roman letter forms, forms become more important than meaning, and feeling more important than legibility.

Above: Yasubumi Miyake, logo for an evening newspaper, 1988. The hiragana characters, turned into pictographs, spell out the word "People."

Tohiyasu Nanbu, logo and packaging for a lacquerware store, 1988. Contemporary packaging combines the elegance of Japan's decorative tradition with modern technology. Nanbu (born in 1951) has his own design shop, Taste, in Osaka.

SHIGEO OKAMOTO ILLUSTRATION

Fukiage Hall, Nagoya City January 25—26, 1986 am.10:00—pm.8:00, 26／am.9:00—pm.5:00 Sponsred by Morisawa Co.,Ltd.

岡本滋夫イラストレーション原画展 1月25日田—26日回 吹上ホール3Fファッション展示場　25日·AM10:00—PM8:00 26日·AM9:00—PM5:00
共催 モリサワ'86新書機材展

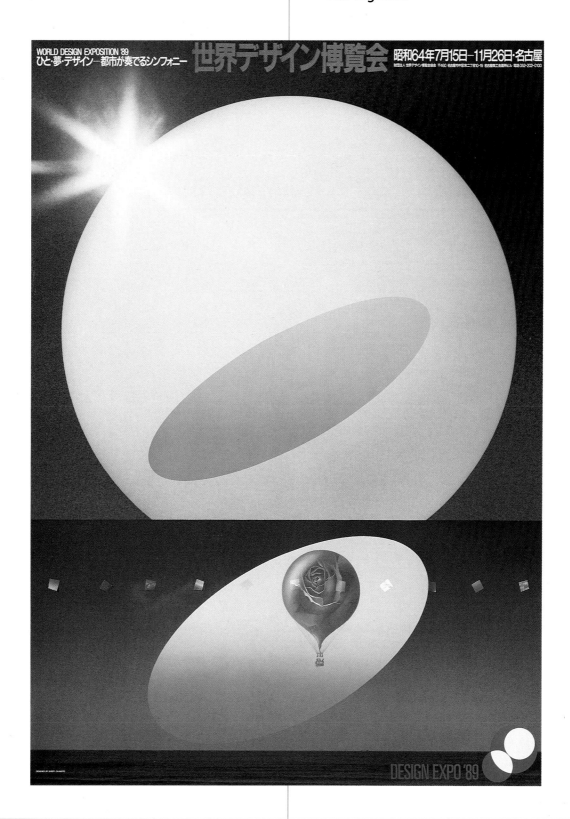

Shigeo Okamoto, poster promoting an exhibition of his own illustrations, 1986 (1030 x 728 mm). An art graduate of Aichi University of Education, Okamoto (born in 1934) received some recognition in the Sixties and early Seventies as an industrial designer, but it was not until the late Seventies and Eighties that his posters became popular and began to win international awards. Many of his designs are limited in their graphic imagery, concentrating on simple geometric shapes or highly structured compositions printed in subtle colours with rich greys and blacks.

Shigeo Okamoto, poster for Design Expo '89, 1987 (1030 x 728 mm). In broad areas of colour, the symbol for the exhibition is repeated in the composition, with a little gas balloon added at the bottom.

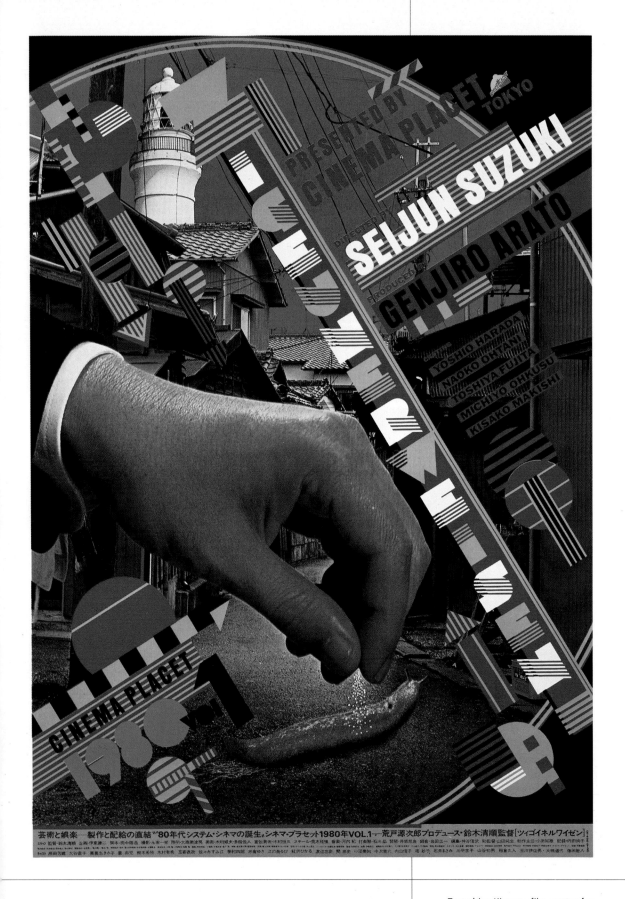

Tsunehisa Kimura, film poster for
Zigeuner Weisen directed by Seijun
Suzuki, 1980 (1015 x 729 mm);
photographs by Makoto Shimizu.
Kimura has experimented since 1969
with photomontages containing both
symbols and connotations, intended
to emulate the visual language
developed by the Russian Formalists.

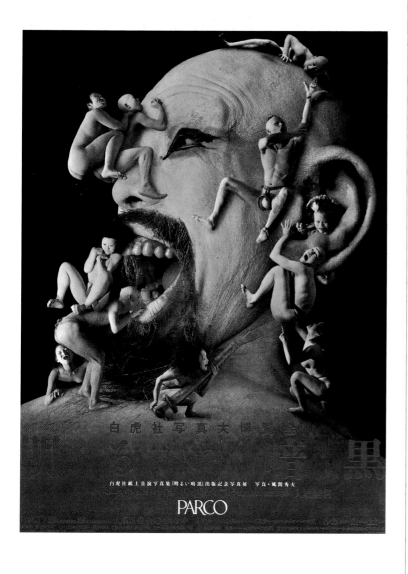

Tsunehisa Kimura, poster for an exhibition of photographs, sponsored by Parco, of the Byakkosha (White Tiger) Theatre Group, 1986 (1033 x 735 mm); photographs by Chichiken Yamano. In this technically beautiful poster, Kimura has combined the image of an actor's head and shoulders with small photographs of other members of the troupe scrambling over him. Their monochromatic painted bodies are surrounded by a brilliant red border to add to the exotic appearance.

Top: Katsumi Asaba, symbol for the Tokyo Designers Space gallery, 1981. The gallery, making exhibition space available for graphic design, is jointly owned by a number of Tokyo designers and is located in the Axis Building in the Rappongi quarter of the city.

Above: Katsumi Asaba, poster for Seibu Department Store, 1988. Young love has only recently been allowed any public expression in Japan; this poster was so popular that it was stolen from all its display sites.

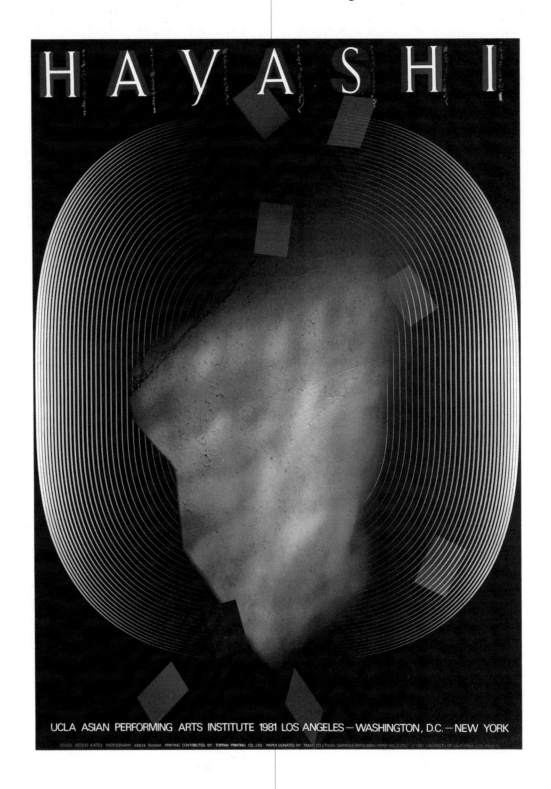

Mitsuo Katsui, poster for the Asian Performing Arts Festival held at the University of California, Los Angeles, 1981 (1030 x 728 mm). Hayashi are small percussion instruments used in Japanese classical and folk music. This was one of a dozen posters by different Japanese artists invited to contribute promotional designs by the coordinator Masaru Katzumie.

Mitsuo Katsui, *Zero*, 1985 (1030 x 728 mm). Katsui has continued his interest in technology throughout the Eighties, and now uses graphic images generated by computer. He describes his philosophy by explaining: "Originality in art is closely related to the technology of design." His abstractions take full advantage of technical developments.

Masuteru Aoba, poster for Seiyu (the supermarket branch of Seibu), 1982; photograph by Takayuki Ogawa. For this poster promoting a summer campaign to exchange gifts purchased at Seiyu, Aoba had a red "ribbon" two metres wide specially made of steel.

第66回ニューヨークADC金・銀受賞作品展　昭和62年9月7日月～19日土　　　G7Gallery　　　第1回NYADC国際グラフィックデザイン受賞作品展　昭和62年9月21日月～10月3日土

Masuteru Aoba, poster promoting the annual exchange exhibition between the Tokyo and New York art directors' clubs, 1988 (1030 x 1456 mm). This poster, in which Aoba has altered his own photograph of the Manhatten skyline, first appeared without lettering in an exhibition of his experimental work; this version won a gold prize at the Poster Biennale in Warsaw.

Conclusion

The heritage of Japan's posters is similar to that of the ukiyo-e woodblock print. Both enjoy a mass appeal for their communicative and artistic value, and both require a unique, multiple-craft production process. Nineteenth-century ekanban shared ukiyo-e's aesthetic and printing process. Once chromolithography was imported in the early part of this century, a series of bijin-ga beauty posters captured Japan's attention. At this period, posters were generally shown inside, framed, rather than pasted on outdoor billboards, which gave them a precious quality, and enabled them to be viewed primarily for their aesthetic value. The product advertised was usually as important as the artist's identity; an attitude that continued during the Thirties when designers followed the style of Europeans and signed their posters. Today, the artist's expression is seen as more important.

After World War II, and a sudden rush for graphic designers to have international recognition, posters became another form of Japanese export. Instead of producing cheap souvenir-style posters as was done before the war, the first generation of designers made a conscious decision to avoid folk-craft motifs and created instead designs based on a modern, European image. Although this decision was not popular with some foreigners, Japanese designers were thus able to break successfully from their past, separating themselves from their economically depressed Asian neighbours and identifying with affluent Americans and Europeans.

These first generation designers were confronted with low-quality paper and poor printing production techniques, which forced them to work with flat colours, hand-lettered type and a minimal use of photography. Posters during the Fifties were, for the most part, still primitive in production and major clients were not convinced of their artistic merits. Many designers were limited to creating *pro forma* posters for cultural events, plays, conferences and Japan Advertising Art Club activities rather than for major corporations.

During the life of JAAC, a majority of the posters submitted to their annual exhibitions were experimental and printed at the designer's expense. Commenting on this in a 1960 issue of *Graphis* magazine, Hiromu Hara explained the prevalence of uncommissioned posters in the annual exhibition. He said it was a tradition for designers, particularly young people who have few opportunities for large four-colour posters, to promote a variety of events as a self-advertisement. Many experimental posters in the Sixties were silk-screened, a print-

Susumu Endo, poster for Kumamoto Prefectural Cultural Festival, 1988 (730 x 515 mm). A photograph of grass has been enlarged and altered with a simple geometric division of space and the placing of a large circle in the centre. Technically superb, the poster looks like a collage but in fact comprises a single photographic image. Endo has recently been concentrating on photographs of natural objects, creating visual illusions with the aid of a computerized airbrush to distort the image before the plates are made.

ing process that provided brilliant colour combinations typical of the Pop and Op styles popular in Japan and the United States. But in the early Sixties, major printers and typesetters made considerable improvements; Dai Nippon and Toppan printers, in particular, worked with designers to improve paper quality and printing techniques. Morisawa Typesetting Company made improvements in phototype in both Japanese kanji and roman letterforms.

The popularity of the poster was reinforced by a significant exhibition, "The Belle Epoch Poster," at Tokyo's Matsuya Department Store in 1965, organized by Masaru Katzumie. He selected over three hundred posters from the collection of the Louvre Bibliothèque des Arts Décoratifs in Paris and prepared descriptive material for the catalogue. These posters were highly influential in moving designers away from the Swiss school towards more individualistic expression. By the late Sixties, young people in most countries were discovering posters as an inexpensive way to decorate their rooms. Printed subject matter as a political or social statement gave youth an identity and comfort in a society that was re-examining its values.

But Japanese posters serve a broader function than just to decorate interiors. Corporations are more dependent on them to promote their image than are Western companies. With leadership from designers in Shiseido, Suntory, fashion boutiques and the advertising sections of large department stores, commercial posters are more experimental and more open to individual expression. Emphasis on posters is demonstrated in various design policies and in design annuals. It is common practice for designers to produce several versions of a promotional poster announcing an exhibition of their personal work. Most major design events are expected to have a series of posters produced by a dozen of the better known designers, with one designated as the "official poster." From the beginning of their publication, Japanese art direction and design annuals usually led with reproductions of the best posters produced in the past year, relegating advertisements, packaging and trademarks to the back.

There are other indicators of the current importance of Japanese posters. Not many years ago, they were freely given to foreign visitors as a personal form of export in order to spread Japan's reputation in graphic design. Now the demand is so great that designers handle posters in the same way as limited-edition prints, making them available only for special exhibition purposes. Some designers, such as Masatoshi Toda and Koichi Sato, produce elegantly printed posters that are clearly limited to a gallery aesthetic and promote no product or service. In the late Seventies and Eighties, posters promoting world peace were frequently accepted in international exhibitions and still receive a wide audience.

There is something inconsistent about the high number and exceptional quality of Japanese posters reproduced in annuals and those that can be found hung outside on the streets. Most posters are large, 40 1/2 x 28 3/4 inches (103 x 72.8 cm) and, in a society that has little free space and no poster kiosks, one wonders where they are all shown. Nineteenth-century ekanbans were hung at major crossroads and in public baths, the social intersections during feudal times. Modern intersections in urban Japan where posters are most often found are coffee houses, train stations and department stores. Many posters for leading department stores and cosmetic firms are reduced to half-size for hanging inside smaller shops, or redesigned for the horizontal nakazuri transport posters. Major train stations have outside boards that accommodate some of the larger sizes, 40 1/2 x 57 1/2 inches (103 x 145.6 cm). But a clear majority of posters seen in annuals and design exhibitions are rarely seen on the street. Probably thousands more people saw the posters Tanaka produced for noh theatre groups *after* the event, in publications and exhibitions, than saw them before the performance.

Very few galleries in Japan's larger cities show posters and other graphic design material on a regular basis. To rectify this, 92 designers – including graphic, industrial, interior, architectural and fashion designers – independently opened Tokyo Designers Space in 1976. As an opening campaign theme, they had "One Day One Show" with daily, individual, solo shows. Dai Nippon printers have recently opened a small but popular space called the Ginza Graphic Gallery, which is set aside in one of their Tokyo buildings for the exhibition of graphic design.

Although some poster exhibitions are held in museums, such as the Tokyo Central Museum, and other small galleries, the chief space for design exhibitions is in the major Tokyo department stores, where anything from 50,000 to 100,000 people will view a poster exhibit. In addition to graphic design, department stores stage major fine arts exhibitions of international art, traditional craft fairs, tea ceremony, and a few even have separate theatres. The Seibu Department Store

"1" "1" "1" 2" 3" 4" 5   "6   "20
  "7   "13   "21   "27"28"29"30" " "
  "8   "14   "22
  "9   "15   "23
  "10   "16   "24
JUNI   "11   "17   "25
  "12   "18   "26
      "19

GEBR. SCHMIDT
DRUCKFARBEN

Susumu Endo, calendar for a German
printing ink company, 1988 (680 x
540 mm). Here the rocks become both
positive and negative shapes. Only in
1883 was the law amended to allow
the publication of calendars;
exchanging them is now a popular
new year's event.

Yoshio Hayakawa, poster for the
Hiroshima Appeals, 1986 (1030 x 728
mm). The ghost-like figure holds a
carefully painted dove.

branch in the Ikebukuro part of Tokyo opened the Seibu Art Museum in 1975. The importance department stores have for cultural life in Japan goes back more than a hundred years to the Edo era, when the merchant class assumed social and cultural responsibilities. For example, when the *Mona Lisa* came to Japan for exhibition in the Seventies, it was shown in a department store. Art museums, with large holdings of historical art, are a very recent addition in Japan. A museum devoted to advertising, however, is currently being proposed, and is due to open in 1992.

Contemporary graphic designers rely on posters to establish their reputation more than any other form of graphic design. First, work has to be noticed and included in some design publications. Once there is some attention, the most popular next step is to stage an exhibition of the designer's work in Tokyo. If successful, the poster for the exhibition would be reproduced in the Japan Graphic Design Association annual *Graphic Design in Japan*. As the exhibiting designer attracts better clients, he or she is invited to participate in more group exhibitions and to design posters for special events.

The historical origin of the Japanese poster is just another example of how Japan was able to absorb a modern technology imported from the West, and alter it to become distinctly Japanese. In examining the progress of Japanese graphic design in the last 150 years it is evident that the goal of designers was not to mimic America and Europe as much as to bring Japan into the modern world. Their success lies in their retention of the original spirit of Japan. In *Graphis* magazine's 1968 double issue, Kamekura wrote about the Japanese spirit found in the word *katachi*. Almost impossible to translate, it roughly means "perfect form," conveying an impression of environmental art, combined with spiritual serenity. It is the essence of the spirit Japanese designers should strive for:

We Japanese designers have inherited a tradition . . . Naturally we cannot accept it uncritically, and many of us feel that to rebel against it is also one of the reactions of the conscientious designer. Yet . . . personally, I believe that while tradition may be a burden to the designer it is something which he cannot entirely reject. Our duty is rather to take our tradition apart and then put it together again in a new way. Perhaps the results will turn out to be the *katachi* we are really looking for.

草月 144
ikebana sogetsu

草月
ikebana sogetsu
144 1982/10

株式会社 草月出版
SOGETSU SHUPPAN INC.
〒150 東京都渋谷区渋谷1-1-4 TEL.407-1828
1-1-4 SHIBUYA, SHIBUYAKU, TOKYO, JAPAN.

Yoshio Hayakawa, cover for *Ikebana Sogetsu* magazine, 1985.
This is a successful magazine largely devoted to the art of
ikebana, flower arrangement, but which also carries general
items about the arts. Hayakawa's softly painted wrap-round
covers were free assignments that allowed him complete
latitude in content and approach. He limited his compositions
to a few household objects placed on an impressionistic
painted field.

Tadanori Yokoo, poster for an exhibition of his paintings, 1984 (940 x 740 mm). The German body-builder Lisa Lyon, painted in Izu-kogen Park in Tokyo, takes on the appearance of a marble monument. By the late Seventies, Yokoo had tired of being a graphic designer and wanted to be considered as a fine artist.

Tadanori Yokoo, self-promotional poster, *Amazon*, 1989 (1030 x 725 mm). Yokoo's latest work refers back to the expressive designs of the Sixties.

Akiyama, Terukazu *Treasures of Asia, Japanese Printing*, Geneva: Albert Skira, and New York: Rizzoli International Publications, 1977.

Allen, Jeanne *Designer's Guide to Japanese Patterns*, San Francisco: Chronicle Books, 1988.

Annual of Advertising Production in Japan, Tokyo: Rikuyo-sha.

Aoba, Masuteru "Intentions, ADC Awards," *Annual of Advertising Art in Japan 85-86*, Tokyo: Bijutsu Shuppan-sha, 1986.

Art Directors Club of Tokyo *Annual of Advertising Art in Japan*, Tokyo: Bijutsu Shuppan-sha, 1959– .

Art Directors Club of Tokyo *Art Direction Today*, Tokyo: Kodansha, 1984.

Art Directors Club of Tokyo *Newspaper and Magazine Advertising in Japan, 1869–1956*, Tokyo: Bijutsu Shuppan-sha, 1967.

Art Directors Club of Tokyo *Packaging in Japan, 1868-1956*, Tokyo: Bijutsu Shuppan-sha, 1969.

Art Directors Club of Tokyo *Posters in Japan, 1860-1966*, Tokyo: Bijutsu Shuppan-sha, 1967.

Aston, W. G. Translation of *Nihon Shoki; Chronicle of Japan From the Earliest Times to AD 697*, London: Allen & Unwin, 1956.

Awazu, Kioshi, ed. *The Posthumous Works of Tadanori Yokoo*, Tokyo: Gakugai-shorin, 1968.

Bayer, Herbert *"Typography and Design," Concepts of the Bauhaus: the Busch-Reisinger Museum Collection*, Cambridge: Harvard University Press, 1971.

Bayley, Stephen *The Conran Directory of Design*, New York: Villard Books, 1985.

Broido, Lucy *The Posters of Jules Cheret*, New York: Dover Publications, 1980.

Brownell, Clarence L. *Tales From Tokio*, Warner & Brownell, 1900.

Chamberlain, Basil Hall *The Classical Poetry of Japanese*, London: Trubner & Co., 1880.

Christopher, Robert C. *The Japanese Mind: the Goliath Explained*, New York: Linden Press/Simon & Schuster, 1983.

Creation, ed. by Yusaku Kamekura, Tokyo: Recruit, 1989– (quarterly).

Day, Barry "The Advertising of Ambiguity," *ADS*, October 1984.

Dorfsman, Lou Introduction to *The World of Ikko Tanaka*, Tokyo: Kodansha, 1975.

Exhibition: 4-G.D. Toyama: Toyama Art Museum Catalogue, 1987.

Friedman, Mildred "Broadside to Billboard," *The 20th Century Poster*, ed. Dawn Ades New York: Abbeville Press, 1984.

Fukuda, Shigeo "Intentions, ADC Awards," *Annual of Advertising Art in Japan 85-86*, Tokyo: Bijutsu Shuppan-sha, 1986.

Fukuda, Shigeo "Annual Review of Graduating Students" *Idea*, 185, 1984.

Gendai Nippon no Poster [Modern Japanese Posters], Toyama: Toyama Art Museum Catalogue, 1982.

Gibney, Frank B. Introduction to *Kanban, Shop Signs of Japan*, New York & Tokyo: John Weatherhill, 1982.

Graphic Design, Tokyo: various publishers, 1959–1986 (quarterly).

Graphis, Zurich: Graphis Press, 1944- (quarterly) .

Hara, Hiromu "Japanese Posters," *Graphis*, 92, 1960.

Haryu, Ichiro "World Expositions at the Crossroads," *Graphic Design, 36*, 1969.

Herdeg, Walter, ed. *Graphis Annual*, Zurich: Graphis Press.

Herdeg, Walter *Graphis Posters*, Zurich: Graphis Press (annual).

Hosoya, Gan "Philosophy," *Gendai Nippon no Poster*, Toyama: Toyama Art Museum Catalogue, 1982.

Hunter, Janet E., ed. *Concise Dictionary of Modern Japanese History*, Berkeley, Los Angeles and London: University of California Press, 1984.

Idea, Tokyo: Seibundo-Shinkosha (bi-monthly).

Igarashi, Takanobu *Igarashi Alphabets*, Zurich: ABC Editions, 1987.

Igarashi, Takanobu ed. *Seven*, Tokyo: Graphic-sha, 1985.

Igarashi, Takanobu *Space Graphics*, Tokyo: Shoten Kenchiku-sha, 1983.

Illustrators Club of Japan, *Illustration in Japan*, Tokyo: Kodansha International (annual).

Imai, Yoshiro "Evolution des Modes d'Expression L'Affiche Japonaise," *L'Affiche Japonaise: Des Origines à nos Jours*, Paris: UCAD Musée de L'Affiche, 1979.

Ishioko, Eiko "Designers' Comments," *Graphics Japan*, Tokyo: Graphic-sha, 1987.

Jaffe, Hans L.C. *De Stijl*, New York: Harry N. Abrams, 1971.

Japan Advertising Photographers' Association, *Advertising Photography in Japan*, Tokyo, New York and San Francisco: Kodansha International (annual).

Japan Graphic Designers Association, *Graphic Design in Japan*, Tokyo: Kodansha International, 1981– (annual).

Kamekura, Yusaku "Advertising Art Today," *Graphis*, 168/169, 1968.

Kamekura, Yusaku "Katachi," *Graphis*, 168/169, 1968.

Kamekura, Yusaku "World Design Conference," *Annual of Advertising Art in Japan*, Tokyo: Bijutsu Shuppan-sha, 1960.

Kanamaru, Shigene "Japanese Advertising Photography," *Graphis*, 168/169, 1968.

Kanda, Akio "Annual Review of Graduating Students," *Idea*, 203, 1987.

Katzumie, Masaru "Japan Style – Yesterday, Today and Tomorrow," *Japan Style*, Tokyo, New York and San Francisco: Kondansha International Ltd, 1980.

Katzumie, Masaru "Lessons from the Japanese," *Adweek, Portfolio of Graphic Design*, 1986.

Katzumie, Masaru "Notes on Starting a Graphic Design Magazine," *Graphic Design*, 34, 1969.

Katzumie, Masaru "Pro et Contra," *Yusaku Kamekura: His Works*, Tokyo: Bijutsu Shuppan-sha, 1971.

Katzumie, Masaru "Tadashi Ohashi," *Graphic Design*, 88, 1982.

Katzumie, Masaru "Tokyo Olympics," *Annual of Advertising Art in Japan*, Tokyo: Bijutsu Shuppan-sha, 1965.

Katzumie, Masaru "World Design Conference," *Annual of Advertising Art in Japan*, Tokyo: Bijutsu Shuppan-sha, 1960.

Kimura, Tsunehisa *Kimura Camera*, Tokyo: Tsuiji Masuda, Parco, 1979.

Kizawa, Kuni "Designers' Comments," *Graphics Japan*, Tokyo: Graphic-sha, 1987.

Kristahn, Heinz-Jurgen and Frieder Mellinghoff *Japanische Plakate*, Vier-Turme-Verlag, 1983.

Lane, Richard *Masters of the Japanese Print*, Garden City, New York: Doubleday & Company, 1962.

Lee, Sherman E. *The Genius of Japanese Design*, Tokyo and New York: Kodansha International, 1981.

Lehmann, Jean Pierre "Madame Butterfly in a Rabbit Hutch. Western Perceptions and Stereotypes of the Japanese," *Japan Style*, Tokyo, New York and San Francisco: Kondansha International, 1980.

Mason, R.H.P. and J.G. Caiger *A History of Japan*, Tokyo: Charles C. Tuttle, 1972.

Masuda, Tadashi *The Design Heritage of Noren*, Tokyo: Graphic-sha, 1989.

Masuda, Tadashi *Works of Masuda Tadashi Design Institute, 1958-1966*, Tokyo: Seibundo Shinkosha, 1966.

Meggs, Philip B. *A History of Graphic Design*, New York: Van Nostrand Reinhold, 1983.

Mitsukuni, Yoshida, Ikko Tanaka and Sesoko Tsune, eds. *The Hybrid Culture*, Hiroshima: Mazda, 1984.

Mitsukuni, Yoshida, Ikko Tanaka and Sesoko Tsune *The Compact Culture*, Hiroshima: Toyo Kogyo, 1982.

Mizuo, Hiroshi *Edo Painting: Sotatsu and Korin*, New York: Weatherhill, and Tokyo: Heibonsha, 1972.

Mouer, Ross & Sugimoto, Yoshio *Images of Japanese Society*, London and New York: Sidney & Henley: KPI Limited, 1986.

Muller-Brockman, Joseph *History of the Poster*, Zurich: ABC Edition, 1971.

Munsterberg, Hugo *The Arts of Japan*, Rutland: Charles E. Tuttle, 1957.

Nadamoto, Tadahito *Nadamoto, Ningen Moyo*, Tokyo: Kodansha International, 1982.

Nadamoto, Tadashito *Women*, Tokyo: Sakoda Kosan, 1966.

Nakayama, Hisayoshi "Transit Advertising," *Advertising Medium: its Function and How to Choose it*, Tokyo: Nikka Advertising Institute, 1983.

Nagai, Kazumasa "Intentions, ADC Awards," *Annual of Advertising Art in Japan 85-86*, Tokyo: Bijutsu Shuppan-sha, 1986.

Nagai, Kazumasa "Joint Exhibition of Tokyo ADC and New York ADC," *Graphic Design*, 40, 1973.

Nagai, Kazumasa "Packaging Design in Japan," *Graphis*, 168/169, 1968.

Nagai, Kazumasa *The Works of Kazumasa Nagai*, Tokyo: Kodansha, 1985.

Nagai, Kazumasa and Yusuke Kaji *Publications and Advertising Work from Shiseido*, Tokyo: Kyuryudo Art Publishing, 1986.

Nippon Design Center, 1960-1965, Tokyo: Nippon Design Center, 1966.

Nippon Design Center, 1966-1970, Tokyo: Nippon Design Center, 1970.

Nippon Design Center, 1970-1979, Tokyo: Nippon Design Center, 1980.

Noda, Ko and Mill Roseman "Japan: The Design Scene," *Communication Arts*, January/February, 1983.

Ohchi, Hiroshi "On Japanese Posters," *1953/54 International Poster Annual*, Teufen AR (Switzerland): Arthur Niggle and Willy Verkauf, 1954

Okumura, Yukimasa "Intentions, ADC Awards," *Annual of Advertising Art in Japan 85/86*, Tokyo: Bijutsu Shuppan-sha, 1986.

Ogawa, Masataka "A Memorandum of One Hundred Years of Posters," *Posters in Japan 1880-1956*, Tokyo: Bijutsu Shuppan-sha, 1967.

Ogawa, Masataka "In Search of the 'Roots' of Graphic Design, Yusaku Kamekura's Resolute Pursuit," *The Works of Yusaku Kamekura*, Tokyo: Rikuyo-sha, 1983.

Ota, Kazuhiko "Designers' Statements," *Graphics Japan*, Tokyo: Graphic-sha, 1987.

Package Design in Japan Tokyo: Rikuyo-sha, 1985- (annual).

Perrin, Noel *Giving Up the Gun*, Boulder: Shambhala, 1980.

Phillipi, Donald L. Translation of *Kojiki: Records of Ancient History*, Princeton: Princeton University Press, 1969.

Poster Nippon Toyama: Toyama Art Museum Catalogue, 1987.

Rand, Paul Introduction to *Shigeo Fukuda*, Tokyo: Kodansha International, 1979.

Reischauer, Edwin O. *The Japanese*, Cambridge, Massachusetts: Belknap Press of Harvard University Press, 1977.

Reischauer, Edwin O. *The United States and Japan*, New York: The Viking Press, 1965.

Richards, Maurice *Posters at the Turn of the Century*, New York: Walker and Company, 1968.

Saito, Mokoto "Intentions, ADC Awards," *Annual of Advertising Art in Japan 85/86*, Bijutsu Shuppan-sha, 1986.

Sakane, Susume "Toward a New Visual Language," *Graphic Design in Japan, Volume 4*, Tokyo: Kodansha International, 1984.

Sato, Koichi "Designers' Comments," *Graphics Japan*, Tokyo: Graphic-sha, 1987.

Schodt, Frederik L. *Manga! Manga! the World of Japanese Comics*, Tokyo, New York and San Francisco: Kodansha International, 1983.

Seidensticker, Edward *Low City, High City*, New York: Alfred A. Knopf, 1983.

Sparke, Penny *Modern Japanese Design*, New York: E.P. Dutton, 1987.

Sudoh, Fumio, ed. *Ten Art Directors in Contemporary Japan*, Tokyo: Seibundo Shinkosha, 1982.

Tanaka, Ikko *The Design World of Ikko Tanaka*, Tokyo: Kodansha International, 1987.

Tanaka, Ikko "Japanese Younger Generation of Designers," *Graphis*, 168/169, 1968.

Tanaka, Ikko and Kozuko Koike *Japan Color*, San Francisco: Chronicle Books, 1982.

Tanchis, Aldo *Bruno Munari: Design as Art*, Cambridge, Massachusetts: MIT Press, 1987.

Tanikawa, Koichi *100 Posters of Tadanori Yokoo*, New York: Images Graphiques, 1978.

Thornton, Richard S. "The Continuity of Tradition," introduction to *The Traditional Japanese Dyeing of Happi and Handtowels*, Tokyo: Shinshindo-Shuppan, 1989.

Thornton, Richard S. "Graphic Design Education," *Graphis*, 168/169, 1968.

Thornton, Richard S. "Japan: Elegant Complexity," *AIGA Journal*, Vol. 5, No. 4, 1987.

Thornton, Richard S. "The Japanese Design Establishment," *Designcourse*, Vol. 1, No. 3, 1969; *Graphic Design*, 36, 1970; and *AIGA Journal*, 13, 1970.

Thornton, Richard S. "The New Generation of Japanese Graphic Designers," *Print*, November/December 1984.

Tokyo: Form and Spirit, New York: Abrams/Walker Art Center, 1986.

Trager, James *Letters From Sachiko*, New York: Atheneum, 1982.

Tsune, Sesoko, ed. *The Wheel: a Japanese History*, Hiroshima: Toyo Kogyo, 1981.

Tsune, Sesoko, ed. *The Rice Cycle*, Tokyo: Japan External Trade Organization, 1974.

Typographics "Tee", Japan Typography Association (monthly).

Wada, Mokoto "What a Marvelous Flamingo," *Terry 100%*, Parco, 1981.

Watanabe, Shinichi "Annual Review of Graduating Seniors," *Idea*, 203, 1987.

Watanabe, Shinichi "Annual Review of Graduating Seniors," *Idea*, 185, 1984.

Weill, Alain *The Poster: A Worldwide Survey and History*, Boston: G. K. Hall, 1985.

West Meets East: California/Tokyo, Tokyo: Japan Creators Association, 1988.

Wurman, Richard Saul, *Tokyo Access*, Los Angeles: Access Press, 1984.

Yamaguchi, Katsuhiro "Histoire de L'Affiche au Japon," *L'Affiche Japonaise: Des Origines à nos Jours*, Paris: UCAD Musée de L'Affiche, 1979.

Yamamoto, Tamesaburo Introduction to *Nippon Design Center, 1960-1965*, Tokyo: Nippon Design Center, 1966.

Yamana, Ayao "An Outline of Japanese Advertising Art," *Newspapers and Magazine Advertising in Japan, 1869-1958*, Tokyo: Bijutsu Shuppan-sha, 1967.

Yanagi, Soetsu *The Unknown Craftsman*, Tokyo, New York and San Francisco: Kodansha International, 1972.

Yokoo, Tadanori *The Complete Tadanori Yokoo*, Tokyo: Kodansha International, 1971.

Yujobo, Nobuaki "Chronological Table" *Posters in Japan, 1860-1966*, Tokyo: Bijutsu Shuppan-sha, 1967.

Yule, Sir Henry *Travels of Marco Polo*, New York: Charles Scribner, 1903.

Yumeji (Takehisa) no Sekai, Gumma Memorial Museum in Edaho, 1986.

Yumura, Teruhiko *Terry's Hitparade*, Tokyo: Bijutsu Shuppan-sha, 1981.

banzuke
A poster dating from the Edo period (1603 to the Meiji Restoration of 1868), issued before a sumo wrestling match to show the status and rating of the participants. Some banzuke were purely calligraphic; others included illustrations.

bijin-ga
Paintings of beautiful women rendered as posters to promote different department stores and commercial products. They were popular from 1908 through to the 1920s, and their legacy continues today in photographic posters for cosmetics and fashion.

bira
A handbill dating from the Edo period that was the precursor of the the more decorative ekanban. It was posted at crossroads and at public baths.

ekanban
A nineteenth-century form of poster that bridges the feudal Edo era and the industrial Meiji period (from the Restoration in 1868 to 1912). The English word "poster" was not adopted until the 1930s.

goshikku
A typographic alteration of Japanese characters that changes the variable thick and thin brush strokes into consistent lines. The name is derived from the European "gothic" or sans serif typeface.

gyosho
An early form of written Chinese kanji characters known for its simple, loose, informal style.

haiku
A 17-syllable poem with three lines of five, seven and five syllables. With direct lucidity, it expresses the writer's deepest emotions by describing nature, and is open to a multitude of interpretations.

hiragana
A 46-character syllabary, representing only sounds, which developed from the cursive written style of kanji. First known as a "ladies' hand" because it was used by women during the Heian period (794-1185), it gradually became the standard syllabary.

kabuki
Popular classical theatre, first performed by an all-female troupe in the seventeenth century. Soon after it changed to all-male, which is how it is still performed today.

kaisho
An early angular, or square, style of writing Chinese kanji characters, which was primarily used for official records. Because of its complicated form it was replaced by the simpler sosho style.

kanban
Hand-crafted shop sign developed by merchants during the Edo era, which continued in use up to the beginning of the twentieth century.

kanji
Chinese-based written characters, or ideographs, that represent objects or ideas. Originally borrowed to represent similar-sounding Japanese syllables, kanji gradually became adapted by the Japanese for their own use and divorced from the meanings of the original Chinese characters.

katakana
A 46-character sound syllabary developed from parts of kanji. First used by men as a form of phonetic shorthand to take notes on science and learning, it grew almost exclusively from writing foreign words.

manga
Originally the name of the rough sketches used by the woodblock artist Hokusai (1760-1849), the name continued in use to refer to bound volumes of illustrated stories. It is used today to mean comic books.

mincho
A form of writing derived from Chinese brush calligraphy, which was translated first to wood and metal type and then to phototypesetting. It is a basic, utilitarian face, corresponding to the West's roman typeface.

monsho
Simple line drawings and designs that were used to identify family clans since the middle of the tenth century; also sometimes abbreviated to mon. They were stencilled on cloth, painted on banners, and carved in wood, stone and metal to identify property.

nakazuri
Transport posters that hang in the centre of the car in a subway or train. Their short lifespan and controlled placement in commuter cars have made them a major form of product advertising.

noren
Fabric banners hung at shop entrances, with the shop's monsho or name painted on the surface. First used in the twelfth century, they remain today in restaurants serving traditional Japanese food.

rimpa
A highly decorative form of art developed in the seventeenth century which lasted until the nineteenth. Its best known practitioners were Ogata Korin, Honami Koetsu and Nonomura Sotatsu.

romaji
A transliteration of Japanese words and text into roman letters. The first form was developed in 1885 and the second, officially backed by the government and widely used today, was introduced in 1937.

shakuhachi
A bamboo reedless flute, about 20 inches long.

shashoku
The phototypesetting process, as differentiated from katsuji, or hot metal typesetting.

sosho
A writing style for Chinese kanji characters which proved popular because its cursive, flowing and expressive lines were well suited to literary notation.

sumi-e
A black-and-white ink painting that uses a sumi or India-ink stick containing a mixture of lamp-black or plant soot, and glue. The stick is rubbed against a wet stone to draw out the ink.

tanka
A verse form unique to Japan, which has five lines of five, seven, five, seven and seven syllables. It is regarded as the country's leading verse form.

ukiyo-e
A school of painting, book illustration and printmaking that developed during the Edo period. The celebrated woodblock prints of popular Edo customs and fashion had considerable influence on Western artists at the end of the nineteenth century.

yoshiwara
A licensed red-light district of the old city of Edo (Tokyo), which flourished from the mid-seventeenth to the mid-twentieth centuries. In the early Edo era (seventeenth century) it was at its height, with as many as three thousand courtesans at any one time; it is now a tame amusement area.

zuan-ka
An early twentieth-century name for a design practitioner, originally meaning only interior and textile designers. Later it came to be used for all designers until it was discontinued in the early 1950s.